AF279484

Shirley Shahan
DOUG'S HEADERS
DRAG-ON-LADY
GOODYEAR

Shirley Shahan
THE DRAG-ON LADY

AMX
AMERICAN MOTORS
390
SS/
EXPER

CarTech®

PATRICK FOSTER

CarTech®

CarTech®, Inc.
6118 Main Street
North Branch, MN 55056
Phone: 651-277-1200 or 800-551-4754
Fax: 651-277-1203
www.cartechbooks.com

Edit by Bob Wilson
Layout by Monica Seiberlich

ISBN 978-1-61325-581-0
Item No. CT675

Library of Congress Cataloging-in-Publication Data Available

Written, edited, and designed in the U.S.A.
Printed in China
10 9 8 7 6 5 4 3 2 1

PUBLISHER'S NOTE: In reporting history, the images required to tell the tale will vary greatly in quality, especially by modern photographic standards. While some images in this volume are not up to those digital standards, we have included them, as we feel they are an important element in telling the story.

DISTRIBUTION BY:

Europe
PGUK
63 Hatton Garden
London EC1N 8LE, England
Phone: 020 7061 1980 • Fax: 020 7242 3725
www.pguk.co.uk

Australia
Renniks Publications Ltd.
3/37-39 Green Street
Banksmeadow, NSW 2109, Australia
Phone: 2 9695 7055 • Fax: 2 9695 7355
www.renniks.com

Canada
Login Canada
300 Saulteaux Crescent
Winnipeg, MB, R3J 3T2 Canada
Phone: 800 665 1148 • Fax: 800 665 0103
www.lb.ca

CONTENTS

DEDICATION

> "Behold, I stand at the door and knock. If anyone hears my voice
> and opens the door, I will come in to him and will dine with him
> and he with me."
> — Revelation 3:20 (Shirley's favorite Bible passage)

This book is dedicated to the memory of one of the finest men I've ever known, my good friend George Lamb. He was a drag racing enthusiast and a genuinely good person in every respect. I miss you, my old friend!

About the AUTHOR

Patrick Foster is one of America's best-known automotive journalists. He is a dedicated historian/author who has been writing for more than 25 years. Foster is a features writer and has regular columns in *Hemmings Classic Car* and *Old Cars* magazines. He is a features writer for *Collectible Automobile* magazine as well. He has written 33 books as well as contributing material for several others. In addition, he has appeared in several automotive documentary films and makes frequent public appearances at automotive events.

Foster has won numerous writing awards, including the Antique Automobile Club of America's prestigious Thomas McKean Memorial Cup Award for the best book of automotive history for 1998. In 1997, one of his works was named Outstanding Periodical Article of the year by the Society of Automotive Historians.

In 2011, Foster was honored with the Lee Iacocca Award, one of the most coveted awards in the car hobby, for excellence in automotive writing. The 2015 International Automotive Media Council (IAMC) Awards saw Foster bring home a Silver Medal for an article on 1930–1934 Nash automobiles and a Bronze Medal for his book *Jeep: The History of America's Greatest Vehicle*. In 2016, Foster took home two awards from the IAMC event when *International Harvester Trucks: The Complete History* won a Silver Medal and an article on George Romney was awarded a Bronze Medal.

The following year, 2017, brought still more awards. Foster was awarded the trophy for Best Book of Automotive History for the year for *Airstream: America's World Traveler*. That book was also awarded a Gold Medal in its category. His book *Willys-Overland Illustrated History* also took home a Gold Medal.

Born in Burlington, Vermont, Foster resides in Milford, Connecticut, with his wife, Diane. His books can be purchased on his Olde Milford Press website, oldemilfordpress.com.

ACKNOWLEDGMENTS

First, I'd like to thank automotive historian and author Bob McClurg for his almost inestimable help in researching this book. Bob very generously gave me permission to reprint segments from an in-depth interview that he did with Shirley Shahan. It included information that I hadn't been able to develop in my own series of interviews and featured valuable insights from Shirley's first husband, H.L. Shahan.

I'd also like to thank Bob Wilson of CarTech books for giving me this book on which to work; it was a sheer pleasure from beginning to end. I'm also grateful to Bob for allowing me some extra time to finish the book when health issues interfered with my work schedule.

Lastly, I'd like to thank Shirley's terrific husband, Ken Bridges, who patiently scanned and copied many of the photos in the book and generously gave of his time to help Shirley and me as we worked our way through her story.

Foreword by Herb "Mr. 4-Speed" McCANDLESS

Resilient. It's the perfect word to describe Shirley Shahan, a charismatic woman who I've had the honor of staying friends with for more than 50 years. I first met Shirley in 1967. Many underestimated her at the time, and many were made a fool. Her incredible skill caught the attention of Chrysler executives, who immediately offered her a factory deal. Her outgoing nature, friendly smile, and competitive spirit made her a perfect ambassador—not only for Chrysler but for the entire sport of drag racing.

She is resilient for choosing the nontraditional path in drag racing, a male-dominated sport, during a time when women were rarely afforded the opportunities of men. It speaks to her talent behind the wheel to overcome such obstacles. She was the first woman to win a National Hot Rod Association (NHRA) major event, to be chosen to do the Mobil Economy Run, and to appear in TV commercials.

She is resilient for creating balance. Shirley has been successful in all aspects of her life: as a wife, mother, and grandmother. I'm incredibly thankful to call Shirley a close friend. We lived during a time that will never exist again. It never felt like work because we did what we loved, and we loved the people we did it with. The drag racing community is a family, and I will be forever grateful that Shirley is part of that family.

— Herb "Mr. 4-Speed" McCandless

Herb McCandless is an American Pro Stock drag racer. With a long career in racing, McCandless won the NHRA's Modified Eliminator title at the 1970 Gatornationals in a Plymouth Barracuda. McCandless also won the 1970 NHRA U.S. Nationals in Pro Stock, driving a 1970 Plymouth Duster for Sox & Martin.

INTRODUCTION

When Shirley Shahan put the hammer down during the last race of the first March Meet ever at the Famoso Racetrack just outside of Bakersfield, California, she made history. Not only was she the first winner of the first March Meet but she was also a woman competing in a man's world.

The Famoso March Meet had been advertised as an East-versus-West showdown with the best California drag racers as well as some heavy-hitters from the East. Then, a slender blonde girl with a bright smile ended up beating them all. As history shows, it wasn't a fluke.

Shirley was young and pretty with blonde hair. She otherwise might have spent her entire life as a stay-at-home mom, but both she and her husband, H.L., loved drag racing, and she enjoyed going to watch him race at the track. One day, fate stepped in, and she had to do the driving instead of H.L. That was when the couple realized a shocking truth: she was the better driver—by far. The rest, as the old saying goes, is history. And Shirley made a lot of history.

Shirley Shahan, a.k.a. "the Drag-On Lady," is a legend in the world of professional drag racing. She's in the history books as the first woman to win a major NHRA drag racing event: the 1966 Winternationals in Pomona, California, in which she outraced such greats as "Dyno Don" Nicholson, Hayden Proffitt, Tom Sturm, and Arlen Vanke. However, her career encompassed much more than that. Shirley drove for Dodge, Plymouth, and American Motors (AMC), and she was a winner with all of them.

I don't actually recall when I first heard of Shirley Shahan, but it was many years ago. I do remember being reminded of her when toy maker Ertl released a $1/18$-scale replica of her AMX/SS drag car back in the 1990s. In addition, I'm pretty sure it was shortly after that when she and I were introduced at an AMC club car show. She struck me as a pert, very good-looking lady with lots of spunk and a good attitude toward life.

After that first meeting, I saw her at other AMC shows around the country, where, like me, she met fans and signed autographs. Often, the show organizers set us up in booths next to each other, which made it easier to get to know her better. Her husband, Ken Bridges, a really nice man, was always with her, and we would chat sometimes as Shirley handled the fans who were lined up to meet her.

Thus, when Bob Wilson of CarTech Books approached me with the idea of writing a book about Shirley, I jumped at the chance. I'll always be grateful to Bob for this wonderful opportunity. In addition, I'm grateful to Shirley for allowing me to relate the story of her amazing career in racing.

So, sit back, pop open a cold one, and enjoy the story.

CHAPTER 1

A California
GIRL (1938–1955)

Shirley Shahan was the first woman to win a major NHRA drag racing event, but her career in professional drag racing encompasses much more than that.

She was a tough competitor, setting records at tracks across America.

(Photo Courtesy Chrysler. Chrysler is a trademark of FCA USA LLC.)

Before there was a Shirley Muldowney, there was Shirley Shahan. Shirley Shahan blazed a trail for women in drag racing as the first woman to win an NHRA national event when she raced at the 1966 NHRA Winternationals. Shirley Shahan is what's commonly known as a living legend. But where do legends come from?

The answer is that they come from all over—from big cities to small towns and from north and south to east and west. That's because a legend is a person, not the place in which he or she was born and not the family in which he or she grew up. A legend is a person who has accomplished something noteworthy or great—something that people will talk about for years to come. Shirley Shahan (universally known as the Drag-On Lady) is a true legend.

Diminutive, quiet, and friendly, she now looks like someone's grandmother, which she is by the way. But in her time, she was a fierce competitor at drag strips across the country. She was a spunky little chick in a short miniskirt and go-go boots with a blonde beehive hairdo, and she regularly showed the guys what competitive drag racing was all about.

Shirley won scores of races, set records, and kicked butt so often that many of the male drivers who couldn't believe that they could actually lose to the petite woman with the bright smile ended up filing protests against her—usually to no avail. Shirley didn't smile her way to fame and success, and she didn't cheat. She was just a faster, better driver than many of her contemporaries, and she has shelves of awards and trophies to prove it. It's been a great life. In fact, it's been one for the record books.

The Beginning

Shirley Shahan was born Shirley Jean Epperson in Visalia, California, on June 2, 1938, to Jacob and Beatrice Epperson. Visalia back then was a pleasant little town with oak-lined streets, situated in the heart of California's agricultural San Joaquin Valley. Jack was a roofer and general contractor, and Beatrice was a housewife.

The family hailed from California because decades earlier Shirley's great-great-grandfather John Jordan captained a wagon train of settlers from Texas to California. John Jordan was an interesting character. He was a former Texas Ranger, and he once owned a salt company called Jordan's Saline that lent its name to the town that grew up around it. Jordan's Saline eventually was renamed Grand Saline, which today is part of the Morton Salt company.

The wagon train that took Jordan and the other settlers to California consisted of 200 hardy pioneers. They traveled the southern route to San Diego, and as they progressed along the way, Captain Jordan would go ahead of them to survey the trail that the wagon train would follow the next day. Along the way, a baby boy was born, and he became Shirley's great-grandfather. Once the wagon train arrived in California, Jordan and his wife put down

Young Shirley watches her baby brother Jackie. When he grew up to be a young man, he was, as Shirley reported, her biggest fan. He attended every race he could and bought every magazine and newspaper that featured a story about her. (Photo Courtesy Shirley Shahan)

permanent roots, eventually settling near Exeter in Tulare County. It was a beautiful area with room to grow and weather that was decidedly pleasant most of the time. It was a good country in which to grow things.

Shirley's father Jacob is pictured here as a young man. When she was still just a child, Shirley worked alongside her dad on his racing jalopies, at first handing him tools and later doing some of the wrenching herself. (Photo Courtesy Shirley Shahan)

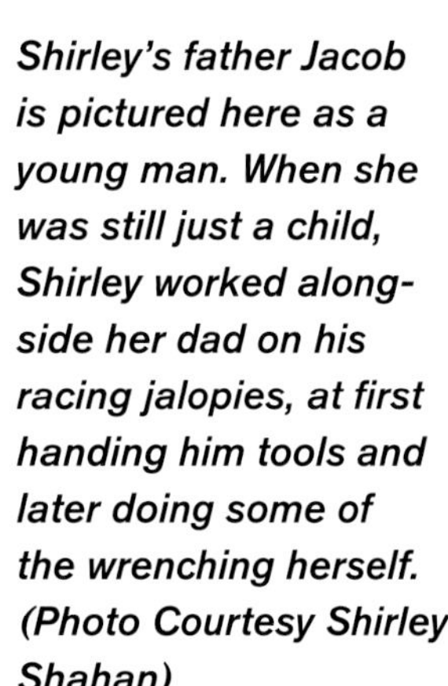

This was the only photo that we could find of Shirley's mom, Beatrice Epperson. It was taken while she was still in high school. Shirley's resemblance to her mother is striking. (Photo Courtesy Shirley Shahan)

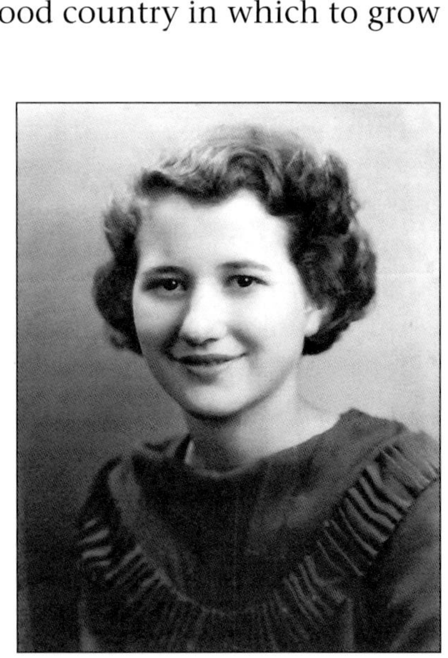

Learning about Cars

Years later, the Epperson family settled in nearby Tulare. Shirley was the oldest of four children: Shirley, Jackie, Jerry, and Kathleen were born in that order. There may be some significance in Shirley being the oldest child. In fact, one could argue that it probably affected how her life turned out.

Shirley's father was an amateur automobile racer, and on weekends, he raced what were known at the time as jalopies. Jalopies were old, beat-up cars that were about one step removed from the junkyard and could be bought for next to nothing and inexpensively raced. Jack Epperson wasn't the driver, however. Other men did the actual driving. Jack found the cars, fixed them up, and kept them running.

Jack worked on the cars in his garage at home, and at a young age, Shirley, being the oldest child, began helping her father whenever he worked on his race cars. Something of a tomboy, Shirley became a sort of mechanic's helper to her dad on most weekends. At first, she held the work light and handed him wrenches and screwdrivers. In the process, she learned about cars and engines.

Here's driver Bill Hester with another of Jack Epperson's jalopies. This one looks like a 1934 Ford. Hester had just won a race, but the track had run out of trophies, so as a joke, the track officials gave him a lightbulb instead. (Photo Courtesy Shirley Shahan)

"At a very early age," she said with a smile, "I knew the difference between a 5/8-inch wrench and a 9/16-inch wrench."

Gradually, Shirley's dad taught her a lot about working on old cars. Jack was a very good teacher, which was not surprising because he'd served in the US Navy as a Seabee, and was very skilled with tools, and had a lot of confidence as a mechanic. Before long, Jack had little Shirley doing some of the minor wrenching as well, such as changing spark plugs, doing oil changes, etc. She quickly learned a lot about cars and the tools to fix them.

"I also remember that when I was about 8 or 9 years old, I took an aptitude test at school, and the results said that I should be a mechanic when I grew up," Shirley remembered with a laugh.

She also became interested in her father's hobby of racing. She saw racing as an exciting activity, and it was a regular part of her life.

One of Shirley's father's racing jalopies is shown with driver Bill Hester and a track clown. Notice the Jack Epperson name on the side of the car. (Photo Courtesy Shirley Shahan)

Shortly after the previous photo was taken, Bill Hester had a serious accident with the Ford, which probably totaled the car.

He ended up being okay.

(Photo Courtesy Shirley Shahan)

As Shirley grew older, she also helped her father with some of his roofing jobs. She often was asked to unload the truck at various jobs, hauling bundles of shingles that weighed 30 to 50 pounds along with all of the other materials, and that helped to build her physical strength. Her strength, in turn, helped her when it came to the athletic activities that she enjoyed so much in school and outside of school. To put it in plain words, Shirley was a lot stronger than most of the other girls in town.

Shirley recalled that the family moved to a new house while she was in the fourth grade. The house was badly in need of painting, so her father put a paintbrush in her hand and taught her how to paint. He himself used a spray gun for the large areas while she wielded the brush.

The family's new home was located on a large lot with about 20 walnut trees on it, and they were the source of Shirley's first paying job. Those walnuts needed to be harvested every fall, and her father paid her $1 for every gunny sack that she could fill with nuts. Shirley actually hated the work because it stained her hands brown, which embarrassed her when she when to school.

Shirley's father was a very likeable character. When her brother Jackie and cousin Walter were

Shirley is sitting on her favorite uncle's knee. Uncle Charlie was a pilot who volunteered for World War II and flew in what was then known as the Army Air Force. He left the service after the war but enlisted again for the Korean War. By that point, the service was known as the US Air Force, and he flew missions in Korea. He remained in the service and flew dangerous missions again, this time in the Vietnam War. (Photo Courtesy Shirley Shahan)

Shirley is pictured with her cousin Chuck and her grandparents on her mother's side of the family, Francis and Charles Coiner. (Photo Courtesy Shirley Shahan)

ABOVE LEFT: *Shirley and her younger brother, Jackie, are in the backyard of the family home in Visalia. (Photo Courtesy Shirley Shahan)* **ABOVE RIGHT:** *Here is a slightly older Shirley pictured in front of the family home. This is the house that she and her father painted. It was originally green, and they painted it white. Her father's advice was "Never paint with a dry brush." The work helped strengthen Shirley, which later helped her when speed shifting race cars. (Photo Courtesy Shirley Shahan)* **LEFT:** *Shirley and her dad ride on the family tractor. Shirley was very close to her father and helped him work on his racing jalopies. She also inherited a love of racing from her dad. (Photo Courtesy Shirley Shahan)*

     SHIRLEY SHAHAN *The Drag-On Lady*

caught smoking behind the shed, Jack made them both smoke big cigars to teach them a lesson. At first, they puffed away like big shots, inhaling the thick smoke and blowing out smoke rings like real wise guys. However, before long, they both got sick to their stomachs and had to go and lie down with pans next to their beds in case they threw up. Shirley remembered it well because she had to stay home from the jalopy races that day to take care of the two boys. Neither of the boys took up smoking after that.

School Days

Naturally, school was a big part of Shirley's early life. She attended the Washington Grammar School in Visalia from kindergarten through third grade, and then she moved to Jefferson Grammar School for grades four through six. From there, she attended

Young Shirley is with baby Jackie and her Easter basket. Shirley thinks the car in the background is the family's Studebaker sedan. (Photo Courtesy Shirley Shahan)

Visalia Junior High School for grades seven through nine, which was followed by Mount Whitney High School, where she attended the tenth and eleventh grades and part of twelfth grade.

As a youngster, Shirley managed to pick up a few scars. She was attacked by a big dog when she was just 11 years old and ended up getting stitches. Her father's partner in the roofing company had three kids: Donnie, Connie, and Bonnie, and Shirley played hide and seek in the roofing company warehouse with them, hiding out among the bundles of shingles and roles of asphalt roofing paper. One time, Shirley accidently stepped on a roofing nail, which became infected and sent her to the hospital with blood poisoning.

As a teenager, Shirley was an outgoing, popular girl with many friends. As with most teens, she enjoyed going to parties and hanging out with her classmates. However, probably her biggest love during her early teenage years was fast-pitch softball, which was a sport that she began playing in the ninth grade.

The team on which she played was called the Visalia Hornets, and it was part of the Valley Softball League. Because Shirley had developed a powerful right arm from helping her dad load and unload the roofing truck, she could reach home plate from center field with one throw. Because of that ability, she was the team's centerfielder.

Grade-wise Shirley performed at a high level, although she failed to apply herself enough to be at the top of her class. She was a good kid. In fact, Shirley remembered getting in trouble just once at school, and even then it wasn't her fault.

She was called into the principal's office for skipping her fourth-period class, even though she actually hadn't skipped it. When she answered the roll call, the teacher had marked another girl's name by accident. Thinking that she was absent, the school called home to report that she was skipping class, and Shirley's mom, not wanting her daughter to get into trouble, told them that Shirley was at home with her! When it was finally established that Shirley hadn't skipped class, it took a little explaining on her mom's part. Eventually, the whole story came out. Beatrice just had a lot of 'splainin' to do.

During Shirley's sophomore year, she helped in the attendance department, and during her junior year, she worked in the guidance counsellor's office.

The year Shirley turned sweet 16 was an exciting

Kneeling in front of her locker is teenage Shirley Epperson. Note the hairstyles as well as the long skirts. This photo was taken around 1953 or 1954, when those styles were all the rage among teenage girls. (Photo Courtesy Shirley Shahan)

It's unknown why Shirley is posed in what appears to be the girls high school shower, but here she is, already a beautiful young woman. Little did she know that very soon she would meet her first husband. (Photo Courtesy Shirley Shahan)

one. One could go to the local theater to see such film legends as Marlon Brando and his stunning performance in *On the Waterfront*, Humphrey Bogart in *The Caine Mutiny* and *Sabrina*, and Jimmy Stewart in Alfred Hitchcock's *Rear Window*. Fans of science fiction could see the weird and scary *Creature from the Black Lagoon*. Rock and roll was just beginning to take hold. Kids could bop to "Sh-boom" by the Cords, and "Shake, Rattle, and Roll" by Bill Haley and the Comets, or listen to "Earth Angel" by the Penguins. Pop music also had some notable hit songs: Frank Sinatra had a big hit with "When You're Young at Heart," Jo Stafford sang "Make Love to Me," and Tony Bennet crooned "Stranger in Paradise."

First Wheels

Growing up, the family car was often the roofing company truck that her father owned, but they also usually had one or two other older vehicles at hand. Somehow, it doesn't seem surprising that Shirley began driving at the tender age of 10 years old in a 1934 Ford pickup truck that her family owned. The area where the Eppersons lived was rural, and Shirley's dad saw no harm in allowing his young daughter to drive his truck, at least within a reasonable distance of home.

The Ford was a solid, dependable machine, but with just a flathead 4-cylinder engine that churned out a mere 50 hp and a clunky 3-speed manual transmission, it wasn't fast. This was probably just as well, considering Shirley's age at the time. However, I have to wonder how a 10-year-old girl was able to steer and use the brake pedal in an old truck with no power steering and no power brakes—not to mention the difficulty of shifting the gears!

Within a few years, that old Ford truck was replaced by a newer, much more powerful Studebaker pickup. Shirley was very happy about the increase in power, and she soon put it to good use. By the time she was 16 years old, Shirley had become a very competent driver. At that point, she earned her driver's license, which meant that she could now drive anywhere she wanted without a hassle.

Shirley soon began to show exactly how good of a driver she was, street racing other teenagers (both male and female) on the roads around Visalia. Any guess as to who usually won? As fate had it, many of the kids in town were into drag racing, and Shirley loved it. She managed to beat many boys and girls with the Studebaker truck, much to the consternation of her opponents.

Naturally, I asked Shirley, "Were you born a car enthusiast?"

Surprisingly enough, she said, "No, not at all. But my dad sure was. He was a weekend jalopy racer, and when he would work on his race cars at home, I'd hang around him as a mechanic's helper, handing him wrenches and pliers. The family would go to watch his cars race on the weekend, and I guess I kind of got initiated that way. I used to love to go and watch the races."

Shirley recalled that her dad eventually bought a pretty nice family car, one of those "which way is it going" Studebakers that were built between 1947 and 1952 (she can't recall the exact year). Why did the family buy another Studebaker? Because one of Shirley's uncles was co-owner of the Switzer and Jordan Company, which was the local Studebaker dealer. The dealer always gave Shirley's father the family discount. And besides, Studebaker always made economical, tough, and reliable cars and trucks.

Looking back, it's obvious that although Shirley received a lot of background and experience from helping her dad, she really got her start as a professional driver by drag racing on the streets of Visalia in the family's Studebaker pickup.

"I was a teenager, and when I got my license, my parents let me drive the Studebaker pickup," Shirley said. "It wasn't long before I was racing guys at traffic lights and winning. Now, usually this wasn't at the place outside of town where we kids did the drag racing, this was more or less racing from stoplight to stoplight in town. That little Studebaker pickup sure

   SHIRLEY SHAHAN *The Drag-On Lady*

had the guts to win races. It was that good!"

Amazingly, Shirley never got a speeding ticket, either.

However, let's face it, many teenagers (usually boys) raced other teenagers back in the day and then went on to become librarians, toll collectors, insurance agents, or some other equally boring occupation. Not many became a top-ranked drag racer with a worldwide reputation and a prominent place in the record books. To enter the top ranks of race car drivers, it takes more than just a fast car or truck and a willingness to take up a challenge. It takes a certain kind of internal drive. It begins with a competitive personality, which is usually something a person is born with. You can't buy it and you can't fake it, and although you may be able to acquire it with experience, in the end, you either have it or you don't.

Looking back, it seems that Shirley Shahan always had a competitive streak, whether it was playing fast-pitch softball, roller skating, running, or whatever. When she was in the sixth grade, Shirley entered a citywide athletic competition and won first place for both the accuracy throw and the long-distance throw. She was passionate about sports, especially softball, and she had the physical strength to excel.

However, when she earned her driver's license, cars became her main focus. Shirley raced any time she could. In addition to stoplight-to-stoplight races, she found other opportunities to compete. She didn't call it street racing. Instead, she said it was semi-organized drag racing that took place on a stretch of highway just outside of town. She considered it semi-organized because the racing was done by a group of regulars with a list of actual rules and regulations. However, she did continue to street race from time to time.

Meeting H.L.

As a typical teenager of the 1950s, Shirley spent most Wednesdays and Saturdays at the local roller-skating rink. It was a great hangout for her and her girlfriends, and she loved to skate. However, on most Sundays, Shirley went to the racetrack with her dad. In between, she and the other kids were in school during the day and then raced each other after school. She loved listening to Elvis Presley and other early rock and rollers on the radio. It was a fun life, a true 1950s kind of life, the kind that just doesn't exist anymore.

Shirley was a good kid who never really got into trouble. So, imagine how her mother felt when the sheriff came to her home one day while Shirley was out and said that he had a warrant for Shirley's arrest! Shirley had received a ticket for jaywalking while downtown shopping for a prom dress. Of course, being a typical teenager, she didn't tell her parents and then simply forgot to show up in court. Luckily, Beatrice knew the sheriff and managed to take care of the matter.

Then, in her junior year of high school, something happened that changed Shirley's whole world. The teenagers in the area often held parties at their parents' homes. At one of those parties, one of Shirley's girlfriends introduced her to an older boy named H.L. Shahan. (The girlfriend was going out with a friend of his.)

The party was actually at H.L.'s parents' house when his parents were out of town. Apparently, H.L. hosted many parties when his parents were visiting friends and family in Oklahoma. I wonder if his parents ever knew . . .

Yes, H.L. actually was his first name. The initials didn't stand for anything else. As Shirley explained, both of H.L.'s parents had the initials H.L. in their names, so when it came time to name their new baby boy, they named him H.L. At the time, it seemed to be the natural thing to do, regardless of the confusion that was bound to occur throughout his life. After Shirley got to know him better, she often called him *H* for short.

H.L. was about four years older than Shirley. He was born on December 29, 1934, in Beggs, Oklahoma. His mother's name was Henry Lee Pyle, and his father's name was Harry Leslie Shahan. Like most women in the 1950s, H.L.'s mother was a homemaker. H.L.'s father did farmwork. The family eventually moved to Visalia, California, where Mr. Shahan got a job on a local farm. According to Shirley, he may have been the manager of the farm.

Shirley was 16 years old when she met H.L. He was young and shy. As Shirley recalled, "He didn't like to socialize very much, but he was a very nice guy. His big interest was cars. He simply loved cars."

Just like Shirley, H.L. loved automobile racing. Apparently, H.L. was able to overcome his shyness enough to ask Shirley if he could see her again, because they began dating. For their first date, H.L. took Shirley to the movies. She doesn't recall what they saw, but the point was the two kids found that they liked each other.

They almost didn't meet. Just before he met Shirley, H.L. had decided to move back to Oklahoma. He and his parents used to go back regularly to visit aunts, uncles, and grandparents. On one visit, H.L. decided that he wanted to stay in Oklahoma and live with his grandparents. He had a relative who worked at Cunningham Chevrolet, which was the local Chevrolet garage, and H.L. also got a job there.

The next time that his parents visited Oklahoma, H.L.'s mother told him that she was worried that his living with his grandparents might get them into trouble with the Social Security Administration and affect their benefits. So, H.L. quit his job at the Chevrolet dealership and made plans to move back to Visalia with his parents. Had he not done that, he may have spent the rest of his life in Oklahoma and never met Shirley Jean Epperson.

Just before H.L. left Oklahoma to move back to California, the local social security office indeed found out about the living arrangements with his grandparents, but the official said that he thought it was a great idea. H.L. could care for grandparents better that way. However, it was too late to change again because H.L. had already committed to move back to California.

So, move back he did, and it wasn't long afterward that he met Shirley. She remembered that H.L. was very good-looking and that he loved cars and drove a pretty nice one. This was during a golden age for American cars, so H.L. had a variety of great cars from which to choose. However, one soon-to-be-iconic automobile caught his eye.

This was taken in the same location as the photo on page 18, but Shirley is posing with her closest friend today, Marian Shippey. Here, Shirley has a very serious look on her face. (Photo Courtesy Shirley Shahan)

In the fall of 1954, Chevrolet introduced an all-new line of cars that were well-made and beautifully styled. For the first time, the new Chevrolet for 1955 also offered a water-cooled V-8 engine that provided good performance and the potential for even more.

H.L. was already partial to V-8s. Before he met Shirley, he had a hot 1947 Ford two-door with the flathead V-8. He was also partial to Chevrolet, so he took a real interest in the division's new car, especially because it appeared that with its introduction, Chevrolet was taking a big step into the performance market. A big feature of this latest Chevrolet was its revolutionary new Turbo-Fire small-block V-8 engine that was available for the first time that year, and H.L. decided to buy one.

A cast-iron pushrod engine displacing 265 ci, the little Chevy V-8 produced a solid 162 hp with its standard 2-barrel carburetor and hydraulic lifters and 180 hp with the optional factory Power Pack that consisted of a Rochester 4-barrel carburetor and dual exhaust. The engine's short-stroke (3¾ x 3 inch) design reduced friction and allowed higher revs.

Better still, H.L. knew there was potential for even more power because the Corvette that year offered a version with the Super Power Pack, which boosted power to 195 hp. Best of all, the Turbo-Fire was a modern V-8 design that boasted a patented new green sand-casting process that allowed it to be relatively lightweight, which was unlike the heavy straight-8 engines that were used by other automakers for a long time.

H.L. showed Shirley how to disconnect the odometer cable so that the mileage wouldn't register.

Because of its unique design and production, the Chevy mill was significantly lighter than its competitors' V-8 engines. The new Chevy V-8 was revolutionary and a dominant performance engine for decades to come. With such great power in the light Chevrolet chassis, H.L. knew that the car was almost certain to be a very competitive racer, and he was right.

The summer of Shirley's junior high school year, H.L. worked for the US Forestry Service in a national park about 70 miles away. Wanting to see him, Shirley often snuck over there, driving her dad's Studebaker truck. Realizing that her father would soon notice the miles piling up on the truck, H.L. showed Shirley how to disconnect the odometer cable so that the mileage wouldn't register. She'd drive a few miles from home, pull over to disconnect the odometer, then drive up to see him. Toward the end of the drive back home, she would reconnect the odometer cable. Her father never knew.

Well, after about a year of dating, H.L. popped the question, and Shirley said yes. They decided to get married as soon as possible. If 17 years old seems a young age to marry, Shirley assured us that it actually wasn't.

"Back then, a lot of us kids got married just out of high school, or even while we were still in school," she said. "It's not like I was pregnant or anything; we just really wanted to get married."

The Young Married Couple

The young couple tied the knot in Las Vegas, Nevada, in November 1955. There was just one little problem: under the laws at the time, Shirley could get married only as long as she had written parental permission, which she received, and as long as H.L. was 21 years old, which he wasn't, at least not quite. However, they had a cousin who was a policeman in Fullerton, and he believed he could help them get married. The couple stayed with him on their way out to Las Vegas, and he agreed to come along with them to help them tie the knot.

The cousin, J.D., went to the local police station and asked the police chief if he could borrow a typewriter. The chief said yes, and J.D. used the typewriter to change the date of birth on H.L.'s driver's license to make him a year older. That should have taken care of things. However, when they went to the clerk, a woman who, according to Shirley, wore eyeglasses about half an inch thick, she noticed that the driver's license looked a little funny.

"Has this driver's license been altered?" the clerk asked the three youngsters.

"Not to our knowledge," they all answered.

And that settled things. Shirley and H.L. got married.

Although he was not much more than a boy at age 20, H.L. was prepared to do whatever was needed to support his new wife. At first, he decided that he wanted to have a job near home, and one of his cousins helped him find employment at a service station in nearby Fullerton, California.

Meanwhile, Shirley, determined to complete her education, enrolled in high school in Fullerton. Then, in December of that same year, H.L.'s uncle in Oklahoma called to say that he'd found a good job for him at the Spartan Trailers company, a travel trailer manufacturing firm in Tulsa. So, during Christmas break, the couple loaded all of their possessions into their 1955 Chevrolet and moved to begin a new life in Oklahoma.

Not long after arriving, Shirley enrolled in Beggs High School in the nearby town of Beggs, Oklahoma, to finish her education (which is why she completed only part of her twelfth-grade school year at Mount Whitney High in California). Of course, going to school also helped Shirley make new friends quickly. With that and a new husband who had a good job, life seemed very sweet indeed.

CHAPTER 2

Married to a
RACER *(1956–1960)*

Here's the 1955 Chevy hardtop owned by Shirley and H.L. Shahan shortly after the accident that wrecked the car and nearly killed her.

With his mechanical skill and lots of friends, H.L. got the car back on the road.

The couple soon decided to trade it in for a newer model. (Photo Courtesy Shirley Shahan)

It was now January 1956, and Shirley and H.L. were comfortably ensconced in Beggs, Oklahoma. Thanks to the kindness of one of his uncles, H.L. had a good job working at Spartan Trailers, which was a small company that manufactured travel trailers similar to those built by the Airstream company. The couple lived with H.L.'s grandmother, and most days H.L. went to work while Shirley went to high school. Things were going fine.

It was certainly a great time to be young and alive. Elvis Presley was releasing one hit record after another, including "Hound Dog," "Heartbreak Hotel," "Love me Tender," and "I Want You, I Need You, I Love You." Meanwhile, Bill Haley and the Comets were still "Rocking Around the Clock," with their year-old hit, and the Platters were singing about "The Great Pretender" while Carl Perkins tried to protect his "Blue Suede Shoes." The flamboyant Little Richard had a big hit with "Long Tall Sally." It was a fabulous era to be a part of.

It was also a time of classic television shows. The top-rated TV show that fall season was *I Love Lucy*, followed close behind by *The Ed Sullivan Show*. Another popular show, the *General Electric Theater*, was hosted by future US president Ronald Reagan. Meanwhile, folks could also try to match wits with contestants while watching the hit game show *The $64,000 Question*.

The top-grossing movie in the theaters that year was *The Ten Commandments* starring the inimitable Charlton Heston as Moses, but most teenagers were more interested in seeing the blockbuster film *Giant* starring the incredibly popular young actor James Dean, a handsome young rebel who sadly was killed in a car accident shortly before the film's release.

A Serious Accident

Overall, things were going well. But early on during her new life in Oklahoma, Shirley was involved in a serious car accident in which she could have been killed. In March 1956, Shirley wanted to use the family car, so H.L. agreed to drive into work with his uncle. To accomplish this, the couple first had to drive over to his uncle's house to drop off H.L. so that Shirley could have the car for the day.

On the way to H.L's uncle's home, H.L. and Shirley were motoring down the road in their '55 Chevy with H.L. at the wheel. He began to pass a slower car that had no brake lights and perhaps even no turn signals. All of a sudden, the other driver turned directly in front of them. Apparently, he had decided to turn left into a private driveway. With the quick reflexes of an experienced racer, H.L. spun the wheel to get back into his lane, but in doing so, he clipped the other car's rear fender. This was just enough to cause his own car to go into an uncontrolled sideways skid.

The force of the skid threw Shirley from the car. Most cars didn't have seat belts back then, and even when they did, most people didn't bother to wear them anyway. Shirley found herself rolling down the highway, over and over and over again. She still recalls wondering when she was going to stop and if she would be alive when she did. Thankfully, she survived, but she was cut, bleeding, and heavily bruised from head to toe, and her beautiful hair was coming out in clumps.

As H.L. relayed to automotive historian and author Bob McClurg some years later, "When I picked her up, she was still rolling. There was blood everywhere. We couldn't get back into the car because the doors wouldn't open. I mean, it scared me to death. But other than being badly bruised up, Shirley didn't get any broken bones or anything, thank goodness. She was really lucky."

The '55 Chevy was banged up too, but they were able to get it fixed.

It's surprising but true that this, the worst car accident in Shirley's life, happened on a rural road in the family car, not at the racetrack. It is perhaps not surprising that Shirley's worst car accident happened when she wasn't behind the wheel. With her razor-sharp reflexes, she may have avoided the crash entirely.

Back in California with a Hot Chevy

That March, Shirley found out she was pregnant with her first child. It was happy news for the young couple, but it was followed in May by some surprising and not so happy news: H.L. was getting laid

For 1956, Chevrolet offered a Power Pack option on its revolutionary 265-ci V-8. H.L. decided he wanted to have one, so he and Shirley traded in their 1955 Chevrolet for a 1956 Chevrolet Delray two-door—she always called it a coupe. Note the sign for Jack Epperson Roofing in the background. (Photo Courtesy Shirley Shahan)

off from his job at Spartan Trailers. There was little work in the area, so the couple turned to her parents for help.

Thankfully, Shirley's dad offered H.L. a job at the Epperson Roofing Company. The couple remained in Oklahoma long enough for Shirley to graduate from high school and then headed West, where H.L. began working for his father-in-law. Of course, the couple also needed a place to live. It so happened that Mr. Epperson owned a small house that Shirley and H.L. rented for $40 a month.

Now reestablished in California, Shirley and H.L. were in agreement about the need for them to purchase a new car, rather than a used one. A new high-performance version of the Chevy 265 V-8 engine had been released, and H.L. wanted it. So, the couple traded the '55 Chevy for a new '56 model.

Here's H.L. and Shirley's new 1956 Chevy Delray with the hubcaps pulled off for racing. The small trophy is the one H.L. won the first time he took it to the track. (Photo Courtesy Shirley Shahan)

In the end, the couple bought a brand-new '56 Chevrolet Delray coupe. The choice of a Delray model was a smart, well-reasoned decision because the Delray was a 210-series two-door sedan. Shirley always called it a coupe, which meant that it was just about the most lightweight of the new Chevrolet models and thus a more competitive race car.

Although the fancier Chevy Bel Air was more attractive and very popular, it weighed more than the Delray and was a lot more expensive. With a base price of $2,176, a Bel Air hardtop was $205 more than the Delray's $1,971 base price (about 10 percent more expensive).

A Delray series meant that the new car was fitted with much fancier interior trim, such as the Bel Air hardtops that everyone was so wild about. However, it was the weight difference that decided the matter in H.L.'s mind; the Delray two-door sedan had a base weight of 3,172 pounds, while the Bel Air two-door hardtop weighed 3,222 pounds in base form. That 50-pound weight difference meant that, all other things being equal, the Delray would be the faster car.

The reason that the car's weight was so important to Shirley and H.L. was because their '56 Chevy wasn't going to be just a family car; it would also be put into service as their race car. They were young and wanted to have fun, and for both of them that meant racing, specifically drag racing at the local National Hot Rod Association (NHRA) racetrack.

The other big reason for buying the '56 Chevy was because it could be ordered with Chevy's ingenious small-block V-8 engine, which displaced 265 ci and was rated at 162 hp when ordered with the standard 3-speed manual transmission. The same engine actually offered more power (170 hp) when ordered with the optional Powerglide transmission. However, H.L. knew that the miserable 2-speed Powerglide gearbox was simply no good for racing because it lost too much power and acceleration to slippage. In fact, there was a joke saying that racers used to repeat back then: "You slip and slide with Powerglide."

Shirley and H.L. ordered their new car with the standard 3-speed manual transmission and the Power Pack engine. With a 4-barrel carburetor, it pumped out an invigorating 205 hp. That was a good starting point, but naturally, H.L. soon went to work to get more oomph out of it.

It's interesting that both Shirley and H.L. were interested mainly in drag racing. But then again, they'd both been raised in the same area, and the kids around Visalia all seemed to love drag racing the most.

H.L. planned to drive the new Chevy to work during the week, and together they planned to drive it to the racetracks on the weekends. After H.L. set up the car for the strip, they raced it there.

At some point, H.L. installed a new dual-quad intake manifold with two 4-barrel carburetors on the Chevy V-8. He had Doug Thorley, the man behind Headers by Doug and later Doug Thorley Headers, install a set of custom header pipes too. While we don't know exactly how much horsepower the little Delray was pushing out after that, H.L.'s tuning skills probably got a lot more than the standard 205 hp. With dual-quads and headers, it wouldn't be hard to figure that the Chevy was pumping out close to 250 hp or even more.

In any event, buying that Chevy was a smart move. H.L. and Shirley knew that they'd made the right choice of cars when H.L. won a trophy with it the very first time he raced it, which was at the Madera, California, racetrack. They had taken delivery of the new car on a Thursday and brought it to the racetrack that Sunday.

The Madera officials put the car in the C/Gas category. H.L.'s friend Buster McGaha warned him, "You can't run in that class, those cars run too fast."

Buster suggested that H.L. run in the D/Gas class. However, H.L. surprised the doubters when he blew off everybody's doors.

"I knew then I had bought the right car," he said later, with a broad grin.

H.L. Shahan knew he'd bought the right car when he won a race the very first time he took it to the Madera, California, racetrack. The couple took delivery of the new car on a Thursday and raced it that Sunday, when H.L. won his first trophy with it. H.L.'s dad chewed him out for racing with a brand-new car, but H.L. didn't care. (Photo Courtesy Shirley Shahan)

H.L. later relayed that his dad chewed him out for racing with a brand-new car. In those days, it was customary to break in a new engine gradually over the course of a few weeks and maybe 1,000 miles by driving it slowly, at varying speeds, and never accelerating flat out until the car had a few thousand on the clock. So, what H.L. did was considered reckless; he could have worn out the engine prematurely. However, he didn't care. If the engine wore out, he'd just rebuild it.

Shirley recalled, "Oh yes, we won several races with that car. We used to win all the time around the valley here. It was a fast car."

Even today, Shirley has fond memories of that '56 Chevy but for a different reason; the first time she raced it herself, which was also at Madera, she was visibly pregnant with her daughter. So, when little Janet Sue Shahan was born on December 5, 1956, in Visalia, she was already a veteran racer.

That '56 Chevy Delray was not only quick off the line but it also had a decent top speed for a car that was spec'd out and geared for drag racing. There was a 100-mph club at the track in Visalia for those whose cars were certified to have topped the century mark on the track. Shirley took the new Chevy and ran it up to 101 mph, so she was able to get in the club. In fact, for a long time Shirley was the only female member in the 100-mph club.

H.L. and a few friends purchased this rail dragster to fix up.

Known at this point as *Gear Eater*, it had a distinctly amateur, home-built look to it.

Note the Swiss-cheesed frame rails and straight-pipe headers. (Photo Courtesy Shirley Shahan)

A Working Mom

Along the way, Shirley found time to continue her education by attending the Whittier Business College.

"I went to Whittier College to learn IBM, and what I learned there helped me to get a really good job with the Southern California Gas Company, which is where I worked for many years in their Visalia office," she recalled.

However, working for the gas company almost didn't happen. In 1957, Shirley accepted a job offer working for a collection agency, and as luck would have it, right after accepting that job, she received a call from the Southern California Gas Company, where she'd applied as well. Being young and inexperienced, Shirley turned down the Southern California Gas Company job, which was the better job by far, because the collection agency had offered first.

"That was a big mistake!" she said recently.

Thankfully, the gas company called again a week later, and this time she took the job. Southern California Gas was a big company with a lot of opportunities for growth, so it was great that she was able to get a job there. She began her career with Southern California Gas in August 1957. The starting pay of $1.85 per hour doesn't sound like much today, but it was a fairly decent pay rate back then. In addition, the company offered benefits, such as health insurance, a retirement pension, and, later on, stock options.

Because Shirley's husband was an amateur racer, her choice of how the family spent its weekends was simple: If she wanted to see her husband, she had better go to the racetrack because that was where he'd be. Of course, if the family wanted to be together, that meant bringing along the kids as well. They didn't mind; the kids loved watching the racing and seeing dad at the wheel. In addition, their mom drove the race car from time to time, which was a real treat for the kids to see.

The Vapor Trailers and a Surprising Discovery

Around 1956 or 1957, H.L. bought a rail dragster named *Strip Tease* in partnership with Bob Brown, Bill Roeben, Larry Roady, and Ed McCulloch. After purchasing *Strip Tease*, there were many, many hours spent at Bill Roeben's shop, working on the Shahan's 1958 *Red-N-Ready*, Bill's 1958 Impala, or the dragster. Revamping the dragster involved many alterations, including those to the engine, roll bar, and chassis.

"Back then, you could buy a new Duntov cam over the counter at Gene Ford Chevrolet for about $20," Shirley said. "I was the gopher girl; whenever a part had to be bought, it was me who went to get it. I also supplied their hunger needs with Taylors Hot Dogs (six for $1) or Roma's pizza ($2 each) along with beer.

"One afternoon, the guys were thirsty and wanted some beer. I said I'd try and get some. I went to my local grocery store, I had my daughter

The rail dragster **Gear Eater** *was transformed into this sharp-looking and very professional dragster known as* **Strip Tease.** *H.L. and Ed McCulloch both raced this machine at tracks around Southern California back in the day. Notice the trophy sitting atop the engine. (Photo Courtesy Shirley Shahan)*

RACING *the Family Car*

Below is a Q&A with author Patrick Foster and Shirley Shahan.

Author: Tell us about that 1956 Chevy you bought. You won some races with it. What was it like racing the family car?

Shirley: Well, you know, we were just average people. We didn't have a lot of money, so we drove it to work every day. We had street tires, and when we got to the track, we'd put on the racing tires and unbutton the headers and race. We usually raced at the Bakersfield track the first Sunday of the month, then at Madera on the second Sunday, and at Visalia the third Sunday. The fourth Sunday was for whatever was running; [it was] usually Fremont, Santa Maria, or maybe Half Moon Bay. We raced them all.

Author: After that 1956 Chevy came the 1958 Chevy with the 315-hp 348 V-8?

Shirley: Yes, that was another car we raced, and I also drove it to work every day. H.L. and I named that car *Red-N-Ready*, by the way. It was a real beauty, a bright red two-door. Once we got that car, we started branching out a little further. We went to Santa Maria, Half Moon Bay, Lodi, and Fremont. We ran that car in the Stock Eliminator class.

After the '56 Chevy came a hot 1958 Chevy Biscayne hardtop. Equipped with the new Chevy 348-ci V-8 engine, it was fast right from the factory. Then, H.L. worked his magic on it to squeeze a bit more juice out of it. Here we see Shirley Shahan and racer Jack Boudakian at the track with recently earned trophies. Both of them won in their class. By this point, Shirley was well-known in local racing circles as a fast and tough competitor. (Photo Courtesy Shirley Shahan)

Both Shirley and H.L. raced the Strip Tease *rail job.*

The transformation from an ugly, homebuilt machine to this sharp, glamorous racer is testimony to the skills of H.L. and his friends.

(Photo Courtesy Shirley Shahan)

Author: We heard you didn't race it much yourself during the 1958 season.

Shirley: That's true. H.L. ended up doing most of the racing that year because I was pregnant with Steven, and after a few months, I couldn't fit behind the wheel!

Author: However, you did race it at the very first March Meet in Bakersfield in 1959, correct? That's the oldest and almost the largest race in California, isn't it?

Shirley: Yes, it is. Back then, it was known as the Bakersfield Fuel & Gas Championships, and I won there at the first race, driving our '58 Chevy in the A/Stock class. But believe it or not, there wasn't any prize money in those days. I think we won a plaque, a T-shirt, and two cases of beer. You didn't race for the money back then; it was just for fun. [Author: And to satisfy that competitive edge, we'll guess.]

Author: Back then, you were racing against the best racers that California had to offer at the time, which is saying a lot.

Shirley: Well, there were a lot of really good drivers back then, yes.

Author: Did you ever drive any other type of dragster?

Shirley: Oh, yes! We also ran a rail dragster with none other than Ed "the Ace" McCulloch. It was a car we called the *Strip Tease*. It was a B/Gas Dragster. The team ran it for about two years. In 1958, I drove the rail at Santa Maria and went about 140 mph.

Come to think of it, H.L. and I also raced boats during the same time we were drag racing. However, I only drove the drag boat a few times. The guy who normally drove it got hit by lightning, and it killed him.

Author: Shirley, we're curious, do you ever go back to the old Bakersfield racetrack?

Shirley: Yes, I do occasionally go there, with my husband, Ken, but not as much as we used to. Bakersfield, along with Pomona, is one of the oldest tracks still in existence, and it has far and away the most history in California. But it's gotten so big and commercial over the years that nowadays you need a golf cart just to get around.

Author: What other tracks did you race at?

Shirley: Oh, a great many. We raced at Visalia, Dinuba, Freemont, Madera, Anna Maria, and Half Moon Bay, just to name a few.

Here we see another shot of **Strip Tease,** *the co-owned rail car, at the track. Even by today's standards it's a sharp-looking machine. Its current location is unknown. (Photo Courtesy Shirley Shahan)*

Janet with me, and bought a couple of six packs—no questions asked. I must have been maybe 18, and the drinking age was 21. Later, the guys wanted some more. I didn't want to go to the same store, so I went to Hayden's Liquor Store, [which was] well-known in our town. As luck would have it, Mr. Hayden himself was there, and when I told him I wanted a six pack, he told me I better get myself out of there or he was going to call my mom! See, he knew my family. How embarrassing!"

Back then, H.L. belonged to a big car club in Visalia known as the Vapor Trailers. It's a legendary organization that still exists today and actually holds the title of the NHRA's longest active car club. The club raced once a month throughout most of the year.

When the Vapor Trailers asked H.L. to serve as a flag starter man, it created a problem. Being the flag starter wouldn't allow H.L. time to also race; he could do one or the other but not both. Shirley was more than willing to serve in his place as the flag lady, but she wasn't allowed to because this person was required to be a member of the club and the club rules at the time clearly stated that no women were allowed membership. Believe it or not, we're told that the same rule applies today.

So, the couple decided to let Shirley drive. At least they wouldn't lose a weekend of racing. Who knows—she might do okay. She'd already tried it a few times, and H.L. had realized that she was pretty good at it. However, what happened next surprised even him.

Years later, H.L. relayed the story to Bob McClurg:

"We had a great big car club, and we raced at Visalia Airport once a month," he said. "I was the official flagman, so every time I went to go race, I had to find somebody to flag for me. One weekend [when I couldn't find anyone to flag for me], I put [Shirley] in the car, and that was it. She became the full-time driver."

There was a simple reason why Shirley became the full-time driver. It turned out she did better than okay behind the wheel. In fact, Shirley consistently set better times than H.L. had done with the same car. Apparently, those early days of drag racing in her family's Studebaker pickup had honed Shirley's reflexes to a very fine point. Well, it was that plus her natural competitiveness and athletic ability.

"The upper-body strength that I had gained from loading my dad's roofing truck, as well as the sports I played in school, really benefited me when shifting gears," Shirley said.

She had strong arms and upper-body strength, which were just the things needed to control a drag car.

Before long, Shirley was racing every weekend at tracks all across the San Joaquin Valley, in Visalia, Bakersfield, Madera, among others. As she did so, Shirley and H.L. realized that there were some other tangible benefits to her being behind the wheel, rather than him.

"We not only found out that I could drive as well as if not better than H.L. but that when I drove, we received a lot more attention from the crowd," Shirley said.

As she piloted the hot Chevy in race after race, she quickly learned her craft as a competitive driver.

H.L. and Shirley campaigned their 1956 Chevrolet Delray with a decent amount of success through early 1958, when they decided to buy a brand-new 1958 Chevy coupe. It was equipped with Chevy's latest engineering masterpiece: the hot new 348-ci small-block V-8 engine that was pushing out a healthy 315 hp in stock form. They picked a bright red color for their new car, so they named the car *Red-N-Ready*. This latest Chevy coupe proved to be another winner for the Shahans.

In 1958, Shirley and H.L. moved into a rental house closer to town. The rent there was $60 a month, but the home had a garage. They both appreciated the garage because prior to this they had to work on their car outside. Yes, Shirley did a lot of wrenching back then.

"A lot of people ask me, 'Did you work on the cars back then?' And the answer is yes, quite a bit," Shirley said. "For example, I remember once H.L. had told me in the morning before leaving for work that he was going to do something major on our '58 Chevy, so I decided to surprise him by getting a lot of the hard stuff done for him. When he came home from work that evening, I had already pulled off the intake manifold and was hard at work removing the heads.

"Now, I never did any of the tuning, I left that to H.L. because he was a perfectionist. But I had the advantage of having smaller hands, so I was able to get into a lot of small spaces where he couldn't. Normally at the drag strip, I would gap and change plugs, check tire pressure, or change tires. If we were running fuel, which we sometimes did later [in the 1960s], I would also do the fuel mix."

As mentioned, Shirley didn't get to race as much as she wanted to during the 1958 season because she was pregnant and couldn't fit behind the wheel of their Chevy. So, H.L. returned to driving, and he proved he was a pretty good driver in his own right.

In a 2004 interview with Bob McClurg, H.L. relayed a story about one particular race:

"Remember Tom Sturm?" H.L. asked. "He had a Chevy with a 4-speed, while ours was a 3-speed on the column, [and we were racing and] I was ahead of him in second gear, but when he put that thing in third gear, he drove right by me, and I figured that it was all over. Then, I put it into high gear, and I drove by him. He followed me back to the pits and said, 'You're cheating!' I said. 'No, I'm not cheating,' and he's all jumping up and down and stuff. After I got to know him, I found out that he was the one who was cheating. He had that thing stroked, had headers on it, and all that stuff, and I beat him with a stocker!"

And the Winner Is . . .

At the time, H.L. was working as a mechanic at a local Chrysler and Pontiac dealership, and he and Shirley continued racing on the weekends. Somewhere during this period was when Shirley returned to the wheel and began driving full time.

In 1959, Shirley and H.L. decided to race *Red-N-Ready* at the very first March Meet ever held at the Famoso Raceway track near Bakersfield, California. The March Meet is an independent drag race held at Famoso, which is actually located in the little town of McFarland, about 10 miles north of Bakersfield.

The Meet began in 1959 under the sanction of the Smokers Car Club and initially was known as the U.S. Fuel & Gas Championships. However, it soon was given the March Meet nickname because it was easier to remember and that was when it was held. Eventually, the event became officially designated as the March Meet after the Smokers Car Club sold the rights to the U.S. Fuel & Gas Championships name.

To add a bit of grit and controversy to the race, the first March Meet was also advertised as an East-versus-West showdown. The best California drag racers were taking on the infamous Floridian Don Garlits, who had been credited with record speeds that some people in the California racing crowd found a little dubious.

So, at the inaugural March Meet in 1959, Shirley ran the *Red-N-Ready* 1958 Super Stock Chevrolet in the A/Stock class. In a full day of competition that shocked and surprised the drag racing world, Shirley won, which made her the first woman ever to win a sanctioned NHRA event. Because it was also the very first March Meet, her victory was especially sweet because it occupies the first mention in the Meet record books, not to mention a prominent place in NHRA history.

To win her place in the record books, Shirley ended up outracing 40 male drivers. The most amazing thing about it was the quality of the competition. Among those 40 men were top-notch professionals, guys who went on to become legends in the world of drag racing, including "Dyno Don" Nicholson, Hayden Proffitt, Don Garlitts, Tom Sturm, and Arlen Vanke, each of whom later became good friends of Shirley and H.L.

At the races, Shirley and H.L.'s daughter Janet poses in front of the family car: a red-hot 1958 Chevy Biscayne with a 348-ci V-8. Notice the hubcaps have been pulled off. It's race day! (Photo Courtesy Shirley Shahan)

It was a highly contentious debate that went on for years and continued on throughout the 1960s, despite that era being one of enormous social change, and it raged for many years afterward. There are probably still a good number of die-hard holdouts that feel a woman's place is in the kitchen. Of course, the simple answer to it all is to point to the number of women in drag racing who have been successful; if they weren't successful, there would be no argument. Shirley had to bear the brunt of it because she was the first to win a big event.

"It's true that some men didn't like being beaten by a female," Shirley said. "They usually were shocked [and] then angry."

One big reason for everyone's surprise at her win, besides the fact that she was a woman driver at a time when there weren't many, was that she was also still relatively unknown in the world of drag racing.

"We had never really raced against any of the Los Angeles crowd until that race," Shirley said. "I know that Tom Sturm, Arlen Vanke, Don Nicholson, and Hayden Proffitt were all at that meet, although I didn't know any of them personally at the time. But my being there ended up being a real eye-opener for quite a lot of people.

"You see, having me driving locally at tracks around the San Joaquin Valley was no longer really a novelty by that point because most people who went to the races had gotten used to seeing me race at the local tracks. But when H.L. and I began to venture further out to the more distant tracks, well, things there were different. Most people weren't familiar with me yet, and they were surprised to see a woman behind the wheel. And when I won, I quickly found out that some of the men really didn't like being beaten by a female. It was a little surprising."

For her part, Shirley never felt she was a "women's libber" as the phrase went back in the 1960s, despite her pioneering wins.

"For one thing, I was doing all this stuff about five years before the women's liberation movement really came on strong," she said.

As Shirley always pointed out, though, she didn't actually outrace each and every one of those gentlemen. In big drag racing events, the winner is determined by a process of elimination. To use a hypothetical example, if Dyno Don Nicholson out-drags Arlen Vanke and Tom Sturm at a particular meet and then gets beaten by Shirley Shahan at the same meet, she actually only raced against one of the drivers, even though it counts as if she raced them all because she beat the guy who had beat the others.

However, one needs to remember today that this all happened in the 1950s, and at the time, the question of whether or not women drivers should even be allowed in drag racing was generally a good way to get into a heated argument. Some male drivers contended that women were simply incapable of driving a high-performance car the way it was meant to be driven (i.e., a man's idea of the proper way).

          SHIRLEY SHAHAN *The Drag-On Lady*

CAROL COX

One woman race driver who isn't nearly as well-known as she should be is Carol Cox. The Whittier, California, home-maker became the first woman ever to win a trophy of any kind at an NHRA national event.

While most people know that Shirley Shahan won the Stock Eliminator title at the 1966 Winternationals and in the process became the first woman ever to win an NHRA national event, very few people are aware that four years earlier at the Big Go West, Carol Cox won her class, S/SA, a feat that she repeated months later on an even bigger stage, at the big Nationals event in Indianapolis.

Like Shirley, Carol Cox was a pioneer in the field of women drag racers.

In any event, Shirley wasn't really interested in breaking glass ceilings because she believed that in her world, at least, they didn't really exist. Shirley's main interest, her driving passion so to speak, was to break records, to beat the other guy, to take home the trophy; it was not to change the world. She had already been driving for years and no one had stopped her then nor was she about to let anyone stop her now. She was competitive in more ways than one.

Getting Hassled

Racing with the Vapor Trailers was good fun, and there weren't too many hard feelings from guys who were beat by Shirley; they pretty much were all friends. However, as she and H.L. traveled around the state to race at different tracks, they often ran against people they didn't know. Sometimes, when Shirley won, there were bitter complaints from the losers.

The NHRA rules at the time provided for handicaps whenever cars from different classes raced against each other. Some drivers loudly complained that Shirley won because the handicap had favored her. That, of course, was nonsense. The handicap rules had been set down on paper years earlier, and they didn't "favor" anyone. In fact, they were in place to make things as equal as possible. However, some hard heads just didn't want to hear about that; they were sore because they'd lost to a girl, and they thought that complaining about it would make it appear as if they had been cheated out of winning a race, rather than the truth, which was that they had

been outdriven.

"I remember a time in 1960 when I won my class, and then when I came back to the pits, I found out that one of the other drivers had formally protested the win," Shirley said. "In those days, all it took to file a protest and have the winner's car subjected to a teardown was $50. When that happened, the engine had to be torn down to see if any 'tricks' had been done to make it more competitive, and the track officials went through the rest of the car as well, just to make sure it was all legal and operating under the official track rules. Well, this fella ended up protesting me, and when I stepped out of the car, the guy's mouth dropped wide open because he could see that I was seven months pregnant. I guess that really shocked him!"

The thought of being beaten by a pregnant woman must have been especially appalling to him. In any event, they did the requested inspection, and Shirley's car was, of course, found to be legal, so the win stood.

Shirley was not alone in getting hassled by a few irate losing drivers. Carol Cox was routinely protested by male drivers who couldn't believe that a woman could actually beat them in a race. With the low cost to protest, it was easy enough for someone to cause trouble, and let's face it, there are a lot of spoilsports in the world, even today.

Anyway, things were different back then; it was another world, really. Today, it almost seems impossible, but just one year before Cox's break-through win, women weren't even allowed to compete at NHRA national events. They had been

---

competing at local tracks for years prior to this, often in a Powder Puff class, but for a long time, women weren't allowed to drive in a national event. In a way, this was merely a reflection of the times. Reportedly in 1961, a woman couldn't get a credit card in her own name if she were single, and for a married woman to get one, she had to have her husband agree to cosign for it. Women couldn't even serve on juries.

Of course, it wasn't always Shirley at the wheel, sometimes she needed an extended breather from racing. Midway through 1960, she had to take a break from racing for a while because, as she later told a reporter, "I was busy having a baby, or something."

On May 20, 1960, Shirley gave birth to her second child; it was a boy named Steven Wayne Shahan.

It was no problem for Shirley to walk away from racing for a spell. H.L. was a really good driver in his own right, so he took over the driving chores while Shirley stayed home with the new baby. In 1960, H.L. was runner-up in the S/S class in the second annual March Meet (a.k.a. Bakersfield Fuel & Gas Meet).

Here's a quick story to illustrate the special camaraderie among the women drag racers and how free and easy things were back in the day at those old racetracks. Shirley had just completed her last run for the day at the Pomona drag strip, and she was the winner. She was driving on the return road, coming around the track to get up to the starting line. The fans were standing up and cheering for her when another well-known lady racer, Paula Murphy, came out to stop her and handed a nice cold beer over to Shirley.

"And then it finally hit me," Shirley said. "Maybe I did something here."

"I never saw myself as some sort of female pioneer," she said. "I just loved to go racing and have fun. I had been racing against the guys for a long time before winning the Winternationals, and I wasn't the only woman doing it, either."

Imagine something like that happening at today's tightly restricted and rule-enforced drag strips!

Shirley remains modest about her wins.

"I never saw myself as some sort of female pioneer," she said. "I just loved to go racing and have fun. I had been racing against the guys for a long time before winning the Winternationals, and I wasn't the only woman doing it, either. There were others. The guys always respected me, so I didn't think much about it."

CHAPTER 3

A Growing REPUTATION *(1961–1964)*

When the Southern California Gas Company finally realized that it had a real celebrity working in its offices, it decided to let the rest of the world know as well.

The company arranged for a promotional photo shoot to highlight Shirley Shahan and her career. This was done in 1963. (Photo Courtesy Southern California Gas Company)

In some ways, you could say that the early 1960s were a blissful time for Americans. The Korean War was over, and the Vietnam War had not yet begun. Rock and roll music was firmly established, and some of the greatest songs of all time were released in 1960: Chubby Checker's "The Twist" was a mega-hit, and everyone loved the hit single "Itsy Bitsy Teenie Weenie Yellow Polka Dot Bikini" by Brian Hyland. Bobby Darin was singing his big hit "Mack the Knife," and the King, Elvis Presley, had a string of hits that included "It's Now or Never" and "Are you Lonesome Tonight."

In 1961, the great Patsy Cline sang "'I Fall to Pieces" and "Crazy," Ricky Nelson had two big hits with "Travelin' Man" and "Hello Marylou," while the Tokens introduced one of the most beloved songs of the century with "The Lion Sleeps Tonight."

In other ways, things were still tense. The Soviet Union was flexing its muscles, the Cold War seemed ready to flare up into nuclear war at any moment, and the horror of that hung over everyone.

Taking a Breather

Shirley's extended breather from racing lasted into 1961, as she gave birth to her third child,

Robert. Her interest in racing never wavered, however. She still raced whenever she could fit it between her duties as a housewife and mom. In the meantime, H.L. did most of the racing, although they both knew it would only be a matter of time before Shirley got behind the wheel of a drag racer on a regular basis again.

The fact was that Shirley was a real crowd favorite, and she was the faster driver of the two. By 1962, she felt that she was ready to get back to racing, at least on a part-time basis. She often found herself winning races while steadily adding more people to her growing fan base. Her driving skills hadn't waned.

As time went on, Shirley continued to learn the ropes of being a drag racer. She learned the best way to launch off the line, when to shift, and when not to, all while gaining a lot more of the valuable driving experiences that go to making a person a more successful competitor in drag racing.

Shirley also learned how to tell by ear when the engine had reached its peak power so that she could shift at precisely the right time and everything else that she needed to learn to become a competitive drag racer.

She began winning more and more races, to the continuing surprise (and sometimes outright anger) of some of the other racers. Not surprisingly, all of the angry ones happened to be men. The crowds, on the other hand, loved to see her win. By that point, Shirley and H.L. were attracting a big following of fans wherever they raced. They loved the idea of a husband-and-wife drag racing couple.

The reputation of the good-looking young woman who could outdrag the boys continued to grow. Shirley and H.L. raced at all of the local West Coast tracks that they could, including Bakersfield, Fremont, Madera, Santa Maria, and Half Moon Bay. By the early 1960s, Shirley was considered a well-established semi-professional racer, and she steadily advanced her career. Many fans considered Shirley to be someone to watch, even at that point, they felt she was destined to be a star.

Shirley and her husband were together for every race. Well, with just one car in the family, it was either go racing or stay home, and both of them preferred to go racing.

It wasn't always easy. After all, with the birth of

Shirley's daughter Janet and son Steve pose for a photo in the family home in Visalia, California, with the family dog Duke, who used to pull the kids around the garage on a creeper. Notice the bookcase of racing trophies behind them. Those were earned by Shirley and H.L. in the early days. Shirley said that the bookcase was purchased with S&H Green Stamps. Do you remember those? (Photo Courtesy Shirley Shahan)

her second son, Robert (Bobby), in May 1961, Shirley was now the mother of three young children. Robert Dale Shahan was named after their friends Bob Brown and Edwin Dale McCulloch. Shirley now had three kids to raise, a household to run, plus cooking, cleaning, and grocery shopping, not to mention holding down a job from 1961 to 1963 at the Electronic Business Service (EBS) where, she said, "I was kind of their Girl Friday." Initially, this was in addition to her day job at Southern California Gas, but in time, she went to work for EBS full time because the gas company had a rule that ladies couldn't work past the seventh month of their pregnancy.

The EBS job was a good one, and the people who ran it liked her, but after three years, she decided that she wanted to just go back to work for the Southern California Gas Company. She could see that it offered her much better opportunities in the long term. EBS management wanted her to stay on with them and even offered her shares of stock in

Here Shirley is seen at EBS. This was a promotional shot to show off the company's new IBM computers, which were run via punch cards. The two towers next to Shirley are file boxes filled with IBM punch cards. At the time, Shirley was a keypunch operator there. (Photo Courtesy Shirley Shahan)

the company if she would stay, but Shirley's mind was made up. She left to return to the gas company.

"It was a good thing I did because about five years after I left there, the EBS company went out of business," Shirley said.

It was all part of a plan, a goal that Shirley and H.L. were working toward.

"H.L. and I had talked it over, and we were working for the day when he could open up his own racing shop, and then I would retire from racing," Shirley said. "But in the end, it didn't work out quite that way for a variety of reasons."

Precision Automotive

As Shirley recalled, it was right around that time that H.L. quit his job as a dealership mechanic to become a partner in a new company called Precision Automotive. It was a high-performance shop located at 316 E. Kern St. in Tulare. It was set up as a partnership between H.L. and a man named Ed Parker.

H.L. had been working for the local Pontiac/Chrysler dealer for a while, but he was always on the lookout for an opportunity to make more money and to be able to work closer to the racing world. To H.L., this new opportunity looked like the way to accomplish just that.

Ed Parker had owned a nice repair shop with another man, but he and his business partner had a falling out and had recently split up. So, after a round of discussions, Parker and H.L. teamed up to open Precision Automotive. The high-performance shop specialized in precision tune-ups for Super Stock race cars to help drivers get more performance out of their cars. H.L. figured that his reputation as an excellent mechanic in the drag racing world should attract more than a few of the local racers and hot rodders. In addition, the business serviced regular cars, doing tune-ups and regular maintenance.

However, since it was a new business, the two men realized that money would probably be tight for a while. Both H.L. and Ed Parker knew that, financially speaking, it was important that they not over-extend themselves, so they agreed to limit their weekly pay initially to just $50 each, and that wasn't very much money even back then, not for a business owner anyway.

To help make ends meet before the baby was born, Shirley had taken on that part-time job working nights at EBS. For a time, that was in addition to her day job at Southern California Gas, raising a family, keeping house, and occasionally racing cars. When she had to stop working at the gas company, she went to work for EBS full-time, then took time off to have her baby, and then returned to EBS just six weeks after that. However, as soon as she could, she returned to work at the gas company; she had come to realize that it was a better job.

From that point on, H.L. and Shirley raced under the Precision Automotive name, and they continued racing on most weekends. As the legend grew

---

H.L. Shahan and Ronnie Broadhead partnered on this 1960 Pontiac Catalina, which was quite a successful race car. With it, they were named the 1963 NHRA World C-Stock Car Champion. Note how "Engines by H.L. Shahan" is painted on the front fender. (Photo Courtesy Shirley Shahan)

of the cute little blonde lady who could outrace the men, Shirley and H.L. became known as the premier husband-and-wife racing duo in the San Joaquin Valley. Fans loved to come out to the track to see if Shirley could beat the best male and female drivers. It was around this time that doors began to open for women racers.

Shirley raced any time that she could, even in borrowed cars. In 1961, Shirley was racing a 1961 Corvette for her friend Maryls Murphy. Maryls worked at a local grocery store and couldn't get Sundays off, so Shirley picked up the Vette with a promise to have it back by 8:00 p.m., when Maryls got off work. Shirley ended up winning several trophies with the borrowed Vette.

Meanwhile, H.L.'s part-ownership in the Precision Automotive garage began to bear fruit. The shop did all sorts of repair work, but it specialized in tune-ups: the kind of real, in-depth, don't-worry-we'll-make-your-car-run-like-a-raped-ape tune-ups for which H.L. was famous. In addition, H.L. got a lot of work preparing high-performance cars for race day. H.L. and Ed Parker managed to attract a good amount of work from racers who wanted H.L. to work his magic on their rides.

"We had anywhere from five to seven drag cars

This photo shows the winning Pontiac Catalina with its Pontiac tow car parked at Bob McLaughlin Pontiac Cadillac Oldsmobile, which was the car's main sponsor. It's sad that two of the dealer's three car brands (Pontiac and Oldsmobile) are no longer built. (Photo Courtesy Shirley Shahan)

running out of that shop, and we raced them," Shirley recalled.

Two of the drivers who used Precision Automotive went on to great fame: Butch Leal, who was still an up-and-coming young man widely known as "the California Flash," and his cousin Ronnie Broadhead. Both men had their race cars tuned and prepared by H.L. at the Precision Automotive shop.

Butch Leal later reminded Shirley of a race in Bakersfield when Precision Automotive had several cars entered. In the finals, there were three cars from Precision Automotive. All three cars won their class; drivers were Shirl Greer, Butch, and Shirley.

Although it was close, Butch lost to Shirley in the Eliminator bracket. (They each won their class and then raced in the Eliminator finals of class winners.) Butch was still a youngster at the time, although he was well on his way to becoming a true legend in the world of drag racing.

As well as things were going at Precision Automotive, it wasn't enough to convince H.L. and Shirley that Shirley should retire from racing. For one thing, the business was still in the early stages and needed to run smoothly for a few years before they could feel confident enough for her to stop racing. In addition, the two of them were having too much fun racing

Sadly, there are not many photos of the Shahan's special 1963 Chevy. It was one of only 57 RPO Z11 Super Stockers that were built. (Photo Courtesy Shirley Shahan)

for Shirley to stop now. It's better to make hay while the sun shines, as the saying goes. She kept racing.

H.L. enjoyed working on cars for Butch Leal and Ronnie Broadhead. It required a lot of knowledge about racing because the two men competed in different classes. Ronnie's car, a Pontiac, competed in the Junior Stock class, while Butch competed in the Top Stock class. Both men were tickled to have H.L. on their team because everybody knew that he was a top-notch race car tuner and preparer as well as a gifted mechanic who really understood drag racing. The team showed some pretty impressive results: in 1963, with H.L.'s help, Ronnie won the NHRA Stock Car World Championship with his red-hot Pontiac.

For their part, Shirley and H.L. continued to race their well-known *Red-N-Ready* 1958 Chevy for more than five years. The car was that good, and H.L. was somehow always able to get a little bit more power out of it. Then, for the 1963 race season, the couple decided to purchase a really special new car that would become a legend: the awesome Chevrolet with the Regular Production Option (RPO) code Z11, which included the incredible Chevy 427-ci V-8. What a machine it was! Shirley loved that car.

"That was really a great car," she said. "It had the aluminum front-end sheet metal for extra lightness and balance, and it was equipped with all the best high-performance stuff right from the factory. You know, I think fewer than 60 of those Z11s were built, so we were fortunate to have had one."

Shirley's memory is correct. In fact, just 57 of the Chevy Z11 road scorchers were produced in all. Shirley would be especially fortunate if she still owned the car today because it could easily sell for $400,000 or more.

Meanwhile, H.L. had been busy. After wrenching for Ronnie and winning the NHRA Stock Car World Championship in 1963, for 1964, H.L. teamed with Ronnie's cousin Butch Leal for a while, preparing and working on Leal's Ford racer. When that job was finished, H.L. took over the mechanical preparation and maintenance of the S/S Plymouth that was driven by a young Hank Taylor, who was known in the racing world as "the Texas Whiz Kid" and who'd held several NHRA records for a spell in 1964.

Wrenching for Hank Taylor required H.L. to move to Dickinson, Texas, for a while. Taylor had bought one of Hayden Proffitt's Plymouth drag cars and needed H.L. to get it tuned and prepared for more racing. As things turned out, H.L. was down in Texas for almost a year, and Shirley visited him whenever she was racing in Texas.

The Awesome 1963 Chevrolet
RPO Z11

The Chevrolet RPO Z11 Super Stockers were built just prior to the announcement of a GM ban on factory racing in early 1963. A reported 57 examples were built, each one featuring a total of 22 lightweight components and powered by the high-performance W-series engine. The 427-ci V-8 was officially rated at 430 hp and was exclusive to this model. In other words, to get the engine, you had to buy the car.

Each car featured dual 4-barrel Carter AFB carburetors, unique Stahl headers and camshaft, 13.5:1 compression, an aluminum two-piece intake manifold, S&S cylinder heads, a reciprocating assembly that was all forged, and special cowl air induction. The body was lightened via aluminum inner fenders, bumpers, brackets, fan shroud, RC bellhousing, and exterior sheet metal. Big, ventilated metallic brakes provided tremendous stopping power. The drive axle boasted 4.56:1 gears and Positraction. The cars were equipped with a tachometer as standard equipment, along with an aluminum-case T10 4-speed transmission with specially hardened nickel gears.

Were they fast? You bet they were. In fact, the RPO Z11 Chevrolet was the first stock drag car to exceed 120 mph in a quarter-mile run.

The base price of an ordinary 1963 Impala was $2,774 F.O.B. Detroit, and the RPO Z11 option cost an extra $1,240 (almost 50 percent additional), which brought the total price to just over $4,000. That was a pile of money in those days—about the cost of a sharp new Corvette roadster.

Years later, H.L. remarked the following to writer Bob McClurg: "If I remember right, there was only 57 of those cars built. Of course, Bill Thomas was the one who got the cars for us. Butch Leal had one and Shirley and I had one. Can you imagine that, having two of those Z11 Chevrolets in a little old town like Tulare?"

On one of the trips, Shirley had a scary experience. She boarded a North American Airlines plane in Los Angeles that was heading to Houston for a race day. The pilot taxied the plane out to the far end of the runway and began to rev his engines to prepare for takeoff. All of a sudden, there was a loud explosion; Shirley had heard enough engines blow at the racetracks to know what that sound was.

As the stewardesses walked the aisles trying to calm people down, the plane quickly began to fill with smoke. Shirley could see the firetrucks and ambulances racing toward the plane, but the stewardesses wouldn't open the doors. Well, they finally did open the doors, but then they told the passengers they had to slide down the emergency ramp to get out.

"Mind you, all the ladies were wearing short skirts at that time," Shirley recalled.

In the end, one of the firetrucks put up a ladder to the door, and she climbed down from the plane that way. They transported the passengers back to the terminal in baggage carts and told them that the airline would fly in a replacement plane from Florida, which was going to take three hours. So, they had to sit and wait. The only good thing about the ordeal was that the captain of the second plane let the passengers (there were only 16 of them in all) fly in the first-class section. The 16 brave souls spent the entire trip eating, drinking, and dancing, and even the captain joined in dancing with the ladies.

Chrysler Comes Calling

By the time that H.L. came back home from his stint in Texas, representatives from the Chrysler Corporation had already begun talking to Shirley about sponsoring the couple with Shirley driving a 1965 Plymouth. Apparently, while they were eyeing Butch Leal and other racers, Chrysler had become aware of H.L., Shirley, and the undeniable popularity of the racing couple.

The story of the pretty blonde gal who could really drive sounded mighty appealing to the powers that be at Chrysler Public Relations. The popular musical duo Jan & Dean had released a hit single

"The Little Old Lady From Pasadena" during the previous June. The song was about an old lady with a "shiny red Super Stock Dodge" who out-drags all the guys in town, and it had been a huge hit. Who knows? Maybe the Chrysler guys wanted to have a little young lady do the same; on that point, I can't say for certain.

The Chrysler people formulated a plan for hiring Shirley to drive for them. She was ready to agree to it. After all, it would be a nice break for her. However, after talking it over with H.L. and Butch Leal, the three decided that the best way to do it right was for Shirley and H.L. to team up with Butch Leal and his 1965 altered-wheelbase Plymouth to form the Leal and Shahan Racing Team. Naturally, H.L. would work on preparing both Shirley and Butch's cars.

However, that was all still in the future. In the meantime, the 1964 season ended up being a fairly quiet year in Shirley's racing career because, as she said, "I was working at the Gas Company and taking care of my rapidly growing kids. I had my hands full."

Shirley match raced on weekends when she could and managed to do a limited amount of traveling.

"During 1964, I drove to L.A. to catch the red eye to Indy," she remembered. "Andy Williams, the singer, came and sat with me! During the flight, we talked, and he sang to me, told me he would leave tickets to his show at the front gate, which I didn't take advantage of, though wish I had. He always played the state fair during Labor Day. Nice man. Fun trip."

However, things were going to change very soon. The 1965 drag racing season was destined to be a lot more hectic for Shirley and H.L. Shahan as her star continued to rise.

This is another publicity shot commissioned by the Southern California Gas Company to show off Shirley's success as a drag racer.

That's the couple's super-rare 1963 Chevy Super Stocker on which she is sitting.

(Photo Courtesy Southern California Gas Company)

CHAPTER 4

The Dodge and Plymouth
YEARS (1965–1968)

In late 1964, Shirley was approached by a manager at Chrysler Corporation's racing program, who asked her if she would become a driver for them. It was a big break for her, and she gladly accepted. Here, she is with her new Plymouth Belvedere two-door sedan. (Photo Courtesy Chrysler. Chrysler is a trademark of FCA USA LLC.)

Between 1960 and the early part of 1965, H.L. Shahan worked as a mechanic for three top drag racers. That work often took him away from his family as he traveled with the teams from track to track and town to town. He was sometimes on the road more than he was at home. He no longer had as much time to spend tuning and preparing Shirley's car.

Shirley was somewhat tied down with three children at home and a husband on the road, and it was difficult to find the time to race. Without H.L. to prep the car, there wasn't much of a chance to get to the track with a race-ready car as often as she wanted. However, things were about to change for the Shahan family.

The Chrysler Deal

As word of Shirley's outstanding driving skills traveled around the drag racing circuit, good things began to happen. In late 1964, a representative from Chrysler Corporation had approached her about driving one of its race cars, specifically a new Hemi-powered Super Stock Plymouth. Earlier, the Chrysler people had approached her good friend

The honor and responsibility of being crew chief for the Drag-On Lady naturally went to H.L Shahan. It was not only because H.L. was her husband but also because he was a gifted mechanic as well as a pretty good driver in his own right. (Photo Courtesy Chrysler. Chrysler is a trademark of FCA USA LLC.)

Shirley watches H.L. use a torque wrench to work on her race car. H.L. enjoyed a great career in NHRA and AHRA racing as an expert tuner and mechanic. Depending on the location of the race and type of racing, H.L. might have to swap out rear ends, switch from gas to nitro, or switch from carburetors to fuel injection, and he had to be able to do it quickly with extreme precision. (Photo Courtesy Chrysler. Chrysler is a trademark of FCA USA LLC.)

This photo, taken at Doug's Headers shop in California, shows the young H.L. and Shirley in the early days of driving for Chrysler Corporation. Doug Thorley and H.L. were best friends, and all of Shirley's Mopars ran Doug's Headers. (Photo Courtesy Chrysler. Chrysler is a trademark of FCA USA LLC.)

Driver Butch Leal was also offered a Plymouth Belvedere race car. Butch, H.L., and Shirley set up the Leal and Shahan Racing Team. Notice the tough-looking hood scoop and chrome wheels on Shirley's car as it blasts past the crowd in the stands. (Photo Courtesy Chrysler. Chrysler is a trademark of FCA USA LLC.)

Shirley was happy to get the hot little Plymouth, and why not? It was a special factory-built performance model equipped with the special lightweight Aluminum Package. The company first introduced this package in 1963 and had enjoyed great success with it. It was improved for 1965. (Photo Courtesy Chrysler. Chrysler is a trademark of FCA USA LLC.)

Part of the Aluminum Package was a specially lightened interior, and we can see evidence of that here in the seat support. For 1965, the weight-reduction package was restricted to the lighter two-door "post" sedans. (Photo Courtesy Chrysler. Chrysler is a trademark of FCA USA LLC.)

In 1965, Shirley Shahan picked up the nickname that would stay with her forever: the Drag-On Lady. It came about as a request from the masters at Chrysler.

Below is a Q&A with author Patrick Foster and Shirley Shahan.

Author: Where did the nickname "Drag-On Lady" come from, and when did you start using it?

Shirley: That was when I was racing the S/S Plymouth. The way it came about was simple enough. One day in 1965, Sam Petok, an executive from Chrysler advertising, said to me, "I want you to use this name the Drag-On Lady." He figured that it was easy to remember and thought it was catchy enough that it would attract a lot of attention, and it turned out he sure was right!

Anyway, the nickname sounded pretty good to me, so I had no trouble using it. They arranged to have the name painted in large letters on the sides of my car in a sort of oriental-looking script, and the whole thing was a real crowd-pleaser.

And you know, that car ran great. In fact, we set the NHRA Division 7 ET [elapsed time] and MPH record for the class with it. We ended up racing all over Division 7 with that car, and I don't remember whether we won the points that year or if we came in second in Division 7, but we were right up there, and we sure were having a lot of fun doing it!

Author: What sort of times was the Plymouth good for?

Shirley: Gosh, you know that little Plymouth would do about 11.17, 11.10, and 127 mph. I think we eventually ran as fast as 132 on carburetors and gasoline. In 1965, I was the runner-up at the 1965 *Hot Rod* Magazine Drag Racing Championships.

The truth is, at that race I would have done better, but the Christmas tree shorted out, and they had to do a flag start. The guy in the other lane, Christian Brothers, got the jump on me. The officials should have called him on it, but for some reason they didn't. In 1966, I was runner-up to Darrel Droke at the AHRA Winternationals at Irwindale Raceway. A week later, I won Top Stock Eliminator at the NHRA Winternationals running an 11.26 and 121.78 mph.

Shirley and H.L. used this color-matched Plymouth station wagon to tow their Belvedere race car to the various tracks where they raced. The couple's friends at Doyce's Paint & Body Shop in Tulare, California, painted both of the vehicles. Shirley liked to bring as much business as she could to her hometown and always had her race cars painted at Doyce's. (Photo Courtesy Shirley Shahan)

Shirley's nickname, "the Drag-On Lady," was suggested by one of the Chrysler Corporation's advertising guys, a fellow named Sam Petok, who figured it was easy to remember and catchy enough that it would attract a lot of attention. He was right, but it was Shirley who made that name a legend in drag racing. (Photo Courtesy Chrysler. Chrysler is a trademark of FCA USA LLC.)

Here are some of the less-glamourous parts of drag racing: loading and unloading the race car from its trailer. Notice the velocity stacks sticking out of the hood of the car. (Photo Courtesy Shirley Shahan)

The Drag-On Lady script was painted in a special oriental-looking script as a play on the Hollywood movie character of the same name. In this photo, we can also see the tachometer showing through the windshield. One of Chrysler's conditions was that Shirley's car had to be equipped with a tachometer, and she had to use it. Up to this point, Shirley had never used a tach; she always knew when to shift by the sound of the engine and the feel of the car. However, she agreed to use the tach, and from that point on added the information it provided to the other sensations to know when to shift. (Photo Courtesy Chrysler. Chrysler is a trademark of FCA USA LLC.)

As part of the Southern California Gas Company's promotion of Shirley as one of its employees, this photo was taken in her race car. (Photo Courtesy Southern California Gas Company)

Shirley and H.L. made a great team. He was one of the best mechanics in the racing scene, and she was a highly competitive, top-notch driver with a fierce determination to win. Matched with the awesome Hemi-powered Belvedere, it was a winning combination. (Photo Courtesy Shirley Shahan)

Butch Leal and offered to sponsor him with a nice Hemi-powered Plymouth stocker.

What Chrysler proposed was a good deal for both Butch and Shirley, and it ended up being a big break for Shirley. It brought her to the attention of a much larger audience and showed that a big company, such as Chrysler Corporation, was confident that she had enough talent to do a really good job for them. This was important because the unspoken truth about corporate sponsorship, regardless of the company, is that there is absolutely no sentimentality involved. The company will sponsor you only because it believes that you can win races.

Dick Maxwell, the Chrysler executive in charge of overseeing the company's racing program, explained to Shirley that he would love to have her as one of their drivers, but he had conditions for her. Chrysler management wanted one of the two race cars to be equipped with the usual 4-speed manual transmission and the other one equipped with a Chrysler 3-speed automatic transmission. Management felt that it would help to demonstrate that true high performance wasn't limited just to cars equipped with a stick shift.

So, the first condition of the deal was that Shirley had to be the one driving the car with the automatic transmission. Why? Probably Chrysler Corporation or Dick Maxwell, it really doesn't matter, had a male chauvinistic attitude, which would have been fairly typical for the time, and felt that Shirley would naturally be more comfortable driving a car with an automatic transmission than with a stick shift.

Of course, that sort of thinking ignored the fact that Shirley obviously could handle a stick, otherwise she wouldn't have risen to the position in which she was (i.e., where Chrysler wanted her to be one of its drivers). It was a little bit like that old joke that goes "I wouldn't want to belong to any club that would have me as a member." In any event, Shirley agreed to drive the automatic-equipped car. It took a little getting used to, but she knew she would be competitive anyway.

The 1965 Season: Driving for Plymouth

The one other demand from Chrysler's Dick Maxwell was that Shirley's race car had to be equipped with a tachometer and that she use it. This again

This photo was taken at the old Riverside International Raceway, which in its heyday was a motorsports racetrack and road course. Established in the Edgemont area of Riverside County, California, just east of the city limits of Riverside and about 50 miles east of Los Angeles, it opened in September 1957 and ran until July 1989. The track hosted major NASCAR and NHRA events. (Photo Courtesy Chrysler. Chrysler is a trademark of FCA USA LLC.)

This photo, which was taken at Indy, shows Shirley checking her tachometer just prior to making another scorching run down the strip. (Photo Courtesy Chrysler. Chrysler is a trademark of FCA USA LLC.)

ignored the fact that Shirley had never used a tach previously in her career and had done pretty well racing without it.

Years earlier, when Shirley was just getting started as a driver, H.L. taught her how to listen to the sound of the engine and gauge the overall feel of the car to tell when the engine power had peaked and it was the optimal time to shift. Shirley understood it right from the start, and that's one of the reasons that she raced so successfully; she knew by the feel of the engine how best to drive the car.

You could say that Shirley needed a tachometer like a fish needs a life jacket, but she went along with the Chrysler man's

Another track that Shirley raced at regularly was the one in Bakersfield, California. In this photo circa 1965 or 1966, we see Shirley at the track in her blue Plymouth Belvedere. By 1965, Shirley's fame had spread up and down the West Coast. She and H.L. were the premier husband-and-wife racing team. (Photo Courtesy Chrysler. Chrysler is a trademark of FCA USA LLC.)

Shirley wears her silver fire suit and stands beside her husband, H.L., at a nighttime race.

The location was Lions Drag Strip in Long Beach, California. (Photo Courtesy Shirley Shahan)

request. Not surprisingly, driving by a tachometer took her some getting used to. In the end, she used a combination of listening by ear, gauging by feel, and eyeing the tach to decide the right shift point. The point is, she didn't really need a tach in the first place because she understood cars. She was a natural racer.

Although Shirley was happy enough with the Chrysler deal, what Chrysler offered her wasn't exactly a gold mine. The company did not pay her any sort of regular salary. Even so, she felt what they did offer was pretty good. Why?

"Although Chrysler did not pay me a regular salary, the company did agree to provide me with a new Hemi-powered race car along with any performance or service parts that I would need during the racing season—all at no cost," Shirley said. "They also provided us with a 1964 Plymouth station wagon to use as a tow vehicle."

As far as income, well, Shirley relied on her winnings, which was a great incentive for her to do her best. Shirley added that besides the car and equipment, the deal was good for her because of where they wanted her to race.

"A big reason why I was pleased with the deal was because I realized we would mostly be racing in California, which meant I would be able to go home most nights," she said. "I was still working for the Southern California Gas Company at the time and had three young children to raise, so that part of the deal was really important to me."

In addition, with the signing of the Chrysler deal, she and H.L. worked together as a team. Shirley did the driving and H.L. was preparing and maintaining her Plymouth race car. For H.L., it became a full-time job.

"During 1965, Chrysler had us running in the Division 7 points race, so we were racing every weekend," Shirley remembered. "My boss at the SoCal Gas Company was very understanding, but naturally he had rules that he was forced to follow. He couldn't let me leave early every Friday; it wouldn't have been fair to the other employees. But he did let me leave early just as often as he could, which was nice of him.

"Traveling to and from the racetracks can get tiring. I remember up near Seattle we raced, and instead of driving home with H.L., I went with someone else because H.L. had to drive the station wagon that we towed the race car with, so he could not travel as fast as someone who was driving a car. By going with someone else, I got home two hours earlier, which meant I got two hours sleep before I had to go into work."

Here we have two shots of Shirley showing her stuff. In the top photo, her car is in the background, well ahead of the dealer-sponsored Plymouth in the foreground.

In the bottom photo, Shirley is taking off. Notice that the front wheels are nearly off the ground. (Photos Courtesy the Patrick Foster Collection)

Another press photo taken at Indy shows Shirley checking out her Goodyear rear tire just before a race. Note the Goodyear sticker in the rear window and the ever-present Doyce's Paint & Body of Tulare, California, lettering on the C-pillar. (Photo Courtesy Chrysler. Chrysler is a trademark of FCA USA LLC.)

When Shirley first began driving for Plymouth, the name of the team was Leal and Shahan, as seen on this early photo. Initially, there weren't many sponsor stickers on her car, but when she began winning on a regular basis, the car blossomed with decals. (Photo Courtesy Chrysler. Chrysler is a trademark of FCA USA LLC.)

One part of racing that is seldom discussed is the extra work that drivers do in support of the people who sponsor them. Here, Shirley mans the booth for Doug's Headers at the big SEMA show. With Shirley, enjoying an ice cream cone, is Colleen Thorley, Doug Thorley's sister. As usual, Shirley is dressed to the nines with a little black dress, matching shoes, dangling earrings, and multiple strings of pearls. Shirley was always very stylish on and off the track. (Photo Courtesy Shirley Shahan)

Because of all that, for much of the mid-1960s Shirley's career was a blur of NHRA competitions, AHRA competitions, match racing, and making personal appearances, along with an incredible amount of driving to and from all of these events. Along the way, she managed to set many NHRA SS/AA track records and win a lot of races.

As proof of her skill and proficiency, *Hot Rod* magazine named her one of the Top Ten drivers, which was an amazing honor for a woman or a man at that time. She was also a consistently popular crowd pleaser; fans flocked to see her race. She was now a celebrity, and a busy one at that.

Having children who needed a mother looking after them was a career handicap that male drivers didn't have to face. To say that she had her hands full juggling being a mom, a wife, and a drag racer while holding down a full-time job would be an understatement. However, she recalled that period with a smile.

"There were lots of times back then when I would leave work on a Friday afternoon, drive many hours to get to whatever racetrack I was scheduled to race at that weekend, race all day, and then drive

Because she was such a rarity—a top-ranked drag racer who was also an attractive woman—Shirley had her photo taken many times in glamourous portraits like the one shown here. (Photo Courtesy Chrysler. Chrysler is a trademark of FCA USA LLC.)

H.L. and Shirley Shahan were the premier husband-and-wife (or is that wife-and-husband) racing team in America. Their picture was taken quite often for use by sponsors. This promotional photo was taken at the Doug's Headers facility in Los Angeles. Doug Thorley was and is renowned for the quality of his high-performance exhaust header systems. (Photo Courtesy Chrysler. Chrysler is a trademark of FCA USA LLC.)

all night to get home so that I could rest a bit before I had to go to work Monday morning.

"But you have to understand that it was a family thing. When H.L. and I were racing, we made sure to have the kids with us as much as possible, despite all the travel that was involved. We both felt it was important to have them with us. A lot of times, we would take all three kids along with us at the same time. Some other times, I'd take just one child with me, then fly home with them, exchange that child for another, and fly back. It was a busy time of life, but it was also a lot of fun."

This glamour shot of Shirley Shahan was taken in May 1966. Shirley was always well-dressed and well-spoken, and she loved to meet the fans at each track. (Photo Courtesy Chrysler. Chrysler is a trademark of FCA USA LLC.)

Mothers everywhere can appreciate this photo of Shirley's son, Bob, wanting to get into the picture by posing on the race car trailer. (Photo Courtesy Shirley Shahan)

Shirley recalled many times at the track when she would make a run and then come back to the pits to check on the kids to make sure they weren't getting into anything before going back out to make another run.

"They had a knack for wandering—especially Bob," she said.

However, Shirley never complained about it, she loved her kids and understood that sometimes children get tired and a little bored. She saw it as just part of the job of being a mom. She was somehow able to thrive in both worlds, motherhood and racing, at the same time.

The Chrysler deal was also important for her because the era of the amateur drag racer was coming to an end. The days of racing the family car were just about over, except of course at the smaller venues. Drag racing was now a big sport, and during the previous 10 years as it grew in popularity, the level of competition had become much more intense.

The cost of purchasing a car and then making all of the necessary modifications to it to have a chance of winning had become much too expensive for most part-time racers. About the only drivers who still managed to stay near the top in their classes were the ones who enjoyed factory backing and had a professional team approach to the business (and it had become a business) along with top-rated mechanics who worked exclusively for them.

Over the years, the growing competition had also boosted average top speeds while lowering elapsed times (ETs) to levels that were once considered impossible. The handful of drivers who occupied the top ranks in the sport had become famous around the country. Track owners loved them because being able to advertise that a race day would be loaded with celebrity drivers meant the grandstands would be full and the gate take very profitable.

In truth, the top drivers now were exactly that: celebrities. Shirley started out well before that happened, so she was one of the early celebrity drivers. The crowds loved them all. At the same time, the purse winnings had grown as well, which made it a lot easier to work as a race car driver full-time, as long as you were fast. However, even though the money was better than it had been, it still was nothing like what today's racers can earn.

The automobile manufacturers also loved the big-name drivers because when they won, it focused attention on the company's cars. There was a marketing man's adage back then that went: "Win on Sunday, sell on Monday." Race fans became diehard Ford fans, Chevy fans, Plymouth fans, or whatever brand happened to appeal to them, which very often was because that car brand was winning a lot of races. When the time came to buy a new family car, those fans would usually buy the same brand that they rooted for at the track. In addition, because the American auto industry was so heavily involved in promoting racing and high performance, people who were interested in racing comprised a significant part of the automobile market at the time.

America's automakers were also in the midst of a historic horsepower race, and power and performance were what most people were looking for in their next new car. This was the golden era of the muscle car, and speed and performance were hot items that were advertised constantly to car buyers. One very big way that the Big Three automakers (Ford, General Motors, and Chrysler) advertised their cars' performance was at the strip on race day. So, winning became extremely important to the Big Three automakers. (At the time, AMC was not involved in racing in a significant way. Studebaker, once known as a high-performance brand, was out of the car business.)

The car Shirley was to race was actually pretty special: it was a 1965 Plymouth Belvedere equipped with the factory Aluminum Package. Chrysler Corporation had first introduced the special lightweight Aluminum Package in 1963 for both Dodge and Plymouth cars. It was targeted specifically at people who were involved in drag racing and

Seeking to shed its image as a solid but boring car, Plymouth hyped its new Hemi-powered models in brochures and advertisements such as this one. As the advertisement says, 470 ft-lbs of torque at a mere 3,200 rpm is not exactly sulky. That kind of locomotive torque could push you back in the seat like a rocket at takeoff. (Photo Courtesy Chrysler. Chrysler is a trademark of FCA USA LLC.)

In her career as a professional race car driver, Shirley drove gas and nitro stock cars and also drag rail jobs. But for getting around the track pits, she sometimes drove a small motorcycle and was dressed in fashionable clothes, as always. *(Photo Courtesy Chrysler. Chrysler is a trademark of FCA USA LLC.)*

Once Shirley signed on as a driver for Plymouth, the division wanted to do a series of press photos to announce its newest star. A photo shoot took place in 1965 at the Indianapolis Motor Speedway, where she was scheduled to race. *(Photo Courtesy Chrysler. Chrysler is a trademark of FCA USA LLC.)*

This photo was taken at the 1965 NHRA Nationals in Indianapolis when Shirley was part of the Leal and Shahan Racing team. *(Photo Courtesy Chrysler. Chrysler is a trademark of FCA USA LLC.)*

     SHIRLEY SHAHAN *The Drag-On Lady*

TOP LEFT: *H.L. Shahan didn't need to do all of the work on Shirley's car; she was more than willing to pitch in with routine tasks, such as removing the valve covers on the Hemi, to save time while H.L. was doing something else. We wonder if she really did that in the expensive outfit that she's wearing. Knowing Shirley, she probably did. She began working on cars when she was about 10 years old, so she knew a lot more about cars than most men did. (Photo Courtesy Chrysler. Chrysler is a trademark of FCA USA LLC.)* **TOP RIGHT:** *This photo of H.L. and Shirley Shahan checking out the undercarriage of their 1965 Plymouth Belvedere Hemi race car shows exactly how a husband-and-wife team work together to be successful. (Photo Courtesy Chrysler. Chrysler is a trademark of FCA USA LLC.)* **MIDDLE LEFT:** *Probably the best-dressed racer in NHRA history to that point, Shirley is shown here cleaning one of the valve covers that she removed from the Hemi. This photo was taken in 1965 at Indianapolis Motor Speedway. (Photo Courtesy Chrysler. Chrysler is a trademark of FCA USA LLC.)* **LEFT:** *Here's the face of a drag-racing champion on her way up the ladder of success. Taken at Indy in 1965, it shows a self-confident Shirley at her best. (Photo Courtesy Chrysler. Chrysler is a trademark of FCA USA LLC.)*

Shirley stands on the fender of the car trailer, talking to H.L., who had just driven the Plymouth race car onto the carrier. (Photo Courtesy Chrysler. Chrysler is a trademark of FCA USA LLC.)

was comprised of a number of aluminum components along with a lightened interior.

For 1964, the number of lightweight parts increased, and it now included the radiator shield and the hood lock brace. To save still more weight, even the factory undercoating was now omitted, as were the dashboard liners and the silencer pads in the front kick panels. These last moves didn't save a tremendous amount of weight, but in drag racing, split seconds count, and every ounce of weight that can be removed from a car is important because it makes it that much more competitive.

The 1965 racing season saw the addition of several more lightweight engine components to the Mopar Aluminum Package, including a magnesium cross-ram intake manifold, aluminum cylinder heads, aluminum water pump and thermostat housings, plus aluminum alternator brackets, all of

The Incredible
HEMI ENGINE

Shirley raced during the Golden Age of drag racing, when manufacturers were turning out some of the greatest cars of all time along with landmark performance engines that would go on to become legends in their own right. The 1956 Chevy 348-ci V-8 with dual-quads was one such mill; the awesome Chrysler 426-ci Hemi V-8 was another.

For the record, "hemi" is a prefix that means half. In the context of the Hemi engine, it refers to its special domed or hemispherical-shaped combustion chambers. The term came into common usage in the automotive vernacular during the muscle car era of the 1960s, when Chrysler Corporation debuted the new 426-ci Hemi V-8 for production vehicles and racing applications.

Actually, the Hemi V-8 engine that was available from 1964 to 1971 was Chrysler's second successful production engine with a hemispherical-headed V-8. The first generation was produced from 1951 to 1958, when it was known as the Firepower V-8, and it helped make the big Chryslers competitive with the Hudson Hornets that dominated NASCAR from 1951 to 1954. The incredibly powerful Hemi engines that are available today on Dodge, Chrysler, and Jeep vehicles were first introduced in 2003.

Besides the Lightweight Package, Shirley's Plymouth Belvedere was equipped with the new 426 Hemi engine, which was introduced to the public in the spring of 1964. The Hemi name came from the cylinder heads, which feature the hemispherical shape that provided room for much larger valves for vastly better breathing, which translated into more power. (Photo Courtesy Chrysler. Chrysler is a trademark of FCA USA LLC.)

Shirley Shahan
DRAG-ON LADY
ROBIN
VISALIA . CALIF.

which were part of an upgraded A990 Hemi racing engine that had been introduced that year. In addition, the front fenders, the hood, and the radiator and grille supports were now made of lightweight stamped steel, rather than aluminum.

Previously available only on the division's hardtop coupes, the weight-reduction package was now restricted to the lighter two-door post sedans. The Aluminum Package proved to be a vitally important ingredient in Mopar's Super Stock package, which was aimed, as its title suggested, at the drag racing community. Being assigned one of these special cars was a sign of the confidence Chrysler had in Shirley's driving ability.

In addition to the Lightweight Package, Shirley's Plymouth racer was equipped with the classic 426 Hemi engine, which was introduced to the public in the spring of 1964. In regular street form, the 426 Hemi was rated at 365 hp, but the factory also offered a hotter version for competing in Super Stock (or on the street) that was rated at 400 to 425 hp.

Chrysler offered its first Hemi V-8 in 1951. Displacing 331 ci, that engine generated a solid 180 hp. For the sake of comparison, the previous year (1950), Chrysler had offered a similar size V-8 of 323 ci (8 ci smaller), but that engine was good for only 135 hp. Obviously, the creation of the Hemi cylinder head was a big advance in performance technology, and to this day, it is one of Chrysler's proudest achievements.

When the company rolled out the 426 Hemi in 1964 and people saw that the engine offered versions of up to 425 hp, they were stunned. That was an absolutely amazing horsepower-to-displacement ratio for the time.

When the company rolled out the 426 Hemi in 1964 and people saw that the engine offered versions of up to 425 hp, they were stunned. That was an absolutely amazing horsepower-to-displacement ratio for the time. That year, cars featuring the innovative engine took first, second, and third places in

Everything counts in drag racing, right down to the smallest detail, including making sure the windshield is clean so that the driver can see where she's going as well as double-checking tire pressure, oil levels, etc. (Photo Courtesy Chrysler. Chrysler is a trademark of FCA USA LLC.)

the prestigious Daytona 500.

Many people ask, "If the Hemi design is so good and offers so much more power for a given engine size, why doesn't everybody build Hemi engines?" The reason is because casting and machining a Hemi head is much more difficult and labor intensive, so it costs significantly more to build a Hemi engine than a conventional head. Chrysler can do it today because it sells its Hemis in premium price segments and also because it has staked a good part of its reputation on the Hemi name. It's now a trademarked and protected brand because it's a valuable part of the company's performance cachet.

Now, about the cars: the previous year's Plymouth Belvedere, the 1964 model, had been considered to be in the full-size car segment but because it was noticeably smaller than the senior Ford and Chevy models it hadn't sold very well. For 1965, Plymouth introduced the big new Fury to vie in the full-size market and assigned a restyled Belvedere to the burgeoning intermediate-size market, where its

SHIRLEY SHAHAN *The Drag-On Lady*

In a promo shot, H.L. appears to be giving Shirley some last-minute encouragement prior to a race. Note the tachometer that was insisted upon by Chrysler managers. (Photo Courtesy Chrysler. Chrysler is a trademark of FCA USA LLC.)

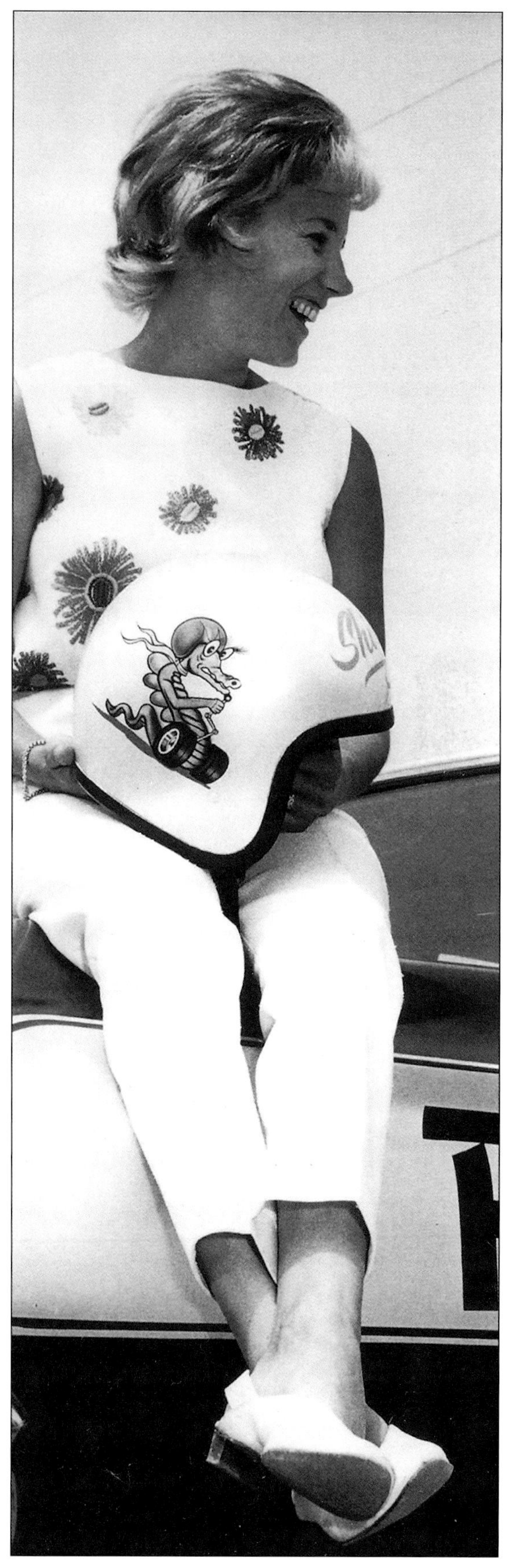

Shirley kills some time between races in 1965. You can tell by her smile how much she loved racing. (Photo Courtesy Chrysler. Chrysler is a trademark of FCA USA LLC.)

larger-than-usual-intermediate size made it a popular choice with buyers.

When it arrived from the factory, Shirley's car, a two-door post sedan, was painted white.

"It was pretty much ready to go racing," she recalled.

Plymouth wanted the car painted special colors, so it was sent at her request to the folks who painted all of Shirley's race cars: Doyce's Body and Paint in Tulare, California. Doyce's painted it a color scheme of teal and white two-tone. The body itself featured a broad white painted section that ran from the hood front to the roof and continued onto and down the deck-lid. To get the exact shade of teal that they wanted, the Doyce crew first painted the bodyside center gold, then put a lighter coat of blue over that, and the resulting look was a very exclusive teal. This color scheme was chosen by the powers that be at Plymouth.

In addition, the Plymouth name was emblazoned in tall letters in the white section of the quarter panels, while the doors bore Shirley's name in script along with the legendary Drag-On Lady in a sort of oriental-look lettering (perhaps a play on the Dragon Lady image promoted by movie star Anna May Wong). On the front fenders were the words "H.L. and Shirley

The Lightweight Package offered by Chrysler in 1965 was only available on the Dodge Coronet and Plymouth Belvedere I two-door sedan bodies, the lightest bodies in the lineup. The rest of the car, including the interior trim and seats, was basically the same as the 1964 Hemi Charger Super Stock cars. For 1965, the package included:

- Lightweight thin steel front fenders (instead of the aluminum ones that were formerly used)
- Lightweight thin steel hood with a Hemi-style thin steel air scoop
- Lightweight thin steel radiator core support and grille support brackets
- Weight-reducing engine parts, including a magnesium cross-ram intake manifold (rather than aluminum), aluminum hemi cylinder heads, aluminum water-pump housing and thermostat housing, and aluminum alternator brackets

The substitution of thin steel fenders, hood, and scoop rather than the aluminum formerly specified was a result of an NHRA rule. The NHRA no longer allowed cars produced with the aluminum parts as had been used on the 1964 Race Hemi cars.

Shahan Racing Team." The rest of the exterior wore the customary logos of various sponsors, including Headers by Doug (Thorley), Champion Spark Plugs, Doyce's Paint and Body, etc. Chrome-spoke Cragar wheels added a nice touch that gave the car a more aggressive look.

Results quickly showed that Shirley hadn't lost her edge in her self-imposed two-year hiatus from racing. With the Plymouth lightened by an impressive 200 pounds and running fuel for a special match race in Vacaville, California, in August 1965, Shirley made the quickest run of her career up to that point. With tires smoking and the engine screaming, she put down an ET of 10.86 seconds and a top speed of 134 mph! What's especially impressive is that she did this with a car she was still just getting familiar with.

Later that same month, at the Palmdale drag strip, Shirley and her Hemi Plymouth set the NHRA MPH record for the S/SA class at 127.30 mph.

With the new Chrysler deal, the only ways Shirley earned money was from winning national events or from running in match races against other drivers. So, there was a strong incentive for her to win or place high because if she didn't, she wouldn't earn a living. As her fame grew and her fan base became larger, she added product endorsements for additional income.

As things turned out, Shirley didn't have any trouble winning and placing. In fact, she was able to get off to a very good start in big-league professional drag racing. During the 1965 season, she raced and beat two of the top drivers of the time: Junior Stock World Champion Mike Schmitt and Top Stock Champion Gaspar "Gas" Ronda.

Her victory over Gas Ronda was particularly exciting because it was a really hard-fought competition held at the big *Hot Rod*–sponsored meet at Riverside, California, that June. Driving her H.L.-prepared Hemi Plymouth, Shirley out-dragged most the field that day, much to the chagrin of many well-known drivers. After a day of smoking tires, screaming engines, and the smell of hot exhaust, Shirley ended up as runner-up for Top Stock Eliminator.

A few of the other drivers (ones who weren't in the race) tried to contend that it was the NHRA handicap system that helped Shirley beat Ronda. In the first race, Ronda drove an A/FX Mustang against Shirley's Hemi-powered S/SA 1965 Plymouth. So, under the rules, she was allowed a slight head start. However, in the race against Mike Schmitt, she had to sit still while he was allowed the head start, and she still beat him. Since Shirley was the winner in both cases, it certainly wasn't the handicap system that determined the winner.

Realizing the very real possibility of hard feelings coming into play, the NHRA experts did everything possible to ensure that the handicaps were fair. Furthermore, since all drivers had to drive under the same rules and the same handicaps, it really wasn't possible for a driver to have an unfair advantage, as Shirley later proved in a series of match races held in Hawaii.

What made the difference in both cases was the combination of Shirley's lightning-fast reflexes, excellent arm strength, inherent driving ability, and a really good Hemi-powered car. There was also the

H.L. Shahan does here what he did best: tuning and preparing Shirley's car for another race, this one was at Indianapolis. Note the Chevy El Camino pickup truck in the background. (Photo Courtesy Chrysler. Chrysler is a trademark of FCA USA LLC.)

During the mid-1960s, Shirley's career was a blur of NHRA and AHRA competitions. There was a lot of match racing and personal appearances, along with a substantial amount of very tiring driving to and from events. (Photo Courtesy Shirley Shahan)

fact that her Plymouth had been tuned by H.L., who was considered to be one of the best drag car mechanics in the country.

In addition, the Mopar performance cars of 1965 were highly competitive entries with a good body, an outstanding Hemi race engine, and of course, the added advantage of the factory Lightweight Package. With proper tuning and the right person behind the wheel, they had an extremely difficult combination for others to beat.

Although the team mechanics were already well-experienced, in April 1965 Chrysler chose to put on a workshop for drivers and crewmembers on the intricacies of servicing and tuning the Hemi engine as well as the other Mopar race equipment. The workshop was conducted at Chrysler's Detroit facilities and actually proved to be quite useful.

Jack Watson, known as Hurst's "Shifty Doctor," gave a presentation on the proper way to adjust the shift linkage. Bob Tarozzi lectured on TorqueFlite transmissions and stall converters, while Dick Maxwell instructed on engine tuning.

The deal with Chrysler meant that Shirley reported directly to Dick Maxwell, Chrysler's director of performance activities. When they said "reported," they meant it literally. All of the drivers who competed under contract with Chrysler, including Shirley, were required to call Dick Maxwell by phone (email did not exist) every Monday morning during the racing season to let him know when and where they had raced the previous week. Maxwell wanted to know who they raced, whether they won or lost, how they placed, etc. That was also the time when they could ask him to send any replacement parts they might need.

Shirley had a close friend at Hurst named Dave Landrith, whom she called when any unusual problems popped up, as they did from time to time. Maybe the worst problem was when Shirley's station wagon was towed away at the Detroit Airport! She had gone into the airport to make sure that the plane was on time as her daughter Janet and racer Steve Bovan were flying home to California. She parked her Plymouth wagon just outside the terminal. She knew she wasn't supposed to, but she said, "I was only gone a minute."

Well, she was gone long enough for the airport towing outfit to tow her car away. It didn't help

that she had no license plates on it; she had just received the car from Plymouth and had a temporary registration (that was expired) pasted to the front windshield, which apparently the tow-truck driver didn't see. H.L. was working at Hurst, so he couldn't help.

Crying, she called Dave Landrith. Quick as lightning, Dave and Dick Chrysler came down to the Detroit airport to help.

"I don't know who they spoke with or what they said, but they gave me my station wagon back," she remembered. "Dave and Dick were really great guys. Dick Chrysler later became vice president of Hurst Performance, and after that president of Cars & Concepts, which I think bought out Hurst."

It soon became obvious that Shirley's initial victories were not a case of beginner's luck because she kept on winning all season. Shortly after her wins at Riverside, she agreed to a special match race in Honolulu, Hawaii. Arranged by a big Hawaiian auto dealer named Jimmy Pflueger, Shirley was slated once again to drive against Mike Schmitt. Pflueger paid to have the cars and the drivers transported to Hawaii for the big event.

As a warmup for the crowd, Shirley was asked to match race against a local fellow named Earl Char, who was considered to be a pretty good driver. Race him she did, winning three of the five races. Then came the big part of the event, the match race against the great Mike Schmitt from Ridgecrest, California (the same hometown as drag race announcer Bernie Partridge). To show how much simpler things were back in those days, Shirley says the two drivers not only came from the same area but they also flew over on the same plane!

The race between Shahan and Schmitt was a much tighter competition than her runs against Earl Char. This competition was a best-of-three race to determine the winner.

Match racing was one of Shirley's favorite types of racing because it paid well and she was very good at it. Soon after her wins at Riverside, she agreed to a special match race in Hawaii. Arranged by Hawaiian auto dealer Jimmy Pflueger, Shirley was scheduled to drive against Mike Schmitt. Pflueger paid to have the cars and both drivers transported to Hawaii for the big event. Here, H.L. and Shirley enjoy some time in Hawaii after the races. (Photo Courtesy Chrysler. Chrysler is a trademark of FCA USA LLC.)

Although Schmitt was a tremendous driver and at the top of his game at the time, Shirley and her Hemi Plymouth were also in top form that day. She ended up as the winner. Although she doesn't remember each of her runs (after all, she did literally thousands of runs in her career), she said that it was all a lot of fun. In fact, she enjoyed the racing so much that she was happy to make the trip when she was invited back to Hawaii for 1968 and 1969. One year, she and H.L. were invited to have Thanksgiving dinner at Hickam Air Force Base, which was quite an honor.

Shirley was red-hot, placing as runner-up in Top Stock at the 1965 Top Stock Finals Hot Rod *Magazine Championship in Riverside, California.*

During one of their trips to Hawaii, Shirley made friends with some local ladies who showed her around the island. They told Shirley about a local superstition of a highway that was cursed by King Kamehameha and said to be haunted by a ghost woman and her dog. The only way to drive safely on the road, they told her, was to bring pork with you. So, the next evening, they bought a pork sandwich to take along, and they all went for a drive on the old Pali Highway with Shirley at the wheel.

"There were six of us in that car, it's dark, there's all these trees hanging over the car, and it's spooky as heck as we drove along," she said. "I waited until we were about halfway up a big mountain and then reached over, unseen, and turned off the ignition. You wouldn't believe the screaming after that!"

From the beginning of 1965 and right to the very end of that exciting season, Shirley was red-hot, placing as runner-up in Top Stock at the 1965 Top Stock Finals *Hot Rod* Magazine Championship in Riverside, California. That's quite an honor, but Shirley still contends that she should have received the top slot.

Shirley learned a lot about life on the road. Initially, she had a friend booking her race appearances, but the man didn't have a good sense of time and distances. He would book her to race in Detroit on a Saturday night and then the next morning in Chicago, so she'd be driving half of the night and then be tired out for the upcoming race. The next year, Shirley began making her own bookings.

"When we began running Division 7 points in 1965, things got very hectic," she said. "The Division 7 race schedule included California, Washington, Nevada, Oregon, and Utah, and I had to get to all the races while still working at my day job. Talk about tiring! I would get off work as early as I could, maybe two hours earlier than usual, drive to the racetrack, race, and drive home the same day, sometimes driving all night, then show up for work again Monday morning. I think it was during 1965 that I came down with the measles and was pretty sick."

Shirley's dad asked her to take along her brother Jerry when she and H.L. were traveling because the boy was starting to hang out with the wrong crowd, and her dad wanted to get Jerry away from there. Shirley gladly agreed and had H.L. put Jerry to work on the team helping to work on the cars.

Jerry was a bit of a wild one, though. Shirley remembered once they were flying back home from Kansas City and Jerry had his suitcase filled with illegal fireworks. He figured that he was going to make a fortune selling them to his friends back home. However, as it turned out, he and a friend in the neighborhood ended up shooting off all the fireworks in one day, so he didn't make a dime on them.

Shirley also brought her sister Kathy with her from time to time. Kathy became Shirley's designated hairdresser while on the road. Back in the 1960s, the big bouffant hairdos like Shirley's meant that you had to get your hair done every week if you wanted to look your best, and Shirley often had a difficult time finding hairdressers.

She usually asked one of the locals for the name of a good hairdresser, but one time, in Bristol, Tennessee, she ended up picking a name out of the phone book. She asked to have her hair bleached and shampooed, but when the hairdresser did that, Shirley's hair started falling out! She was horrified at the outcome. Shirley ended up having to get her hair cut down to a 2-inch length and wait for it all to grow back.

THE ROAD *Part I*

By Shirley Shahan

H.L. and I were coming home from Texas one time after spending a weekend racing in Mexico City. We were driving the station wagon and towing the race car behind us on a trailer. H.L.'s friend George was at the wheel of the truck when all of a sudden the whole outfit starts swerving. H.L. told George, "Don't fight it," but I looked around behind us, and I could read the lettering on the side of the car that we were towing, which was not a good sign.

So, I convinced H.L. and George to pull over. We thought maybe we had a flat tire. But no, it was not a flat tire; instead, the entire wheel and tire were gone! We had to turn around, find the wheel and tire, and then limp into the nearest town, which was a small place in West Texas called Marfa.

We asked a gas station attendant if there was a welding shop nearby, and he said, "Nope, there isn't. But there's a

One thing about Shirley Shahan that was true back in the day and is still true today—she's always smiling. But her biggest smiles were when she was racing and winning. (Photo Courtesy Chrysler. Chrysler is a trademark of FCA USA LLC.)

farmer nearby who does welding."

So, we went out to see the farmer, and he said that he could have it ready in the morning.

We managed to get a hotel room (there was only one available), and lucky for us it had two beds in it because besides me, H.L., and George, we had Bette Thorley with us. She and I shared one bed and H.L. and George took the other. In the morning, the farmer had the wheel ready, but after a short drive it broke again. We had to limp back to his farm, where he re-welded it, and this time it held.

The 1966 Season

In the January 1966 issue of *Super Stock* magazine, writer Howard Pennington posed a rhetorical question. He asked: ". . . are women really capable of driving high-performance machinery in the way it should be handled?"

He then answered the question by noting, "Shirley Shahan and her 1965 Plymouth Super Stock may not end all the arguments on that point, but she's sure brought some new evidence before the court."

As a matter of fact, when the article was written, Shirley was tied with Gas Ronda in points (450 points each) in the NHRA's Division 7 competition for the World Points Top Stock Eliminator title.

When asked about her racing technique, Shirley explained, "It mostly comes naturally. You either have it or you don't. This is the first year that I've used a tach for shifting. I still shift by feel as much as by tach. If I'm pulling up on my opponent, I just leave it in that gear a little longer."

Shirley and H.L. did a lot of match racing during 1966.

"To be competitive in match racing, H.L. would install fuel injectors, and [he] moved the rear wheels forward just like they do on Funny Cars," Shirley said.

Shirley especially enjoyed the 1966 racing season. In an interview with Bob McClurg, Shirley explained, "When we went on tour in '66, all we did was match race. We left April 15 and didn't come back until after the US Nationals in September, so

This posed publicity shot shows H.L. and Shirley pushing the Super Stock Plymouth off its trailer. (Photo Courtesy Chrysler. Chrysler is a trademark of FCA USA LLC.)

five full months on the road. We raced every weekend and sometimes two times."

Her husband, H.L., added, "During that time, we ran fuel injectors. We put 30 percent nitro in it, and we altered the car's wheelbase by about 2 inches. After that, we won almost all of the match races we were in. That '66 was just a fantastic car; it ran a best time of 9.70 seconds and 132.54 in match-race trim. Let's face it, that's some going."

But it was a hectic life for both of them. Shirley raced or was on her way to a racetrack pretty much every single day. She ran at NHRA national events in Bristol, Tennessee; Englishtown, New Jersey; and Gainesville, Florida; as well as dozens of smaller tracks.

"One of the promoters who liked to have us come out to his town several days early was 'Broadway Bob' Metzler, the owner of the Great Lakes Dragaway in Milwaukee, Wisconsin," Shirley recalled. "You

The Drag-On Lady takes a break, sipping an RC Cola while reading an advertisement for Mr. Norm in which she is featured. As a co-owner of Grand Spaulding Dodge in Chicago from 1962 through 1977, Mr. Norm's focus on high performance helped it become the biggest Dodge dealership in the world. He recently passed away. (Photo Courtesy Shirley Shahan)

Dick Carvalho (left), the Shahan's best mechanic and friend, along with Ronnie Broadhead (third from left) and other racing friends enjoy the view from the top of Ronnie's truck. (Photo Courtesy Shirley Shahan)

Shirley has a trackside conversation with Jack McFarland, the man who convinced her to switch from Plymouth and come drive for Dodge. McFarland was a Dodge public relations representative and a great guy, Shirley said. (Photo Courtesy Chrysler. Chrysler is a trademark of FCA USA LLC.)

have to understand, Bob was a great promoter. We always raced at his track over the Fourth of July weekend, as he always put on an especially big show then. One time, we were scheduled to be racing for him, it was in 1966, and he had us come out a whole week early to help promote the racing.

"That man had us on every TV station, every radio station, and every newspaper there was in the entire Milwaukee area. To make one scheduled appearance on a TV show, we had to drive right through downtown Milwaukee with our station wagon towing our trailer. After that, we raced all weekend long. I remember it was unbelievably hot and the roads were so bad that weekend that we ended up getting five flat tires on our trailer."

In late 1966, H.L. remembered, "Sometimes we would race San Antonio at the Alamo Dragway on one night and then race at Houston the next day, or Detroit one day and then Chicago the next day. We sure put a lot of miles on that station wagon of ours!"

One minor hassle that H.L. always faced was the need to swap out rear ends on the race car, depending on where they were racing and whether they needed 4.11 gears or 4.88 gears (for eighth-mile tracks). However, he got to be pretty fast at it.

While on the road, Shirley would fly home every month to pay the bills and exchange kids so that they all had a chance to travel. Janet liked to brag that she always got to go to Indy.

SHIRLEY SHAHAN *The Drag-On Lady*

DRAG CAR

Below is a Q&A with author Patrick Foster and Shirley Shahan.

Author: Shirley, can you tell us what it's like inside a drag car? It must be very hot, noisy, and scary, right? Is it claustrophobic?

Shirley: No, really, it's none of those things. Despite the big powerful engine and having no body insulation, there's not all that much noise because you're wearing a helmet, and it's not too hot inside the car, either. As far as being scared, I was never really scared while I was racing, although I did have a few close calls in the shut-off lanes. That's only because the amount of room you have for decelerating once your run is over can vary a lot from track to track, and if you happen to be racing at nighttime, it can be a little unnerving because a lot of time the shut-down area isn't well-lit, and the return road might not be straight.

Author: There must be a strong smell of gasoline in the car, right?

Shirley: Actually no, and anyway, that wouldn't bother me at all. What was difficult was when you were running nitro fuel. You see, before we'd race, we'd do a few burnouts to get the tires warmed up for better traction. You do a short burnout run going forward, then back up and do another, and when you were backing up, you'd get all the nitro fumes in the car, and they would burn your throat and your eyes—really unpleasant. It wasn't so bad if you had your asbestos face mask on because that would filter out a lot of the nitro fumes. The fire suits and safety equipment are about 200 percent better now than they were in the 1960s, eliminating a lot of the nitro fumes.

Author: What goes through your mind as you're racing?

Shirley: Well, naturally you're wondering if you got off the line quick enough and you wonder what your time is going to be. In match racing, you can't help but sneak a peek out the corner of your eye to see if your opponent is right beside you or not, and you're saying to yourself, "Come on, baby, just a little bit more."

One story I can tell you is about the time I was match racing in Colorado in my 1968 Dodge when I blew an oil pan going through the lights at 130 mph! What happened was a bolt blew off one of the connecting rods at speed and it went right through the oil pan. The oil drained out, but thankfully it didn't blow all over the track. Otherwise, I could have been in serious trouble, going into a slide or spin out at that speed. The oil just drained directly underneath the engine, so I was able to stop the car without losing control.

Of her 1967 Dodge race car Shirley said, "It was a pretty car to look at and even came with air-conditioning, a vinyl roof, a really nice interior, and of course it had a big Hemi engine under the hood. But as pretty as it was, that thing was just a lead sled. It never ran nearly as fast as the '65 Plymouth did." (Photo Courtesy Chrysler. Chrysler is a trademark of FCA USA LLC.)

Shirley raced mainly in the West Coast for much of her career, although she did make it East quite a few times. She also raced in Hawaii three years in a row at an invitational event and raced several times at a racetrack in Mexico City, which is where this photo was taken. (Photo Courtesy the Patrick Foster Collection)

Author: You must have blown the engine though.

Shirley: No, actually, I was able to shut the engine off really quick, so it didn't suffer any more damage. I was lucky, I guess.

Author: I'd say you were thinking pretty fast. We're curious about something, though. In my personal car, when I put my foot into the carburetor, the traction control takes a few seconds to take hold, so the car twists and turns out of shape like a wild animal trying to get traction. Did your drag cars try to push themselves out of shape getting traction?

Shirley: No, not usually. They grab right away and go down the track nice and straight. At times, though, one lane might be slicker as a result of oil residue, and that might pull you to one side.

Author: I'm guessing the Detroit Locker rear ends you were using were a lot more serious than the traction control that comes from the factory.

Shirley: Well, gosh, I would hope so!

Author: You've driven both stick shift and automatic transmissions in your career. Is there a difference in driving techniques between them?

Shirley: Yes, there is. With the automatic, it's harder to launch as quick as you want to, so sometimes you do a neutral-gear start, where you rev up the engine in neutral [and] then dump it into drive. That puts a lot of stress on the transmission, but it helps you get going a lot faster. With the automatic, you drive it in each gear until you can feel the valves are about to float, then you shift.

You don't want to wait until the valves begin to float because that's when you begin to lose power. With a stick shift—and I've driven both the 3-speed on the column and the four-on-the-floor—you can feel when the engine reaches peak power, and that's when you shift.

Shirley drives during a nighttime race. The location is unknown. Drag racing takes place at tracks all around the country, and sometimes the days turn into night before the racing is over. Although the tracks were usually well-lit, the slow-down lanes sometimes weren't, and that could be dangerous, especially if the track didn't run straight. (Photo Courtesy Chrysler. Chrysler is a trademark of FCA USA LLC.)

The Winternationals

In early 1966, Shirley followed up her 1965 *Hot Rod* win with a final-round finish at the 1966 AHRA Winternationals in Irwindale, another big important win to add to her list of successes. However, the race that really assured her place in the record books was her amazing win at the 1966 NHRA Winternationals in Pomona, California.

The three-day meet was an incredible event with more than 500 entries competing. The show had a late start due to reduced visibility caused by low-lying fog. But once the soup cleared up, the teams quickly got to work. By this time, most of the drivers were accustomed to the Christmas tree starting system and were able to time it to the split second. Shirley had kind of an off day that Satur-

day, but then on Sunday she was full of competitive juices and ready to rock and roll.

At the wheel of her *Drag-On Lady* Plymouth, Shirley defeated contestants round after round as the crowd roared its approval. She made the final matchup for the Mr. Stock Eliminator title, facing the great Ken Heinemann of Daytona Beach, Florida, driving his new 1966 Brand X Eliminator Hemi Plymouth Belvedere. Heinemann even had the advantage of a slight head start due to the handicap system.

Once the starting lights ran down to green, Shirley punched the gas pedal and took off in a roar of smoke and screaming rubber. She quickly caught up with Heinemann, and the two Mopars ran side by side down the track! Just moments before running through the finish lights, Shirley managed to pull ahead to win! Heinemann's run was clocked at 12.01, and Shirley was clocked at 11.26.

The race day announcer had a lot of fun working the crowd throughout the day, describing the races and steadily hyping Shirley's achievements as she advanced in the standings. The announcer periodically wondered out loud if Shirley was going to end up winning the meet. It was obvious that she was at the top of her game that day.

As the hours wore on, his announcements grew louder as he steadily dialed up the suspense. "Can she do it?" he'd yell into the microphone. "Will she do it?"

The crowd was getting wound up to a fever pitch by the excitement. Every time Shirley drove an elimination race, the announcer further added to the anticipation, building excitement by the hour until pretty much every race fan there knew that they were witnessing something special. The mood was exciting and almost unbearably tense. After coming this far in the day's races, would Shirley be able to pull off something that had never been done before?

The last match-up came, and Shirley blasted through in the lead. All eyes were on her when, finally, it was announced that Shirley was the overall winner. The crowd stood up and roared in a thunderous response. There was applause, yelling, screaming, and many hats thrown in the air. It was one of the really great days in drag racing history.

Her surprise win made drag racing history. Never before in the history of the National Hot Rod Association had a woman won a major drag racing event. Shirley went into the record books as the first. It was a ground-breaking, pioneering win that people still talk about today.

"What a thrill that was," Shirley said. "It was a really great day for me. I'll never forget especially the fans who stood up in the stands as I passed by after my final run, cheering for me. I'll never forget them and their amazing support. So, it was a really good day and a really good feeling.

"It had a direct effect on the path of my racing career because it was right after that when we started getting phone calls from several organizers who wanted us to go back East and race. They were interested because I was the first woman who'd won a major event, and they realized I'd be a good draw.

On February 20, 1966, Shirley made history yet again when she became the first woman to win a major NHRA drag racing event. On a bright, sunny day at the sixth annual Winternationals Drag Racing Championship at Pomona, 28-year-old Shirley Shahan took on the best of the boys in racing and won the title as Top Stock Eliminator. The part-time secretary blasted her way to the top with a stunning performance of driving ability. Shirley stayed cool as she beat the other racers one by one. (Photo Courtesy UPI)

Up to that point, I can honestly say I did not realize what an impact I had made in the sport of drag racing. You see, I'd been doing it for so long it just seemed ordinary to me, and then suddenly people were sitting up and paying attention."

After the race, Shirley was mobbed by journalists and photographers and did an on-the-spot interview with the popular *ABC Wide World of Sports*

Shirley displays the enormous trophy that she won at the Winternationals in 1966. With her is, of course, Miss Hurst Golden Shifter Linda Vaughn. The gentleman standing with them is the legendary entrepreneur George Hurst, inventor of the famed Hurst shifter and many other pieces of performance equipment. (Photo Courtesy Chrysler. Chrysler is a trademark of FCA USA LLC.)

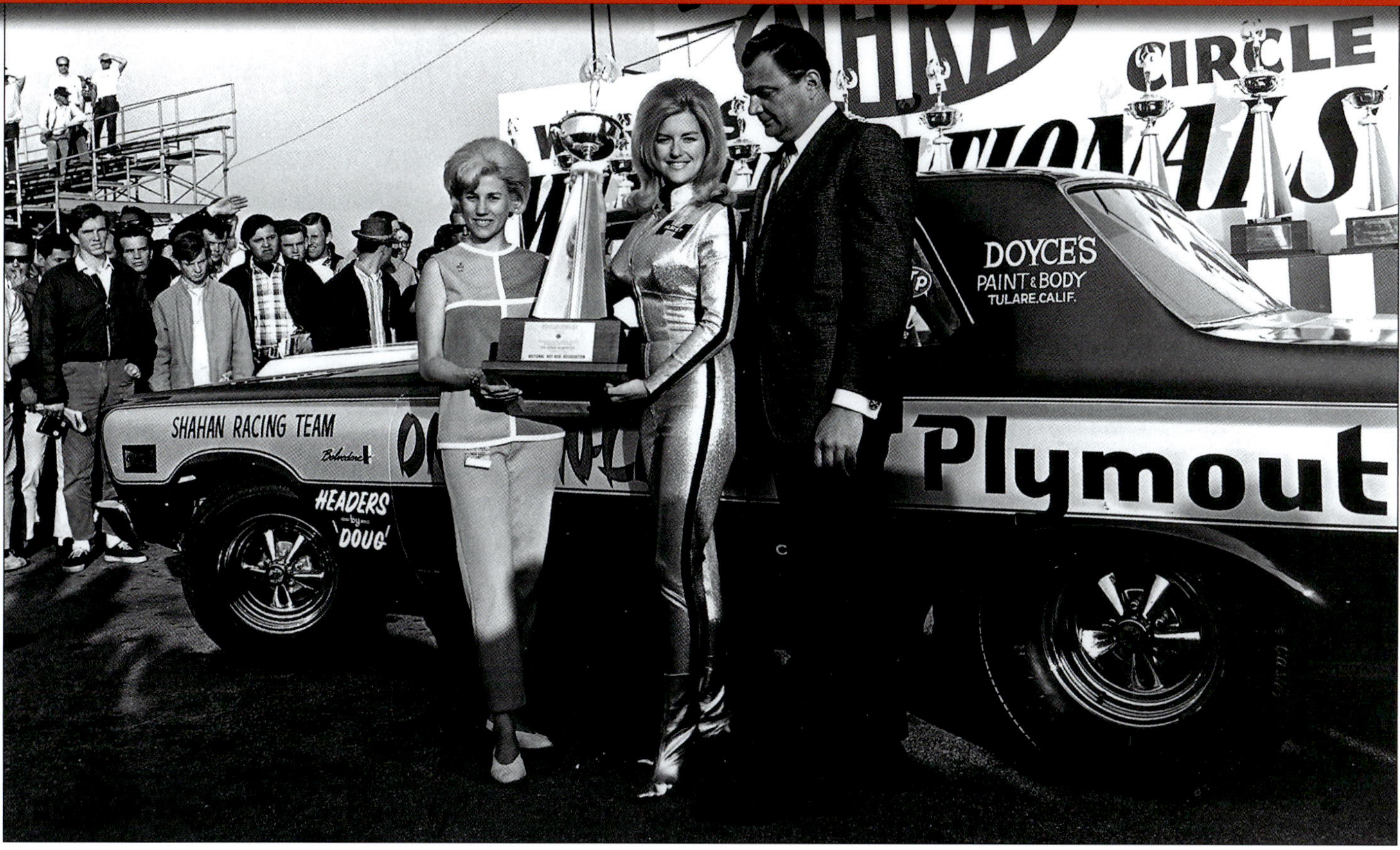

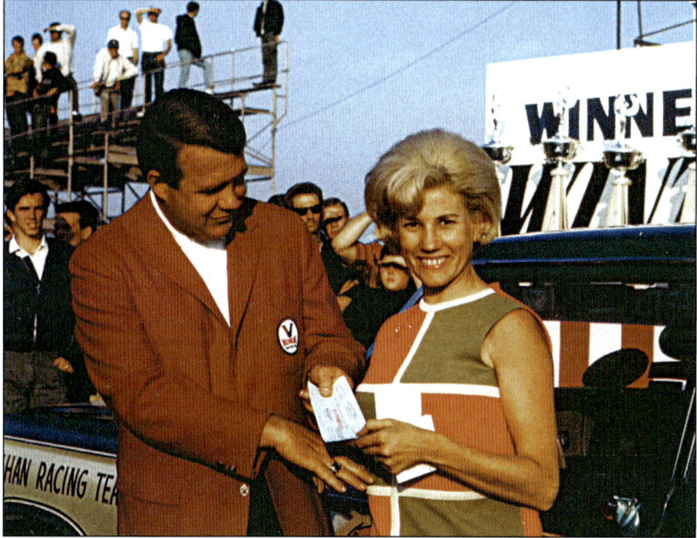

Shirley not only won fame at the 1966 Winternationals but she also took home a bag of money as well. She received a check from a representative of the Valvoline Oil Company, which was one of the event sponsors. As time went on, Shirley and H.L. won additional sponsors that were eager to have their name displayed on a winning car. (Photo Courtesy the Patrick Foster Collection)

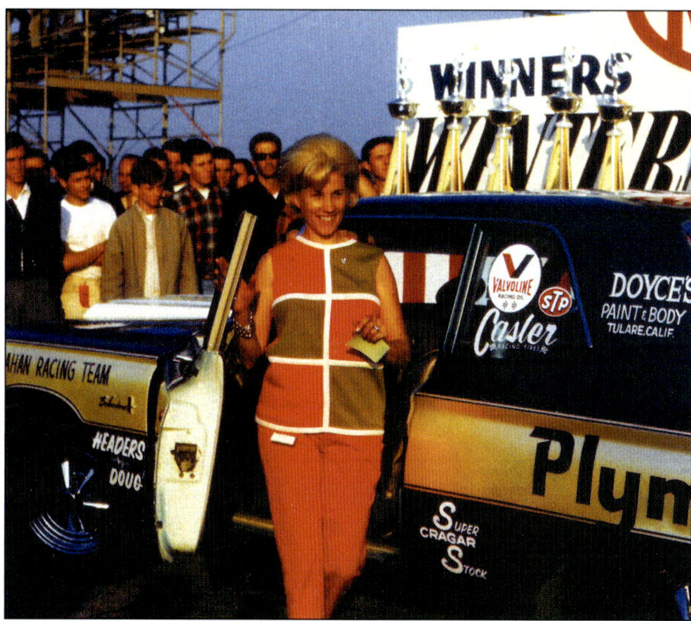

Shirley poses with her car and her check from Valvoline at the 1966 Winternationals. Note the Valvoline decal on Shirley's car along with the Casler Racing Tires decal and the Cragar Wheels sticker. (Photo Courtesy the Patrick Foster Collection)

Champion **again** sparks the...

Winners at the Winternationals!

TOP FUEL Winner of the 1965 NHRA Nationals and Winternationals, the "Hawaiian" does it again! Mike Snively drives Roland Leong's rapid rail to victory in just 7.54 seconds—at 209.78 mph! And the potent Keith Black Chrysler again gets its spark from Champions!

TOP STOCK The Drag-On Lady strikes! Shirley Shahan pilots her H.L. Shahan-tuned, Champion-sparked Plymouth to Top Stock honors with an 11.26-second run at 126.76 mph!

TOP GAS Gordon "Collecting" Collett takes another big one! His Champion-sparked Chrysler pulls him to 189.86 mph and victory in just 8.33 seconds!

SUPER ELIMINATOR Victory in this new bracket for all blown cars is won by Hugh Tucker in his Chrysler-powered, Champion-sparked AA/Street Roadster.

JUNIOR STOCK The hotly contested Junior Stock battle sees 23 class winners battle for honors, with final victory going to this '66 B/S Chevrolet. Entered by Bill Casler and driven by Wiley Cossey, its 427-cube mill is sparked by Champions.

COMPETITION ELIMINATOR

Arnold Chaves drives the Dos Palmas Machine D/A, powered by a Champion-sparked Chevrolet, to top a field of 14 class winners.

The 1966 NHRA Winternationals is the biggest and best winter drag meet yet! And six big Eliminator titles are won by Champion-sparked cars! It's more proof that—no matter how tough the going—you can depend on *Champions*. So next time *you* install spark plugs, make sure they're BOSS plugs—*Champions!*

CHAMPION SPARK PLUG COMPANY • TOLEDO, OHIO 43601

Not to be outdone by Shirley's other sponsors, Champion Spark Plugs ran this print advertisement for the winners at the 1966 Winternationals. Shirley and her Hemi Belvedere are seen in the second row with the following: "Top Stock—The Drag-On Lady strikes! Shirley Shahan pilots her H.L. Shahan-tuned, Champion-sparked Plymouth to Top Stock honors with an 11.26-second run to 126.76 mph!"

LEFT: *Shirley received checks from several sponsors for winning the 1966 Winternationals. George Hurst presented her with a check for her win. Shirley and H.L. got to know Hurst pretty well, and she admired his business skill and his inventiveness. In addition to his performance equipment, Hurst invented the famous Jaws of Life rescue tool that is used by so many fire departments to rescue people stuck in cars after a bad accident. (Photo Courtesy Chrysler. Chrysler is a trademark of FCA USA LLC.)* **RIGHT:** *To say that Chrysler Corporation was pleased with Shirley being named Top Stock Eliminator at the NHRA Winternationals would be a gross understatement. Chrysler was thrilled! Not only had a Plymouth won but it won with a woman driving, which was the first time a woman had ever won a major NHRA event! The publicity they received from that double-win situation was worth a fortune. (Photo Courtesy Chrysler. Chrysler is a trademark of FCA USA LLC.)*

television program. Her record-book win also put her on the cover of *National Dragster* magazine. In time, Shirley's win would open up opportunities for more women to compete in professional drag racing because she proved that it could be done.

It proves how quickly life can change. In the space of less than 12 seconds, Shirley Shahan went from being a highly competitive driver in a field of other highly competitive drivers to being an undisputed champion, the winner, and a major celebrity in the field of drag racing. National news wires spread the word across the country and around the world, and it brought tons of free publicity for her as well.

Shirley receives a hug from beloved comedian/actor Red Buttons. Becoming Top Stock Eliminator at the 1966 Winternationals brought an abundance of free publicity for Shirley. She won a free trip to Las Vegas, where she got to see Diana Ross at her opening show at the Frontier Hotel. Shirley was invited to Diana Ross's backstage party, and one of the people she met was Red Buttons. (Photo Courtesy Shirley Shahan)

"Due to my winning the Winternationals, I appeared on the *Hollywood Squares* and *To Tell the Truth* television shows in New York City," Shirley recalled. "One of the prizes I won was a free trip to Las Vegas, and when I went there, I got to see Diana Ross at her opening show at the Frontier Hotel. I was also invited to her backstage party, which was great fun, and one of the people I got to meet was comedian/actor Red Buttons. A nice man—he gave me a big hug!"

As noted, H.L. had modified Shirley's racer with fuel injection and had it running on nitro during

After her historic, record-smashing win at the 1966 Winternationals, Shirley was almost immediately whisked away to be interviewed for the popular ABC Wide World of Sports television program. This may have been her first appearance on television, but it would not be her last. (Photo Courtesy Chrysler. Chrysler is a trademark of FCA USA LLC.)

The Plymouth Division of Chrysler Corporation showcased the top drivers of its cars in this somewhat snarky advertisement that thanks the competition for showing up. Bragging about the great year that Plymouth was having in racing, it says, ". . . ask the man who didn't own [a Plymouth]; he finished second a lot." In the upper left-hand image, Shirley Shahan and her Drag-On Lady Hemi Belvedere is shown, which, according to Plymouth, ". . . shut down all the stocks to become the first 'Mrs. Stock Eliminator.'" It's nice to be recognized. (Photo Courtesy Chrysler. Chrysler is a trademark of FCA USA LLC.)

'66 NHRA Winternationals, Pomona, Calif.—Shirley "Drag-On Lady" Shahan, in her specially prepared Hemi-Belvedere, shut down all stocks to become the first "Mrs. Stock Eliminator."

'66 NHRA Springnationals, Bristol, Tenn.—Jere Stahl, in a specially prepared Hemi-Belvedere, blew off everybody in A/S, then went on to take Top Stock Eliminator.

We'd like to thank our competition.
For showing up.

Let's just say 1966 was a very good year. For Plymouth, that is. And if you don't believe us, ask the man who didn't own one; he finished second a lot. Which, in a drag race, is about as low as you can get. Too bad, fella. But thanks for showing up.

Moral: Buy The Boss—Belvedere GTX. 440 cubes, standard; 426 Hemi, optional. For street or strip. You'll never love another. Hear us: Plymouth is out to win.

Plymouth

'66 NHRA Summernationals, Indy.—Jere Stahl and said Plymouth did it again, walking away with Top Stock Eliminator (i.e., if you can call an 11.73 ET walking.)

'66 NHRA World Championship Finals, Tulsa—Make that three in a row for ol' Jere, as he and his Plymouth took Top Stock for the third time in one season!

the head-up match races, but it was then converted back for the NHRA Winternationals.

Up to this point, Shirley still considered herself to be a part-time racer and a semi-professional. This was mainly because she still had a full-time job with the Southern California Gas Company and that was her primary source of income, although it was being rapidly surpassed by her earnings as a top-ranked driver. With her rise in the standings, it was clearly time for her to make a big decision: should she remain a semi-professional, keeping her day job even though that meant giving up a lot of important racing opportunities, or should she cut her last ties to "the regular life" and become a full-time professional driver?

That decision was easy. Shirley loved racing, and that's what she wanted to do for a living. So, on April 15, 1966, Shirley quit her job at Southern California Gas to concentrate all of her time and attention on Super Stock racing. She made sure she left the gas company on good terms because she realized that she might want to return to it someday and because, well, Shirley is just a nice lady.

As mentioned, in 1965, H.L. had been working with Butch Leal on the famous *California Flash* Hemi Plymouth before deciding to devote all of his time working on Shirley's racer, which by now sported the already famous "Drag-On-Lady" lettering on the sides.

Some years later, Shirley relayed the following to Bob McClurg:

"After we won the Winternationals, drag strip promoters started calling us to go and race on the East Coast as well as the West. So, we had to make the decision: am I going to keep my job and is H.L. going to continue running the shop, or are we going to go racing full time? In the end, I decided that I was going to quit my job and become a full-time professional racer. Meanwhile, Dick Carvalho, who was a friend of H.L. and me, ran the shop while H.L. was gone on the road with me.

"That April 15, I quit my day job. Our first race was at Memphis, Tennessee. H.L. left a couple of days earlier with Bob Rehfeld and our son Bob, driving out with the race car. Then, I flew on ahead, arriving there first. I told him that he could meet me there, and I said I would be staying at the Holiday Inn, where I had a reservation.

"However, when he got to Memphis, H.L. found out that there were actually seven Holiday Inns in the area, and I hadn't [specified] which one I would be at. Here we were, 27- and 30-year-old young kids, and we lacked the sort of traveling experience where we would make sure to let each other know the address and phone number of the particular hotel we were staying at.

"Well, it took H.L. a little while to find out which Holiday Inn I booked into. I guess we were so inexperienced as travelers we just didn't know what was going on!"

Match Racing

So, Shirley began to tour. Talk about a liberating feeling! She competed all that summer, match racing all over the United States and even into Mexico. Match racing was important for her because, as she explained, "That really is how I earned my living after I quit the gas company, and I have to tell you, match racing was quite an experience. You ran on bumpy tracks, narrow tracks, eighth-mile tracks four cars abreast with short shutoff areas, and dark night tracks.

"To be competitive in match races, H.L. installed fuel injection for the engine and moved the rear wheels two inches forward. That altered the weight distribution and gave us much better traction. The way things worked was that we'd race all day then sometimes drive all night to get to the next racetrack. But you know, looking back on it, it was a lot of fun. Along the way, you'd see old friends, meet new ones while driving on bumpy, unsafe tracks and try to match wits with the other drivers—not to mention with the race promoters, TV and radio stations, newspaper offices, flag starters, and track

This press photo was taken at the headquarters of Doug's Headers. Most of the other sponsors' decals have been removed from the car to highlight Doug's Headers sponsorship. (Photo Courtesy Chrysler. Chrysler is a trademark of FCA USA LLC.)

managers, and try to get paid, which sometimes became contentious.

"H.L. and I raced all over the United States, including Hawaii, and even traveled down to Mexico City. I'm proud to be able to honestly say that we won the majority of the races. It sure was an exciting time; you were living completely on the edge, and you had to win to earn. Sure, it could be stressful at times, but we also had a lot of fun.

"One time, I raced against Tom McEwen at Lions Drag Strip when he was running a really fast jet-powered car. Because of the difference in power between his car and mine, he gave me a half-track head start, and he still managed to blow past me just before the finish line. He was traveling at over 300 miles per hour!"

Endorsements

Among the many products Shirley endorsed were Buco racing helmets, which were made by the Buco Products Division of the American Safety company. In one advertisement, Shirley explained her choice of helmets this way: "My Buco helmet isn't exactly the thing to wear over a bouffant hairdo, but I know I can depend on the protection." The advertisement then went on to say, "Take the advice of the Drag-On Lady and look to Buco for safety helmets, competition belts, harnesses, and other important safety products."

In 1966, the Casler Tire Company used Shirley in its advertisements, one of which noted that the three top winners at the Winternationals had all

Becoming a
TOP ELIMINATOR

Not having anywhere near enough skill to be a competitive racer, I've often wondered what a professional driver thinks are the most important attributes needed to be a winner. So, below is a Q&A with Shirley Shahan.

Author: Exactly what does it take to become a Top Eliminator?

Shirley: It takes a lot of things. Number one, you have to have a competitive personality; that's really important. Number two, you also need to have very good reflexes. Number three, you have to know that you are a winner. Number four, you have to have the best crew chief.

Author: Why good reflexes?

Shirley: (Laughs) Well, you need to have fast reflexes because in racing your car might be 1/10 of a second slower than the other guy's car, so to beat him, you need to make up that 1/10 of a second plus a little more. The way you do that is by being a little faster hitting the gas pedal and a little faster working the shifter. In addition, knowing exactly when to shift gears is very important.

Author: Anything else?

Shirley: Well, you really have to have a competitive car, obviously, and that car has to be tuned and prepared by someone who knows how to get every last bit of speed out of it. Ultimately, everything matters, because it's a combination of things that make the difference between winning and coming in second or third or way back in the race results. In my case, H.L. was the best mechanic.

Author: The time you spend behind the wheel of a typical drag race is only mere seconds. How does it feel during that time as you accelerate from 0 to maybe 130 mph? Does time seem to slow down?

Shirley: Well, mostly the time feels like what it is, 10 seconds or less. Except maybe when you look out the corner of your eye and your opponent is pulling up beside you; then it seems like an awful long time to the end because you're worried that he's going to pass you.

With a big win like the Winternationals, there are always lots of press photos taken, and this is one of them. The beautiful young lady next to Shirley is Miss Winternationals. (Photo Courtesy Shirley Shahan)

In this Plymouth sales brochure from 1966, Shirley Shahan is highlighted for setting a new S/SA top speed mark of 129.30 mph at Palmdale, California, that August. That wasn't her fastest speed ever, of course. We asked Shirley what her fastest top speed was, and the answer was 142 mph! This was in the days before four-wheel-disc brakes and all of the safety equipment that modern race cars enjoy. (Photo Courtesy Chrysler. Chrysler is a trademark of FCA USA LLC.)

11 cars . . . all Plymouths . . . qualify for Top Stock Eliminator at NHRA Winternationals.

And speaking of fast, the Hemi (and some of its smaller-inch cousins) manages to get specially modified Plymouths from one end of a ¼ mile to the other ahead of its competition in some really hot elapsed times.

Like the last NHRA Winternationals. The only cars to qualify for Top Stock Eliminator were Plymouths. Eleven of them. And Plymouth took nine class wins at the meet.

And two of these class wins were scored by Plymouth Barracudas, relative newcomers to big-time drag racing. The Barracudas also made a big dent in the NHRA Springnationals, where Richard Petty won the B/Altered class with his Hemi-powered Barracuda. This was where the season's most unusual exhibition car made its debut. The rear-engined wheel-standing Hurst "Hemi Under Glass," a Plymouth Barracuda powered by the Plymouth 426-cubic-inch Hemi engine and driven by Bill Shrewsberry.

"Drag-on-Lady" hits 129.30.

Among the records set by Plymouths in drag races is the S/SA top speed mark of 129.30 set at Palmdale, California in August by Shirley Shahan with her Hemi-powered Plymouth "Drag-on-Lady."

Plymouth won two classes and tied another at the premier running of the SUPER STOCK Magazine Nationals at York, Pennsylvania in August.

At the CARS Magazine meet at Cecil County, Maryland, August 21, Hemi-powered Plymouths won in three classes.

Hemi-Cuda: 171.85 in 8.88.

And, before we forget the quick-quarter machines, remember that the "Hemi-Cuda" campaigned by the Southern California Plymouth Dealers has been eating up the competition. Last November it became the quickest and fastest stock-bodied, stock-wheelbase drag machine going. At Carlsbad (Calif.) it cranked off a 171.85 in 8.88!

So, any way you count it . . . drag strip, super stock track, or the Salt Flats, you're going to find Hemi-powered Plymouths out in front. You may not need quite as much as the Hemi turns out, but whatever you're looking for in a car, Plymouth probably has more of it than anyone else.

Any time you're in doubt, remember things like torsion bars, the Hemi, the TorqueFlite transmission . . . every one of them available in Plymouths. And the standard safety equipment: padded instrument panel and sun visors, inside and outside rear-view mirrors, back-up lights, anti-windlift windshield wipers and electric washers, safety inside door-release handles. All of these safety features, combined with proving-ground safety research and the actual on-the-race-track testing are what make the '66 Plymouth synonymous with safe, dependable performance. And make the Plymouth the great road machine it is.

In addition to "the hot ones," we do make a variety of luxury cars . . . and some surprising economy models too. You can check them out at your nearest Plymouth Dealer along with the hot machines. But if your real dream is a Hemi-powered Plymouth Belvedere, check the next page.

Fun on
THE ROAD *Part II*

I asked Shirley to tell a story I'd heard once before but didn't know if it was true. She relayed this story:

"One of the stupidest things that ever happened to us actually happened in California. We had raced in Long Beach one Saturday night, this was in August of 1965, and Richard Schroeder—he later drove an SS/AMX too—invited us to stay at his home. Little did we know that to get to his house we would have to drive by the Watts neighborhood, and this was right in the middle of the Watts Riots. Remember them? They consumed that part of Los Angeles for nearly a week and some 34 people died, and more than 3,400 people were arrested. It was the worst rioting in America in decades.

"Well, I have to tell you there were exactly two cars on the freeway that night: ours and Richard's. We could see the lights of police cars and flames from burning buildings. To this day, I don't know why we weren't stopped or shot at."

Shirley raced all summer and didn't come home until after the Nationals in September. Along the way, there were quite a few funny things that happened. Once, for a match race in Houston, Texas, Shirley was scheduled to race against her good friend and racing rival the great Hubert Platt, a.k.a. the Georgia Shaker. Platt had a well-earned reputation as a joker and prankster; in fact, the motor press often referred to him as "the Clown Prince of Drag Racing."

For this race, Platt borrowed her blonde wig, which he put on, along with his silver fire suit. Then, just before the match races were to begin, Platt drove Shirley's Hemi Plymouth right up to the starting line. No one thought anything was different or unusual, they just thought it was Shirley at the wheel, until Platt stepped out of Shirley's car dressed in drag and wearing a big grin. He raised his hand, waved to the crowd, and all of a sudden, they realized who it was. Platt, and Shirley, got a huge laugh from the stands along with a standing ovation.

Once the comedy was over, the two competitors got down to the business at hand. Well, Shirley put Platt in his place by winning the first two rounds, but then Platt came back strong and won rounds three and four. The fifth run would have decided the winner, but before it got going, the transmission in Shirley's Mopar broke, and track officials ended up calling it a tie.

THE CHRYSLER *Years*

During her career, Shirley drove a series of *Drag-On-Lady*-themed Mopar cars that were tuned by her husband, H.L. Shahan. These included three SS/BA classed cars: the first was the 1965 Plymouth Belvedere I, which was followed by a 1967 Dodge Coronet and then a 1968 Dodge Dart. Each one of them was powered by the famed Chrysler 426 Hemi engine.

"The '65 and '68 models were both limited-edition cars from the factory," Shirley said. "I think my favorite of the three was the '65 because it was a really fast car and it got me an awful lot of good press."

Looking back on it, the year 1966 proved to be a great one for Shirley. She was still driving for the Chrysler factory team and doing quite well. She had followed her 1965 *Hot Rod* Championship win with a final-round finish at the 1966 AHRA Winternationals. In the racing world and out, Shirley was becoming something of a media star. She was asked to appear on TV shows and do radio interviews, and the enthusiast magazines all covered her in detail. It was all pretty exciting for a young woman from a little town in Southern California.

Buco Puts **SAFETY** where the **ACTION** Is!

Shirley Shahan, "Drag-On-Lady," is one woman driver who has earned the respect of thousands of male drivers all over the country. Shirley has lots of savvy and go that has made her a consistent winner at drag strips everywhere. She also has lots of savvy when it comes to selecting protective equipment. "My Buco helmet isn't exactly the thing to wear over a bouffant hairdo, but I know I can depend on its protection." Like many racing drivers, Shirley Shahan realizes the importance that research has played in Buco's safety helmet design.

Take the advice of "Drag-On-Lady" and look to Buco for safety helmets, competition belts, harnesses and other important safety products. Write today for Buco's free '67 Speed Sport Catalog, decal and Safety Helmet Research Booklet.

Buco Products Division

BOX 1063, NORTHLAND CENTER STA., SOUTHFIELD MICH. 48076

DARBY, PENNSYLVANIA   **SOUTHFIELD, MICHIGAN**   **FRESNO, CALIFORNIA**

Buco Products Division of the American Safety company hired Shirley to appear in ads for their popular racing helmets. The closing lines advise readers to "Take the advice of the Drag-On-Lady and look to Buco for safety helmets, competition belts, and other important safety products."

PERSONALITIES

During her career, Shirley Shahan met and became friends with some of the greatest legends in drag racing, as well as some pretty odd types. Below is a Q&A with author Patrick Foster and Shirley Shahan.

Author: You knew Buddy Martin pretty well. Tell us about him.

Shirley: Buddy Martin was the crew chief and the brains behind the Sox & Martin racing team, while Ronnie Sox was the driver and a pretty flashy personality. They also had a man by the name of Jake King as their mechanic. We got to know them all pretty well because in 1965 they got a '65 Plymouth like we did.

When we would go to North Carolina, we'd go stay at Buddy Martin's house, and over the weekend he'd take us to country fairs and things like that. Buddy was the kind of guy you could rely on for anything, really. I remember one time we were at a fair, and all of a sudden, I saw a guy fall on the ground, like he was having a seizure or something. I yelled for Buddy to come help because I knew that whatever it was that was wrong with that poor man, Buddy would know what to do. He was just that kind of guy.

Author: You became good friends with Doug Thorley and his wife, correct?

Shirley: Yes, that's right. They were wonderful people—always friendly. H.L. and Doug were best friends. They would go to Utah to hunt together. We'd visit them at their house. Doug kept a small burro on his front lawn.

Author: Like a garden statue?

Shirley: Goodness, no, it was a real live burro. You know, a small donkey, named Barney. It was sort of a pet. Doug had a white picket fence around his front yard and the burro stayed there all day, perfectly content. They had him for years. It was a residential neighborhood, but apparently the neighbors didn't mind.

Author: We've heard that some of the track owners could be difficult to work with.

Shirley: Well, there sure were a few characters. One of them was Bobby Starr in Greensboro, North Carolina. Bobby was known for walking around barefoot like a good ole boy, and also for hosting Ku Klux Klan meetings the night before the racing. I remember going to his track one Sunday and asking where Bobby was and being told that he was out in the

One of the benefits of being the child of a famous person is that you usually get to meet other famous people. In this photo, Shirley Shahan's young daughter Janet is with the great performance icon Miss Hurst Golden Shifter Linda Vaughn. Vaughn made personal appearances at racetracks all over the country as a symbol of and spokeswoman for Hurst Performance Products, usually dressed in eye-catching outfits. (Photo Courtesy Shirley Shahan)

*Another well-known driver fielding a Hemi Mopar was Dick Landy, who is seen next to his **Landy's Dodge** and with his trademark cigar. (Photo Courtesy the Patrick Foster Collection)*

woods chopping down the cross they'd used for a meeting the night before. That's just how things were in the South back then. It was kind of shocking.

When we were on a racing tour in the South in 1966, I could not believe they didn't let the Black people into the races. They actually had to stand outside. Being from California, that was a shock for me. We raced with Malcom Durham and Corky Booze, and they were good friends. Corky raced a Javelin, I believe, and Cloy Fitzgerald, who was a NHRA tech official, was and is a good friend. One time at a race, Norma Kempton, Cloy, and myself walked up to the front desk of the motel and asked for a room. Talk about shock.

Author: Tell us some more stories, please!

Shirley: Some of the best people I met were Carl and Marie Gay. Carl ran the racetrack in Dickenson, Texas. It's called the Bay Area Raceway today. His son Don was a racing legend known as the "Texas Teenager." The great thing about driving for the Gays was that you were treated like family.

As a racer, you stayed in their home. They had a cook, I think her name was Esther, and she cooked all day long on race day, which was Saturday. After the match races, we would all go back to the Gays' home to eat. Esther would prepare roast beef, chicken, and pork, plus salads, breads, all kinds of cakes and pies, ice cream, anything you could think of they had set out for us. All of the track hands, racers, and friends were invited. In fact, it was over at their house where I met Dave McClelland, who became a legendary racetrack announcer and also a good friend.

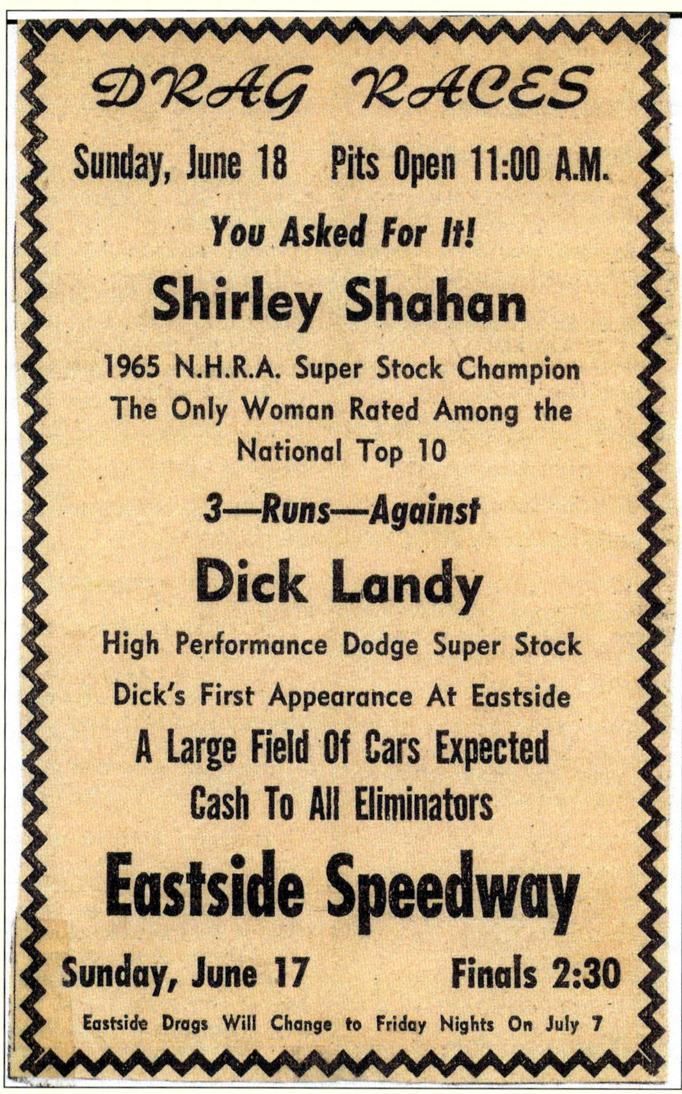

This is an advertisement from 1966 for a series of three match races between Shirley Shahan and Dick Landy at the Eastside Speedway. It was Landy's first appearance there.

Linda Vaughn was a big part of the sparkle and glamour of the drag racing world in the 1960s. Seeing each other at tracks around the country, she and Shirley became good friends. (Photo Courtesy the Patrick Foster Collection)

Jim Tibbets was another old drag racer friend who was a bit of a character. He was always promoting something! Jim was on the Ford Racing Team as well as building and managing various drag strips. Jim is the man who ran the Circle Track Circuit in Denver. In 1972, he asked H.L. to run the AMC Hornet after we left American Motors. They ran a Chevy, a Ford, and the AMC out of their shop.

Author: We've seen a photograph of you and H.L. with Mark Donohue and Roger Penske.

Shirley: Yes, but the truth is that was the only time I met them. They were just starting out with American Motors. Mark Donohue was very nice, and you know, Roger Penske has certainly become a huge success in business since then.

Author: Tell us about George Hurst.

Shirley: Well, he was just a brilliant man. You know, in addition to all the high-performance stuff he made, he also designed and built the Jaws of Life rescue tool, which is still used today to rescue people who are trapped in their smashed-up cars after a bad accident. In addition, he's the one who hired Linda Vaughn and made her a superstar attraction in the racing world. But it became a sad story. George got forced out of his company, and I think he later committed suicide. A sad ending for such a great man.

Author: You were friends with Linda Vaughn, right?

Shirley: Yes. When I met her, it was at the Winternationals in 1966, [and] she was just this sweet little thing. She was from Georgia originally. She's a great person and has a great memory. She's the kind of lady who can meet your children once and then 10 years later see them with you and remember each of their names. An amazing memory. She's a really nice person. You know, early on her mother made all of her clothes for her; that's why they fit so well. She had to because Linda's, uh, natural endowments meant that most store-bought dresses and blouses would have been too tight at the top.

Shirley got to know and respect George Hurst for his business acumen and nice personality. He built a big high-performance equipment business only to lose it in a deal gone wrong. The man on the left is J.C. Agajanian, who was an influential figure in American motorsports history. He was a promoter and race car owner, among other things. (Photo Courtesy the Patrick Foster Collection)

Author: How about Walt Czarnecki?

Shirley: He was a nice young man working for George Hurst when I first met him. After a while, Dave Landrith at Chrysler realized Walt had a lot of potential and helped him get a job at Penske Racing. He ended up as the executive vice president at Penske Racing.

Author: Any others you'd like to mention?

Shirley: Yes. Hubert Platt, who was known as "the Georgia Shaker." Hubert was a real personality. Every time he'd come up to see us, he'd bring a few bottles of genuine Georgia moonshine! And Herb and Marie McCandless became good friends. Herb is still involved in the racing world. Sadly, Marie passed away a few years ago.

used Casler tires. Shirley's picture topped the page because she was the big winner: Top Stock Eliminator and also Super Stock runner-up.

Another product that she endorsed was Fram oil filters in an advertisement that proclaimed, "Shirley Shahan wins with Fram Filters!" Not to be outdone, Chrysler's Plymouth Division also devoted advertising space to Shirley and the other Plymouth drivers, although one might wince a little when reading her described as "the first Mrs. Stock Eliminator."

Shirley also promoted Doug Thorley headers, Valvoline oil, and Iskenderian cams. Like Shirley, Ed Iskenderian was originally from the San Joaquin Valley. Goodyear Tires asked her to promote its tires, and she did some great advertising for Cragar wheels, appearing in a miniskirt in one advertisement and wearing just a jacket in another. She also

The DRAG-ON *Lady on TV*

Below is a Q&A with author Patrick Foster and Shirley Shahan.

Author: From 1966 through 1968, you became very well known around the country. We heard you even made some television appearances around that time; is that true?

Shirley: Yes, actually it is. In 1968, I was a contestant on the popular TV programs *Hollywood Squares* and *To Tell the Truth*. If you don't know how *To Tell the Truth* worked, it went like this: myself and two other ladies were introduced to a panel of three people. Each of us introduced ourselves as drag racer Shirley Shahan, and then the panelists were allowed a few minutes to question each of us about our expertise, trying to guess which of us was the real deal. In the end, panelist Bill Cullen was able to guess I was a drag racer! It was a lot of fun!"

At the *Hollywood Squares*, I was told to bring along three outfits, as they filmed several episodes at one time. The said no stripes and no checks—they don't show up well on TV. So, I brought three outfits but two of them were the same color, and boy did I get chewed out!

Author: The Winternationals win also got you some pretty good attention, didn't it?

Shirley: Oh, yes, actually quite a bit. ABC's *Wide World of Sports* interviewed me on the spot, right after the race, and that was very exciting!

did endorsements for B&M transmissions and a safety commercial for Dodge.

A New Dodge for 1967

Toward the end of the 1966 racing season, Chrysler gave Shirley and H.L. one of the new 1967 Dodge R/T Street Hemis to drive.

"They sure did, but, you know, it was a real sled!" Shirley said. "It was a pretty car to look at and even came with air-conditioning, a vinyl roof, and a really nice interior and of course it had a big Hemi engine under the hood. But as pretty as it was, that thing was just a lead sled. It never ran nearly as fast as the '65 Plymouth did.

"Jack McFarland is the one who got us that car, and I'm sure he meant well. It wasn't a special edition or specially built unit like the '65 was, and it just couldn't move fast enough. Part of the problem was that it weighed about 3,700 pounds, [which was] roughly 300 pounds more than the previous car, and I think because of that it was just not competitive, especially with the automatic transmission.

"We found we just couldn't get that Dodge R/T to launch off the line quick enough simply by flooring the gas pedal, so we started doing neutral-gear starts. I would rev the engine up to something like 5,000 to 6,000 rpm in neutral and then slam it into gear. It would launch a little better that way. I wasn't the only one doing this; other drivers were doing it too. The only problem was that the cars started breaking—actually more like exploding—transmission parts.

"Chrysler's Dick Maxwell got mad at us and said, 'If we hear that you guys are doing neutral-gear starts, that's it. No more free parts for you!' Well, I suppose besides the considerable expense of replacing a blown transmission, Chrysler was also concerned about its image. I guess it never looks good to have the public see you blowing transmissions on race day. The Chrysler automatic back then was a pretty tough transmission, but those neutral-gear starts could blow them up sometimes. But thankfully I never broke anything on my car. Some of the other drivers ended up blowing their transmissions, which naturally made the Chrysler corporate people really angry."

Chrysler also gave Shirley and H.L. a new Dodge D500 truck to haul the race car. They had the truck customized in Tulare. Thankfully, sometime later, Chrysler also gave Shirley another new car to race. This time, it was a 1968½ Hurst Hemi Dart. When Shirley took the wheel of that hot little number for the first time, things began to change again, this

The main problem with the new Dodge Coronet drag car that Shirley was given was that it didn't launch well off the line, and that is a very big problem in drag racing. H.L. put everything he had into making the car faster but was never entirely satisfied with the results. Note the Carlsbad Raceway sign in the background. (Photo Courtesy Chrysler. Chrysler is a trademark of FCA USA LLC.)

Here's a press photo of Shirley and H.L. with a writer from Car Craft *magazine. Shirley added the note on the photo, which is just an indication of how eager they were to get out of that 1967 Coronet R/T and into something lighter and faster. That was coming soon. (Photo Courtesy Chrysler. Chrysler is a trademark of FCA USA LLC.)*

time for the better.

"I think that Hemi Dart was probably the best race car we ever had," Shirley said. "It was a really fast car. I didn't win any big races with that car because we weren't chasing the points back then, but we match raced it quite a lot, and it was very competitive.

"When we started touring in 1966, doing a lot of match racing, we sort of got out of the NHRA spotlight, and we didn't get as much press notice as we had before. We were winning our match races and stuff and earning very good money, but nobody in the press ever seemed to notice. Well, once in a while someone from the track would phone in a story, but we just didn't get much notice from the press back then. Their focus was always more on the points races."

When asked about how fast she was able to run with the Dart, Shirley answered, "Well, we ran 10.90s at 133.00 mph. It was a really fast little car. But we didn't set any records because, like I said, we weren't chasing the points."

Shirley said that the wild wheelies and sometimes the erratic behavior of her various race cars never scared her.

"The only time I ever got really scared was on those Southern drag strips that weren't made all that great," she said. "To give you an example, at Memphis, there were lights just to the end of the track, and then the track ended in a sweeping curve. Now, your car doesn't always have working headlights, so if it was dark you had to just kind of feel your way around the track.

The Drag-On Lady's new dragster for 1968 is shown. The 1968 Hemi Dart was compact, light, and extremely fast, which of course made Shirley happy after struggling with the sluggish Coronet so long. (Photo Courtesy Shirley Shahan)

This color photo shows the new color scheme used for the Dart with the blue swirl lacework stenciling and new graphics. This shot was taken at the Winternationals. (Photo Courtesy Chrysler. Chrysler is a trademark of FCA USA LLC.)

"I remember once I was following the side of the road around, to get back for another run, when all of a sudden there wasn't any road under me. It ends up the rain had eroded all that side of the track and there I was hanging over the side of the road. I was stuck there, and nobody came out to get me unstuck. I could see guys were down at the other end of the road and were talking and yakking and ignoring me.

"Finally, I got hold of someone and said, 'Tell them to send someone to get me out of here!'"

It ended up that Shirley was extremely lucky that her car didn't roll down the embankment. There was an old fence post sticking up that went through the front tire and fender and that was the only thing that prevented her from a much more serious accident. She might have ended up rolling down a very steep ravine.

There were other incidents of the non-accident type that made life on the road more interesting. Early one Friday morning in 1967, Shirley and H.L. were at Doug's Headers in Los Angeles, getting new headers installed on their Dodge pickup truck, which at the time served as their tow vehicle. They were about to start another road trip and knew they had to be in North Carolina to race that

Thankfully, Chrysler finally gave Shirley another new car to replace the Coronet; this one was a 1968½ Hurst Hemi Dart. (Photo Courtesy Shirley Shahan)

Shirley makes a nice launch at a race at the Orange County International Raceway in California. She was ranked as one of the 10 best drivers in the country at the time and was a formidable competitor. Notice the different paint scheme used this year. (Photo Courtesy Chrysler. Chrysler is a trademark of FCA USA LLC.)

SHIRLEY SHAHAN, Top Stock eliminator, also Super Stock Automatic runnerup

WILEY COSSEY, "B" Stock Class winner
and Junior Stock eliminator

JOE SMITH, Super Stock Automatic
class winner

A way that Shirley earned extra money during her racing career was by promoting performance products for various companies. In this vintage print advertisement from May 1966, we see her at the Winternationals, where she drove on Casler "Spraling" Cheaters, which were popular high-performance tires. The advertisement describes Shirley as the Top Stock Eliminator and also Super Stock Automatic runner-up.

After campaigning the 1965 Belvedere for two years, Shirley and H.L. Shahan switched to racing for Chrysler Corporation's Dodge Division. They were given a new racer; this one was a beautiful white 1967 Dodge Coronet R/T hardtop equipped with the hot 426-ci Hemi V-8. It was a nice car, but as H.L. noted, it was a "lead sled" that was not nearly as quick as the Plymouth. (Photo Courtesy Chrysler. Chrysler is a trademark of FCA USA LLC.)

Shirley wears her silver fire suit in December 1966 buckling on her helmet in preparation of another run. Just 28 years old at the time, she was already a sensation in drag racing. (Photo Courtesy UPI)

Shirley has a discussion with Buster Couch, the official NHRA starter. (Photo Courtesy Chrysler. Chrysler is a trademark of FCA USA LLC.)

Sunday. They finally took off around 10 a.m.; H.L. drained a tank of gas while driving and then Shirley took over.

After two days, they stopped one night to fill up their truck, which had two gas tanks. In a hurry, they decided to fill just one tank. Unfortunately, the gas station attendant mistakenly pumped diesel fuel into their truck instead of Hi-test gasoline, and neither Shirley nor H.L. noticed it.

As they drove down the road, the truck's engine started misfiring like crazy, so they pulled over to try to determine exactly what the problem was. H.L. was able to figure it out pretty quickly, and got underneath the truck, opened up the petcock on the gas tank, and drained a tankful of diesel fuel onto the road. They switched to the other tank and drove back to the station to fill the truck again.

Bobby Starr was the promoter at the North Carolina drag strip. Shirley stopped to call him when they had reached the North Carolina border around 2 p.m. on race day and told him they wouldn't be able to make it in time.

"You better come on; we've got the people waiting in the grandstands," Starr replied.

Shirley and H.L. finally arrived around 3 p.m., and Starr was right. The grandstands were full of people who were waiting to see the Drag-On Lady race.

They weren't disappointed because, as Shirley recalled, "That day we had to race a Ford, a Chevy, and a Dodge, and we ended up beating all three of them."

Bobby Starr asked Shirley to race two more cars, but H.L. said they couldn't because the transmission was just about worn out.

"In the end, I think that Starr docked us $300 for being late," Shirley said.

As Shirley remembered, it was somewhere around this time that she received a phone call from none other than Al Turner, an executive in the performance division of the Ford Motor Company. Turner, who later was nicknamed "Big Smoke" Turner, wanted to know if Shirley would consider making a switch and become a driver for Ford.

Although she was happy enough at Chrysler, Shirley figured that it couldn't hurt to see what Ford had to offer. She agreed to meet with Turner at Ford headquarters in Dearborn, Michigan, known as the "Glass House." After a friendly discussion with Turner, she decided to stay with Chrysler for the moment. But it probably got her to thinking about making a move to another company if she could get the right deal. It would be perhaps a year or so later that just such a deal was presented to her.

During the 1967 and 1968 racing seasons, many women race drivers noticed that they were getting more attention, as well as respect, at the track. This was because the prior year Shirley Shahan had enjoyed such a big win at the Winternationals. It began to change some drivers' opinions of their female competitors.

All in all, the Chrysler deal wound up being a good one for Shirley. She and H.L. raced for them full time until the end of 1968, when a new deal was offered to her by another company that had watched what she was able to do for Plymouth and Dodge. For Shirley, there was a certain level of professional risk because the car company that wanted her to drive for them was none other than AMC, the maker of the car that every grandmother loved: the little Rambler.

Anyone who knew anything about racing knew that AMC had precious little experience in the field of motorsports. That was precisely why it wanted to have someone like Shirley on its team in the first place.

One thing that AMC had was guts, along with a few really good guys running its brand-new performance program. It also had some very good cars that had been recently introduced. In addition, AMC really wanted Shirley to drive for the company. The executives made her an offer that she couldn't refuse. So, she made the big decision to leave the Chrysler camp and drive for AMC.

"H.L. had the shop, we had the kids, I had quit my day job, and Chrysler wasn't paying us any sort of salary," Shirley said. "So, we lived off of what we earned from the shop and from match racing. That was fun, but it could also be scary at times; you were living by your wits and by your driving skill. There was no certainty that you would earn a paycheck in the coming week. In contrast to that, AMC offered us a lot more stability in our lives. So, we decided to make the move."

This press photo taken in late 1968 or possibly early 1969 shows that a new hood scoop was wide open this year and the paint graphics were different as well.

The use of lace stencils was popular back then, as a matter of fact, the author did lacework racing stripes on his 1962 Mercury.

(Photo Courtesy Chrysler. Chrysler is a trademark of FCA USA LLC.)

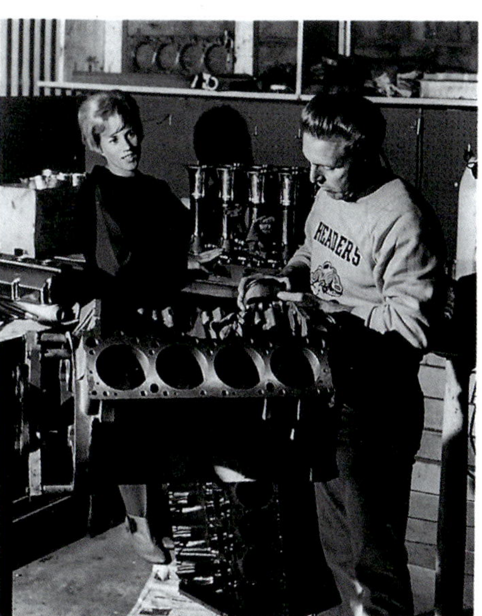

This photo collage was taken by photographer Chan Bush. The pictures were taken at the Shahan home as well as at the track. Not many women had a fire suit hanging in their clothes closet back then! (Photos Courtesy Chan Bush via Shirley Shahan)

H.L. tunes the quads on the Hemi Dodge. H.L. was a natural mechanic, a genius with his hands, and he was recognized throughout the racing world as a top wrench. He was a vital part of Shirley's racing success. (Photo Courtesy Chrysler. Chrysler is a trademark of FCA USA LLC.)

This is a hot little Dodge Dart tribute car that Shirley's son Bob built and raced. (Photo Courtesy Shirley Shahan)

Shirley's Dodge blasts down the track to another win. After struggling with their previous Dodge, the new Dart was a refreshing change of pace. (Photo Courtesy Patrick Foster Collection)

During the 1968 season, Shirley and H.L. toured the country doing match racing, which was always a big money-maker. Shirley was at the top of her game, and around this time, Ford Motor Company tried to recruit her to drive for them. (Photo Courtesy Chrysler. Chrysler is a trademark of FCA USA LLC.)

Shirley races at Cecil County Dragway in Rising Sun, Maryland. Her car is in the background and ahead of the Plymouth Barracuda at takeoff. Cecil County Dragway is still in operation today. (Photo Courtesy the Patrick Foster Collection)

Go-go boots were the style for young women in the 1960s, and Shirley was a very style-conscious young lady.

During the mid-1960s, many women race drivers noticed that they were getting more respect at the track. (Photo Courtesy Shirley Shahan)

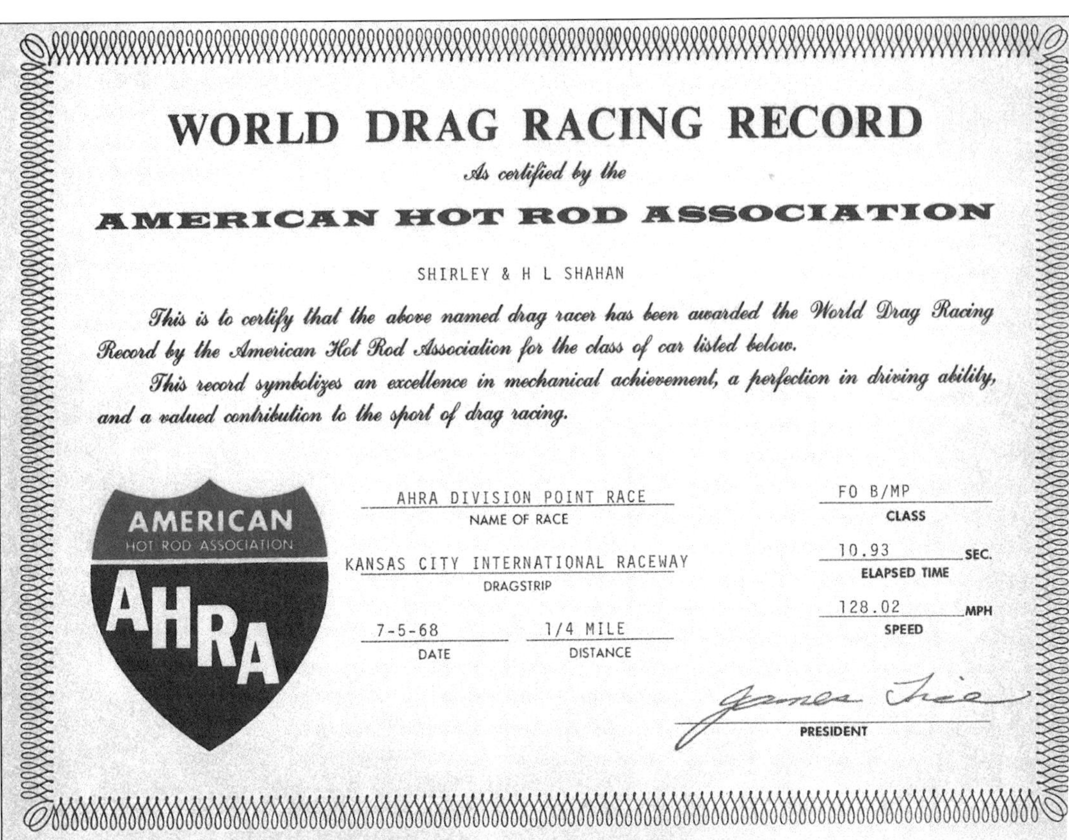

An AHRA World Drag Racing Record award certificate was issued to Shirley on July 5, 1968, for an ET of 10.93 and a speed of 128.02 mph in the quarter mile at the Kansas City International Raceway. This is one of many issued to Shirley during her career. (Photo Courtesy Shirley Shahan)

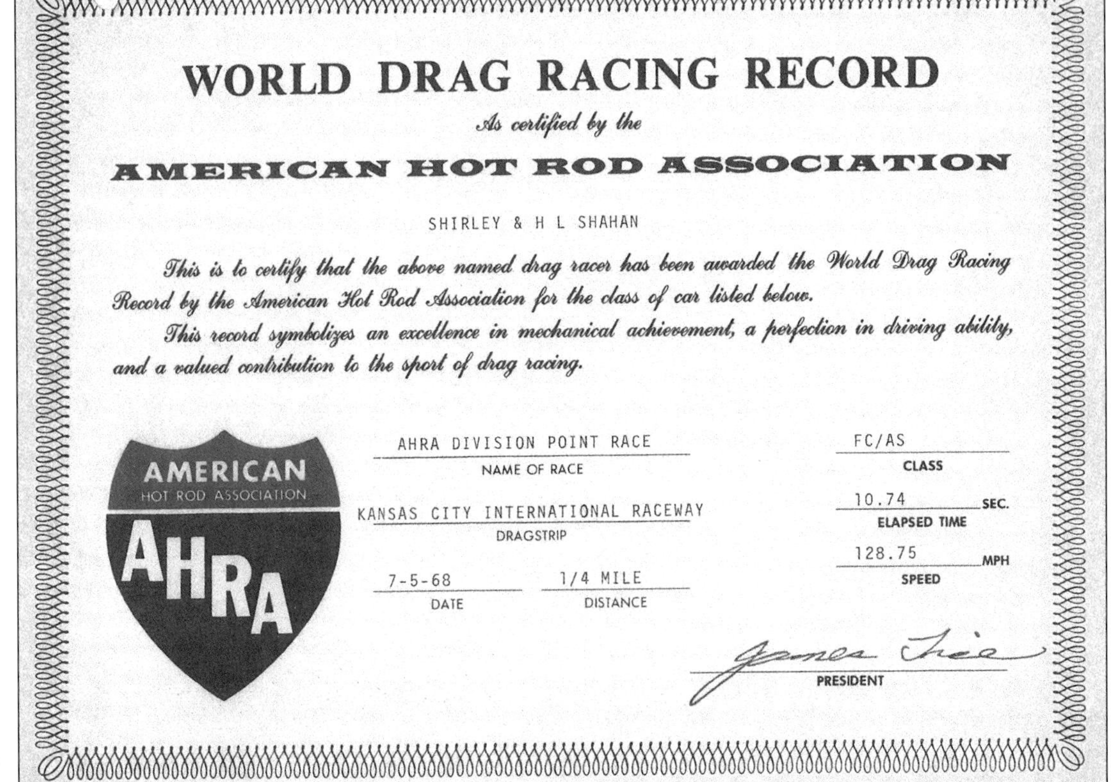

Another AHRA World Drag Racing Record was set by Shirley on July 5, 1968, at the Kansas City International Raceway. She was credited with setting a new record in class FC/AS by burning through the quarter mile in 10.74 seconds at a speed of 128.75 mph. (Photo Courtesy Shirley Shahan)

With tires smoking and engine screaming, Shirley set yet another AHRA world record in Kansas City, this time in the FC/BS class for an ET of 10.83 seconds and 126.76 mph. (Photo Courtesy Shirley Shahan)

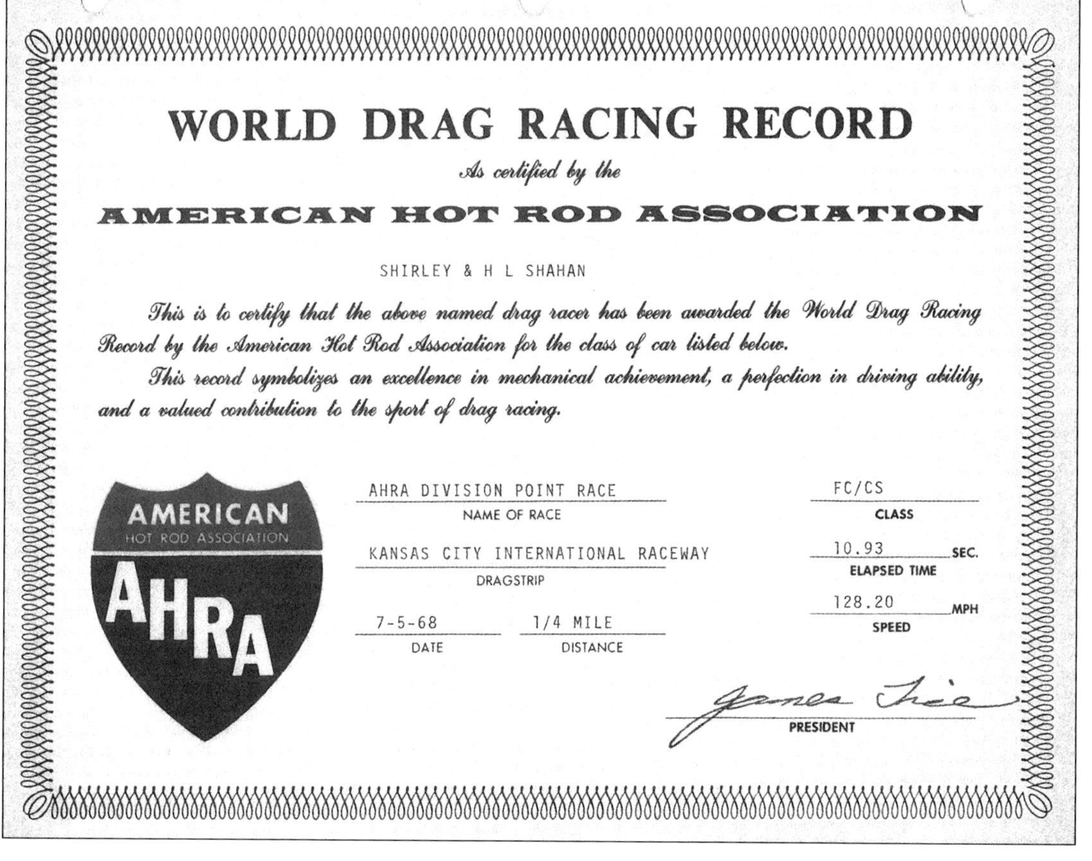

Shirley was obviously at the top of her game on July 5, 1968, because she set several world records, including this Class FC/CS record for 10.93 seconds and 128.20 mph. It was one of literally dozens of awards that she won. (Photo Courtesy Shirley Shahan)

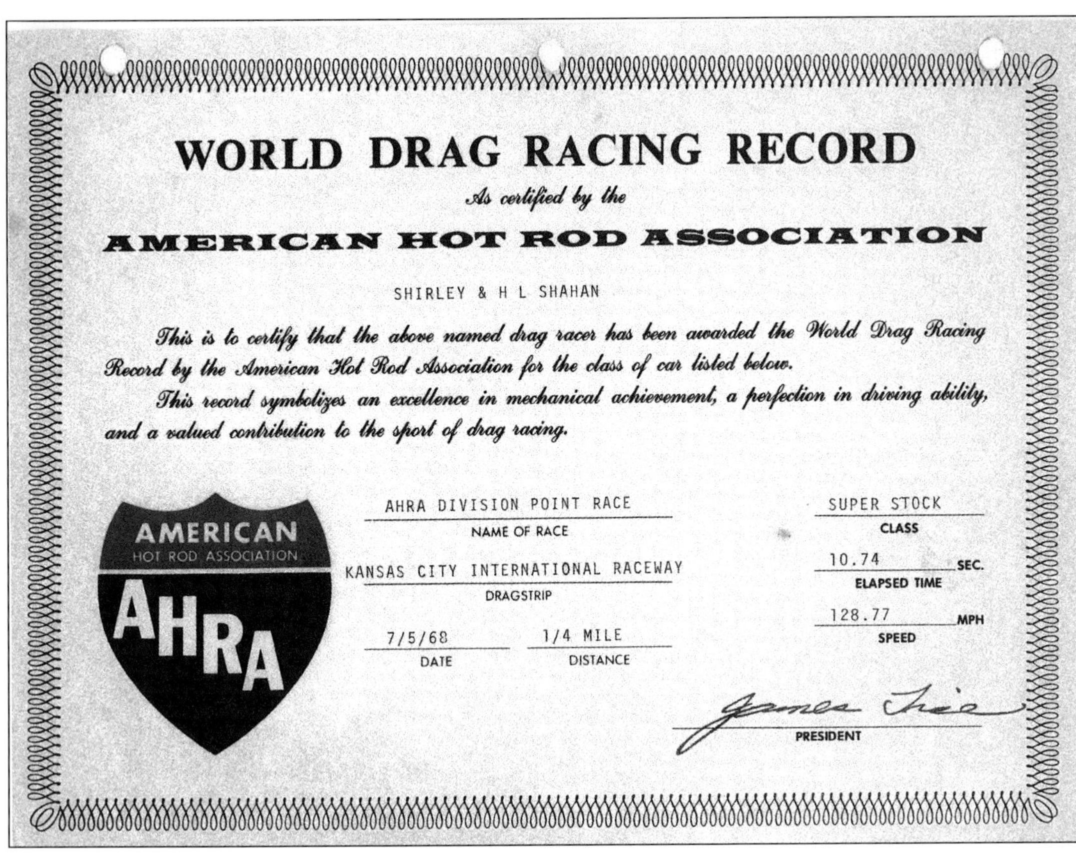

Another world record was set on July 5, 1968. This one was in the Super Stock class with an ET of 10.74 and a top speed of 128.77 mph. Notice how the AHRA awards are in the names of both Shirley and H.L.

Still racing at the top of her form, Shirley Shahan set a new track record at the Orange County International Raceway on October 12, 1968, in the SS/BA class for an ET of 10.71 seconds and 131 mph! (Photo Courtesy Shirley Shahan)

   SHIRLEY SHAHAN *The Drag-On Lady*

CHAPTER 5

The Mobil
ECONOMY RUNS

Chrysler Corporation asked Shirley to drive one of its entries in the 1966 Mobil Economy Run.

Intrigued by the challenge, Shirley accepted and was assigned a new Plymouth Fury I two-door sedan equipped with the standard slant-6 engine.

(Photo Courtesy Chrysler. Chrysler is a trademark of FCA USA LLC.)

Some folks may not believe this, but Shirley Shahan, the one and only Drag-On Lady, actually competed in the Mobil Economy Run—not just once but a total of three times!

So, what business does a professional drag racer have driving in a fuel economy run? Isn't that a little like asking the chef at LeCinq restaurant in Paris to cook up a serving of beans and franks or asking Superman to open a jar? Well, working as a professional driver and being sponsored by an automobile company means that you may be required to participate in events in which you may not necessarily be interested. During Shirley's time driving for Chrysler Corporation, she was asked to also compete in the Mobil Economy Runs—those once-famous annual contests to demonstrate the fuel economy of factory-stock automobiles.

Background

The Mobil Economy Run was a big event that took place every year from 1936 to 1968, except during the World War II years when gasoline rationing was in effect. The runs were designed to provide consumers with optimal, real-world fuel efficiency numbers that were developed during a coast-to-coast drive on public roads with each car and driver facing regular traffic and weather conditions. The cars had to be certified as bone-stock and equipped only with regular factory equipment.

Sponsoring the event was the Mobil Oil Corporation (known today as the ExxonMobil Corporation), while the United States Auto Club (USAC) operated the runs and sanctioned them. These runs were well-known in their time, and the fuel economy results were reviewed and talked about by thousands of motorists, who often used those figures to help decide which new car to purchase. So, to a manufacturer, it was important to try to be in the number-one or number-two position in your class, if at all possible. There were several classes, and they were changed from time to time.

It wasn't until 1957 that women were allowed to drive in the Mobil Economy Runs, despite the fact that even back then they comprised more than half the driving population in America. By the time Shirley Shahan was asked to pilot a car in the Mobil Economy Runs, it was no longer completely unusual to see a woman at the wheel, although women were still very much in the minority.

Seen here at a nighttime stop in St. Louis during the 1966 run, Shirley's navigator, Burt Sisson, put a handmade sign in the back window of her car the **Drag-Less Lady** *as a joke. (Photo Courtesy Chrysler. Chrysler is a trademark of FCA USA LLC.)*

The event was in essence a marketing contest that pitted the Big Three US automakers and the remaining independent brands against each other. The object was to win the coveted title as the Mobil Economy Run winner within the class your car competed.

Originally, the contest used a rather complicated "ton-miles" formula, which included the actual fuel mileage as well as the weight of the vehicle in its calculations to come up with a miles per gallon per ton of weight fuel economy rating. This complex formula tended to favor bigger, heavier cars, so one sometimes saw a big Lincoln sedan coming in first place while a 6-cylinder economy coupe would be farther down the list.

It was done that way to placate the Big Three automakers, whose cars tended to be on the larger size and thus otherwise would have consistently lost to smaller cars like the Aero Willys, Henry J, Hudson Jet, and Nash Rambler. However, starting in 1959, entries were judged on an actual miles-per-gallon basis.

To make things fair for all, there were multiple categories, so big cars competed with other big cars, and small cars competed with small cars. Naturally enough, the new compact cars just beginning to appear on the market were usually the top fuel economy champs, while the Big Three builders could point to whatever wins they were able to score in their own respective categories. So, just about everyone was happy. Breaking the run down into different classes was a much more equitable way to compare each car, and although the small cars were usually the overall winners, it didn't matter to most buyers. They were looking to see how cars fared in the size range in which they were interested.

Of course, this also meant that there were a lot more winners than in earlier years because they named a winner for each class and also an overall winner. For 1959, the new compact Studebaker Lark debuted to give some serious competition to the Rambler line of compact and small cars that were

 SHIRLEY SHAHAN *The Drag-On Lady*

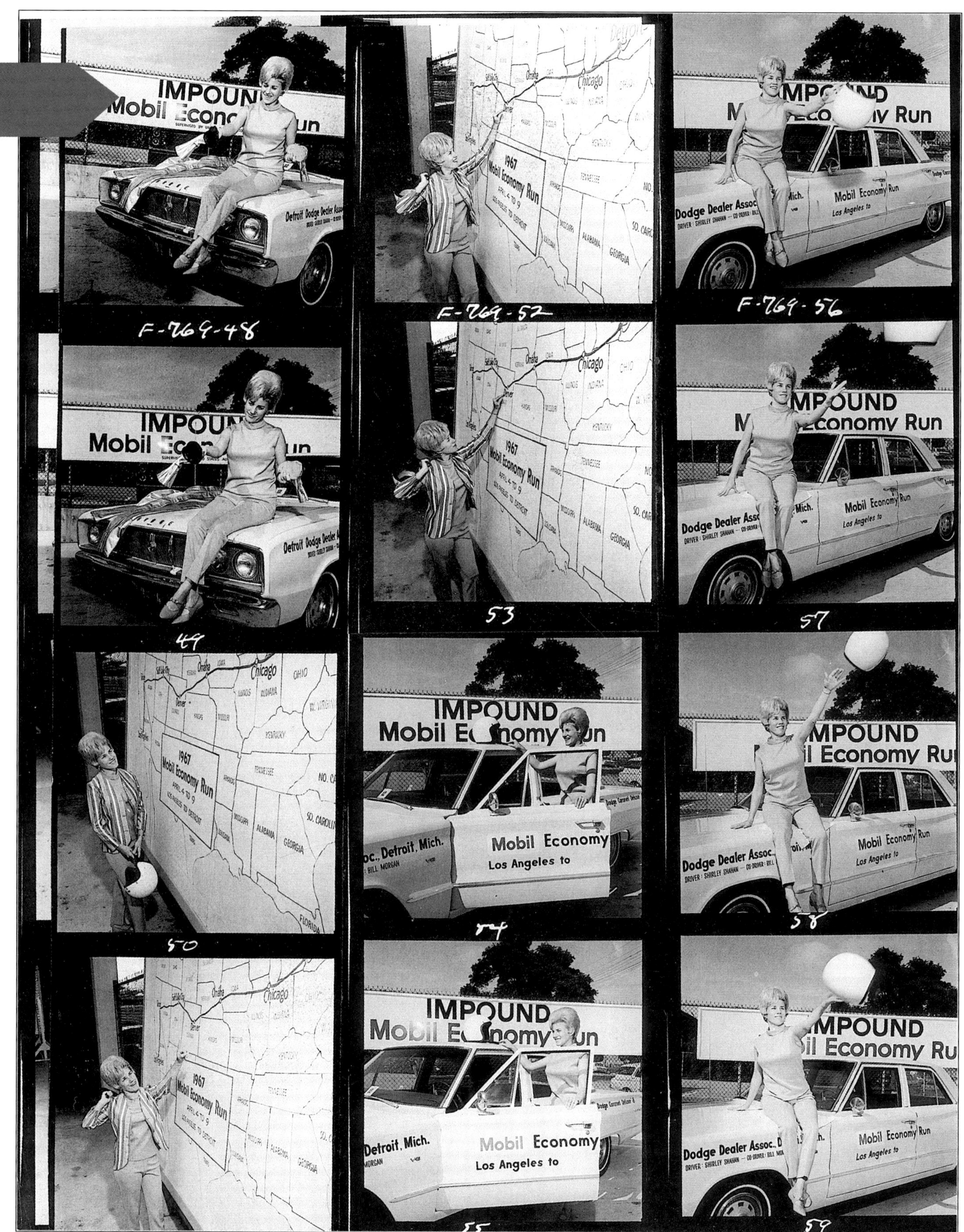

IMPOUND
Mobil Economy Run
Detroit Dodge Dealer Assoc
F-769-48
IMPOUND
Mobil Economy Run
Detroit Dodge Dealer A
49
1967
Mobil economy Run
APRIL 4 TO 9
50
1967
Mobil Economy Run
APRIL 4 TO 9
1967
Mobil Economy Run
APRIL 4 TO 9
F-769-52
53
IMPOUND
Mobil Economy Run
Mobil Economy
Los Angeles to
54
IMPOUND
Mobil Economy Run
Detroit, Mich.
Mobil Economy
Los Angeles to
55
IMPOUND
Mobil Economy Run
Dodge Dealer Assoc. Detroit, Mich.
DRIVER: SHIRLEY SHAHAN — CO-DRIVER: BILL
Mobil Economy Run
Los Angeles to
F-769-56
IMPOUND
Mobil Economy Run
Dodge Dealer Assoc.
DRIVER: SHIRLEY SHAHAN — CO-DRIVER: BILL
Mobil Economy Run
Los Angeles to
57
IMPOUND
Mobil Economy Run
Dodge Dealer Assoc.
DRIVER: SHIRLEY SHAHAN — CO-DRIVER: BILL
Mobil Economy Run
Los Angeles to
58
IMPOUND
Mobil Economy Run
Dodge Dealer Assoc. D
DRIVER: SHIRLEY SHAHAN — CO-DRIVER: BILL M
Mobil Economy Run
Los Angeles to
59

known as fuel economy champs. The Larks and Ramblers were joined in 1960 by the Chevrolet Corvair and the Ford Falcon, and by 1961, a flood of small compact cars entered the US market.

Because good fuel economy was a major selling point among the compact cars, it was doubly important for a manufacturer's compact to win its class or at least come very close to the top. AMC in particular had built a reputation for outstanding fuel economy in its Rambler cars and put extra effort into winning its class, and in most of the years in which it competed, it did win. The engineer who did the most driving for AMC, Les Viland, was one of the best economy drivers in the world.

Within the various classes, one could pretty much use whatever stock factory engine and transmission combination that was desired, as long as it was regular factory equipment in that particular model and not some special setup that the automaker produced strictly to win the run. In truth, some companies did attempt to offer special fuel economy equipment strictly to give their cars an advantage in the runs.

Cars were recognized for best fuel economy rating with both six and V-8 engines and with manual or automatic transmissions, which was important because even back then, the majority of new cars sold were equipped with an automatic transmission. Although the winning factory liked to trumpet its stick-shift fuel economy, it wasn't really pertinent to the millions of buyers who drove only automatic-transmission cars. The same line of thinking applies with the engines as well. Although a full-size Chevrolet equipped with the standard 6-cylinder engine could achieve some pretty respectable fuel economy numbers, the V-8 numbers were more important to most drivers because most full-size Chevys were sold with a V-8.

In 1955, officials changed the rules to allow only cars equipped with automatic transmissions to compete because, as they noted, the use of an automatic transmission had become typical rather than the exception. In 1954, some 58 percent of cars sold in America were equipped with an automatic; by 1955, that figure was expected to exceed 60 percent, and most people figured that it was bound to continue to increase year by year, as in fact it did.

The idea behind the economy run was that it could determine the optimum fuel economy (gas mileage) potential of ordinary passenger cars under the sort of driving conditions typically encountered by average motorists. Naturally, such an important event was likely to attract cheaters who could modify the engines to produce unusually good fuel economy. To prevent special preparation or modifications of the participating automobiles, the United States Auto Club (USAC) purchased the cars at dealerships and thoroughly checked them before certifying them as stock.

The participating team's mechanics could go over the vehicles to make sure the timing, carburetion, etc. were set to provide the best fuel economy possible, but everything had to be within factory specifications. Otherwise, they would be disqualified. In 1955, a rule change was made to limit such preparation time to no more than 24 hours.

It's safe to assume that before the cars were turned over to their respective drivers, they had been gone through from stem to stern to make them as competitive, fuel-economy wise, as possible. Valves were adjusted with a degree of precision that only an expert mechanic can achieve. The carburetor would be adjusted to be as lean as possible, spark would be adjusted to maximize economy, and tires would be pumped up to their maximum recommended pressures to reduce rolling resistance.

Every tuning specification would be gone through to ensure the best possible fuel economy while also making sure to stay within the factory guidelines because doing otherwise would mean getting disqualified. Thus, if the tire manufacturer recommended tire pressure of 26 to 30 psi, it would be set at 30 psi, not a pound greater or lesser. The engine idle speed was set at the lowest end of the

The Mobil Economy Runs had a wide variety of classes so that the competition was as fair as possible.

Shirley's 1966 car, a big Plymouth Fury I, competed in the standard-size 6-cylinder class.

(Photo Courtesy Chrysler. Chrysler is a trademark of FCA USA LLC.)

factory range. Even the coolant thermostat would be checked and, if desired, replaced by the hottest one the factory recommended because a warmer engine generally gets better gasoline mileage than a colder one.

Once each car was inspected, the cars' hoods and chassis were sealed by USAC officials to ensure that no further modifications could be made on the sly. Before the run each factory gas tank was disconnected so that fuel use could be accurately measured by using a special tank that was mounted inside the trunk. Then, prior to the initial fueling and each refueling thereafter, each car would be leveled via portable hydraulic jacks for precise topping off of the fuel tank. Once the vehicle was perfectly level, gasoline was added to a level line drawn inside the filler neck. Every possible effort was made to keep each factor exactly equal for each car.

Classes

Because of the wide variety of automobile types, the Mobil Economy Run during the late 1950s initially had eight classes based on wheelbase, engine, and body size, as well as vehicle price. The leading automakers provided the drivers, and an official USAC observer was placed in each car to prevent any deviations from the official route, as well as to penalize for traffic or speed limit violations.

In the end, because each of the cars had been tuned and adjusted for optimal fuel economy, it pretty much came down to two things: the basic economy of the car and, more importantly, the skill of the person driving the car. The drivers selected were usually chosen because they were known to be particularly proficient at driving economically, or it was believed that they possessed the skill and patience needed to wring every last bit of mileage out of each gallon of gasoline. Hot foots were not welcome; economy racing called for an easy foot on the gas pedal.

The 1966 Mobil Economy Run

The first time Chrysler asked Shirley Shahan to drive in the Mobil Economy Run was during 1966. The reason Chrysler wanted her as a driver probably was simply because she was such a guaranteed crowd pleaser and was sure to attract attention. The Chrysler people told her that she wouldn't be paid anything extra for doing the run, other than her expenses, which was a little unfair since they didn't pay her a regular salary and there was no opportunity to win any money (as there was in drag racing).

Despite the prospect of driving slow rather than fast, Shirley was actually quite excited to be competing in the run.

"I saw it as another form of competition, and I was really happy to be doing it," she said. "I felt it was something I might be able to do well.

"Chrysler's Bob Cahill gave me the job of driving in the economy runs, and I did that for three years. Chrysler always ensured that we had a 'practice car' for the Mobil Economy Run, and we would use it to prepare for the actual run. Even though we didn't know what the actual route was going to be because

The routes selected for the Mobil Economy Runs were supposed to reflect a wide range of driving experiences and traffic conditions. They were not always on smooth highways. In fact, they sometimes went on dirt roads through small towns. (Photo Courtesy Chrysler. Chrysler is a trademark of FCA USA LLC.)

Shirley, H.L., and Janet discuss Shirley's upcoming first drive for the Mobil Economy Run for 1966. It was a week-long affair, and unlike drag racing she wouldn't be able to come home during the week or even be able to call during the day. (Photo Courtesy Chrysler. Chrysler is a trademark of FCA USA LLC.)

the run officials kept that a well-guarded secret until the last minute, we did know what our first destination stop would be and, as a team, we would drive that route ahead of time to get a feel for the car as well as some idea of route conditions.

"For example, the first day's scheduled journey might be Los Angeles to the Grand Canyon, so we would drive that route to get a good feel for the road and the automobile, see where the hills were and plan our driving strategy accordingly."

The planned route for the 1966 Mobil Economy Run was from Los Angeles to Boston, a distance of exactly 3,301.4 miles. Shirley competed in Class E, which was for standard-sized cars equipped with 6-cylinder engines. She was assigned a new Plymouth Fury I two-door sedan with the standard slant-6 engine. Shirley had no problem driving for economy, and she learned a big lesson that first year.

"For my first time out as a rookie in the economy run," she said, "I drank too much coffee just prior to all of us taking off. In time, I realized I really had

For her first year in the Mobil Economy Run, Shirley finished second in her class. While that was an excellent showing for a first-time effort, she feels she could have won first place if not for an incident in which she allowed her navigator to take the wheel. He pestered her to drive right from the start. Almost immediately, he got into a fender bender that cost them valuable time and forced her to speed up to stay on schedule, which cut her fuel economy. (Photo Courtesy Chrysler. Chrysler is a trademark of FCA USA LLC.)

Here's a publicity shot of Shirley, who came in second in her class in the 1966 Mobil Economy Run. This photo was taken in Detroit. (Photo Courtesy Chrysler. Chrysler is a trademark of FCA USA LLC.)

     SHIRLEY SHAHAN *The Drag-On Lady*

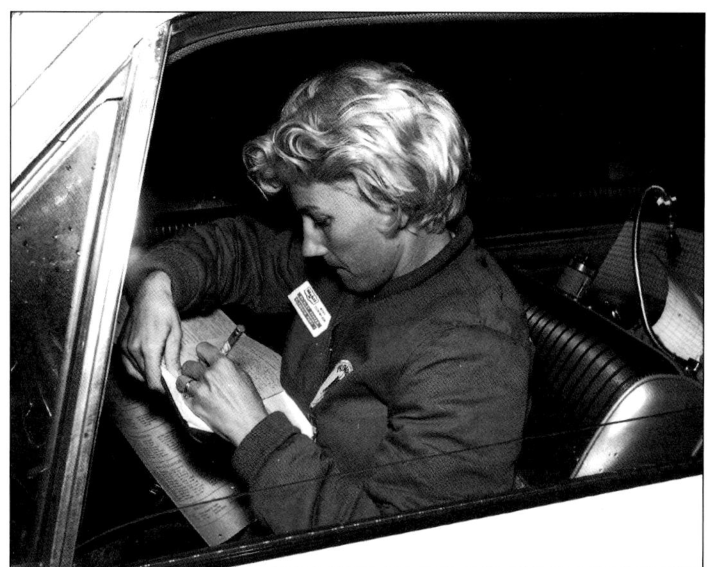

Shirley is at the wheel of her Fury I, marking the route directions in preparation for another stage of the run. Her navigator sat in the rear seat, and you can see his reading lamp and route guide in this photo. (Photo Courtesy Chrysler. Chrysler is a trademark of FCA USA LLC.)

to go! But you can't really make a stop along the way other than the scheduled stops; you're just not allowed to. I thought I would bust a gut before we got to our first stop, but thank goodness I made it! Needless to say, I didn't make that mistake again."

Each car that was entered had a driver, a navigator to make sure that the driver drove the correct route, and a USAC official who made sure that safety rules (i.e., speeding, red lights, the correct route) were not violated.

"You had a navigator sitting in the back seat, and if your navigator told you that you had to drive at 57 mph, then you drove exactly 57 mph—not 56 or 60," Shirley said. "The navigator had a route map that was handed out the night before by officials of the economy run, and so the navigator knew exactly where you had to go and how fast you should be going to maintain the proper average speed, and he would brief you all day long to help keep you on course. He had an important job.

"The USAC official sat in the front seat. These officials changed at lunch break and you never had the same official twice."

Shirley was asked if she found it difficult to get used to driving slow and for maximum fuel economy compared to the way she had to drive while racing.

"No. Actually, I really enjoyed driving in the economy runs," she said. "It was a challenge, an effort to do your best against a field of competitors. Sure, at times it was stressful, but it was something you accomplished on your own without the help of anyone else, other than your navigator."

Controlling gas usage was important.

"It was like driving with an egg under your gas pedal," Shirley said. "You had to be careful every second because there might end up being a tenth of a mile per gallon difference between first place and second."

At the end of each day, there was a meeting of drivers and run officials when the day's fuel economy results were posted, and specially prepared route maps were handed out so that drivers could acquaint themselves with the next day's travel directions. Drivers were also told what the open road speed would be the next day, which was important because they had to stay on schedule. Otherwise, they could be penalized or even disqualified.

The driver meetings were long and tiring, especially after a long day of driving.

"It might be 10 p.m. before the meeting ended and we were allowed to go to our rooms," Shirley said. "The following morning, you had to have your luggage packed and waiting at the front door by 5 a.m."

To add to the misery, the run traveled across several times zones.

"Eventually the time changes start to catch up with you," Shirley said. "You get tired."

That first economy run went pretty well for Shirley. Even though she was new to the run and a drag racer, not a fuel economy driver, in her first attempt, Shirley managed to place second in her class with a score of 20.5574 mpg over the challenging route. Her results placed her about half a mile per gallon less than the class winner, Ms. Patricia Sawyer, who drove a Chevrolet Biscayne six to achieve 21.0454 mpg, and half a mile per gallon ahead of the third-place finisher, Ginny Sims, who piloted a Ford Custom 6 that got 19.9196 mpg. Not surprisingly, the overall winner of that year's run was veteran economy driver Les Viland from American Motors at the wheel of a Rambler American 440, from which he was able to wring 23.8063 mpg.

Shirley would have done better that first time, but she had a navigator who kept pestering her to let him drive for a while.

"I finally gave in and let him take the wheel," she said. "That was a big mistake because he almost immediately got into a fender bender. We had to stop, wait for the police to come, and then exchange information with the other driver, so it was quite a while before we got back on the road with me driving now, of course. I had to drive faster than usual to catch up on our time, and that cost us gas mileage. I think if it wasn't for that, I might have won first place in my category."

The 1967 Mobil Economy Run

Apparently, Chrysler was pleased with the results because the following year, 1967, found Shirley driving a factory-sponsored Dodge. The reason for the change in makes was because of her switch from racing for Plymouth in 1966 to Dodge for the 1967 race season. For her part, Shirley was happy enough to go take another crack at the Mobil Economy Run.

"I really liked the economy

At a stop during the Mobil Economy Run, Shirley looks over the route map with a lady cab driver who entered the run every year. The fellow to the left is unidentified; the man on the right is racer Bill Golden. You can see his famous **Little Red Wagon** in the background. (Photo Courtesy Chrysler. Chrysler is a trademark of FCA USA LLC.)

SHIRLEY SHAHAN *The Drag-On Lady*

runs," Shirley told Bob McClurg. "On the run itself, you got up about 5 in the morning, put your suitcase outside the door because a truck would come and pick up your suitcase, but you didn't leave until about 7 or 8 a.m. If they said you were leaving at 7:15 a.m., then you were leaving at 7:15 a.m. sharp, and that was that. You had to be in your car ready to go, no excuses.

"At about 2 minutes prior to your departure time, one of the run officials would come along with a stopwatch and then stand next to your car. At the proper moment, he would begin to count down to 7:15 a.m. When the watch hit precisely 7:15, you turned the ignition key, hit the gas, and were on your way. It was that tightly controlled. So, it was a lot like drag racing in the sense that when it was time to go, it was time to go!"

The Mobil Economy Run route was quite a bit different this year and was 463.6 miles shorter as well. This time, Shirley competed in Class D, which was for intermediate-sized cars equipped with V-8 engines, and her car for this run was a handsome new Dodge Coronet Deluxe V-8.

However, it was a disappointing run for Shirley because her Dodge suffered carburetor problems throughout the entire run, which is the absolute worst sort of problem to have in a fuel economy contest.

Shirley managed only to come in fourth place in her class, recording a respectable 18.9898 mpg. The first-place winner in her class achieved an impressive 20.0111 mpg driving a Plymouth Belvedere II V-8.

The 1968 Mobil Economy Run and a Big Trophy

Chrysler asked Shirley to drive again in the 1968 Mobil Economy Run, and it proved to be the high point of her career in fuel economy driving. There were some rule changes in 1968: all cars in all classes (except for the two compact classes) were required to be equipped with power steering and power brakes, this was in recognition of the popularity of those options. In addition, the cars were now equipped with the rudimentary exhaust emissions control equipment that was now mandated by law and air-conditioning was required for medium-price

As Shirley traveled across the country during the Mobil Economy Runs, she made sure to call her family to see how they were doing. In this press photo, we see sons Bob and Steve and daughter Janet listening in as H.L. talks with Mom. Whether racing or driving the economy runs, Shirley spent a lot of time on the road away from her family. (Photo Courtesy Chrysler. Chrysler is a trademark of FCA USA LLC.)

and luxury cars, since the majority of cars in those categories were purchased with factory-installed air-conditioning.

Shirley was again driving a Dodge, specifically another mid-size Coronet Deluxe V-8. As she later recalled, "Our team mostly consisted of Chrysler engineers like Bob Cahill and Bob Checkley. There were about four or five of us in all. The last year I drove in the economy run, when I won my class, drag racer Mary Ann Foss also drove on our team. We had a total of six cars on our team. Mary Ann drove a small compact Dodge V-8, a Dart I think, while I drove an intermediate-size Dodge Coronet, also with a V-8. It was a big event, and they had several different classes. They had a 6-cylinder class. They had a small V-8 class and a large V-8 class. There was an economy car class. There was something like 50 to 60 cars participating in the event on a yearly basis, so it was a big thing!"

The 1968 Mobil Economy Run was unique in that special and unforeseen circumstances caused the officials to terminate the run well before the cars reached the planned finish location. As originally

For her third running of the Mobil Economy Run, Shirley was assigned a 1968 Dodge Coronet V-8 equipped with power steering, power brakes, and air-conditioning. Drag racer Mary Ann Foss was also on the Dodge team. (Photo Courtesy Chrysler. Chrysler is a trademark of FCA USA LLC.)

The official hostess for the City of St. Louis greets Shirley upon entering the city during the Mobil Economy Run. Note the extravagant hairdo that was so typical of that era. (Photo Courtesy Chrysler. Chrysler is a trademark of FCA USA LLC.)

scheduled, the route was to go from Los Angeles to New York City, traveling via the Grand Canyon, Colorado Springs, Kansas City, Indianapolis, and Washington, DC.

Covering more than 3,000 miles in 5½ days, the drivers were required to maintain an average speed of more than 54 mph, which was the fastest in run history. The competitive divisions were basically the same as in 1967. As mentioned, joining Shirley as a Dodge driver was fellow drag racer Mary Ann Foss. The two ladies made a friendly bet as to who would end up with the highest fuel economy score.

The run began just before sunrise on April 2. A light rain was falling, and it continued on into San Bernardino. There, the drivers picked up Interstate 15, heading to the dry, hot Mohave Desert. The drivers crossed into Nevada, heading for Las Vegas for the first stop of the day. At the Tropicana Mobil service station, each car was topped off under the watchful eye of USAC officials. After a 40-minute lunch break at the Aladdin Hotel, they continued on south toward the Hoover Dam and crossed into Arizona. Along the way, drivers encountered 35-mph winds, which cut into fuel efficiency, then it was snow and ice on the way to the Grand Canyon.

The next day's run of more than 600 miles and 12 hours to Colorado Springs was marked by more challenging weather. The first stop on the route was at Blake Hick's Mobil gas station, which was followed by lunch at the local junior high school. By this point, Shirley was in first place in her class, leading by 0.17 mpg. It was a slim lead indeed, but it was still more than enough!

Then, it was on the road again, crossing into Colorado and on to Wolf Creek Pass Summit (later made famous in a song by C. W. McCall), which was the highest elevation on the run at 10,850 feet above sea level. The weather was pretty bad; a Colorado spring blizzard was laying down ice and snow on the ground and making things so much more difficult that a stop was made so drivers could put chains on their tires. It was only the second time in run history that had happened.

After passing the summit, they drove on to Pueblo, Colorado, where they stopped at the Sunrise Mobil gas station for refueling. Shirley recalled that her fellow Chrysler driver came over to talk with her.

"Just after Wolf Creek Pass, Scott Harvey, driving for Plymouth in the same class as me, came over to brag about how little gas he had needed," Shirley said. "But, when my car was topped off, it actually took less gas than his. I think he felt a little defeated."

　SHIRLEY SHAHAN *The Drag-On Lady*

Shirley Shahan crosses the finish line for the 1968 Mobil Economy Run.

She did pretty well the first two years and came in first in her class in the third year, which was quite an accomplishment for anyone, let alone a lady who was more used to burning rubber than saving gas. (Photo Courtesy Chrysler. Chrysler is a trademark of FCA USA LLC.)

The following day, April 4, was another long one: nearly 600 miles to Kansas City. Starting out, temperatures were near 0°F, and once again the roads were icy. However, by the time they reached the state of Kansas, weather conditions were greatly improved.

Upon entering Kansas City, several drivers heard a stunning announcement on the radio: civil rights leader Rev. Dr. Martin Luther King Jr. had been shot in Memphis, Tennessee. By the time the last car arrived, word came in that he had died of his wound.

Before long, protests and riots sprang up in several cities across the country. Although things remained quiet in Kansas City and were reported to be calm in Indianapolis, the situation in Washington, DC, where the run was scheduled to be in just two more days, was becoming serious. Run officials began to discuss possibly changing the route or even ending early.

The next day, April 5, drivers took off in an orderly fashion, headed for Indianapolis, stopping along the way at Elmo's Mobil gas station in St. Charles. Traveling on Interstate 270, they bypassed St. Louis, crossing the Mississippi River into Illinois and stopping in Edwardsville for brunch at the Holiday Inn. Then, it was once more back to motor-ing down the highway, pulling for the Indiana state line, and heading into the Eastern Standard Time Zone.

Just outside of Indianapolis, drivers pulled into the Speedway Mobil gas station for refueling and then continued on to the Indianapolis Speedway, where another stop was scheduled. There, the drivers made a one-lap run around the famous Indy Brickyard before going on to the Indianapolis Motor Speedway Motel impound area.

Inside the motel, drivers gathered around televisions sets to watch the latest news regarding the assassination and its aftermath. They learned that President Lyndon Johnson had proclaimed Sunday April 7 as a national day of mourning for the fallen civil rights icon. That was the same day the run was scheduled to end in New York City.

Around 9 p.m. came an announcement from the run's chief steward Art Rene that the run was being terminated there in Indianapolis "in deference to President Johnson's proclamation," he said.

Rene's announcement went on to say that the final results for the run would be calculated that evening and would be announced the following morning, April 6. A schedule of events for Saturday would be announced as soon as possible.

The following day, officials announced the run

results and, as things turned out, Shirley took home first place in her class. It was quite an accomplishment for a drag racer, right? It had been a close thing the entire way, with Chrysler's Scott Harvey breathing down her neck most of the way in his Plymouth Belvedere, which, for all intents and purposes, was nearly identical to Shirley's Dodge Coronet. Both were equipped with the same Mopar V-8 engine and automatic transmission combination.

How close was it? Scott managed to record 20.5154 mpg. Shirley's car, being a Dodge, actually weighed slightly more than Harvey's Plymouth, so her overall result of 20.5744 mpg was all the more impressive. The results clearly illustrate how close the difference is between first and second place. In drag racing, the difference may come down to split seconds, but in fuel economy driving, the difference comes down to mere hundredths or even thousandths of a gallon.

Interestingly, Shirley's mid-size V-8 fuel economy score in the 1968 run was actually a little bit more than 1 mpg higher than any of the smaller compact V-8 cars, which proved once again that the driver often makes the difference.

Each year that she drove in the Mobil Economy Run, Shirley was given a handsome plaque that illustrated the route that year. However, for her winning effort in 1968, Shirley took home a nice big trophy and the heartfelt thanks of Chrysler Corporation.

The following year, 1969, Shirley was signed on to race for another company, AMC, and they didn't ask her to drive in the economy run. It had a well-trained team already and didn't need to add to it. Shirley could focus instead on drag racing.

It was quite an honor to come in first in her class at the 1968 Mobil Economy Run, and you can tell that by the size of the trophy. Shirley stands with navigator Al Shadbourne. (Photo Courtesy Chrysler. Chrysler is a trademark of FCA USA LLC.)

Happy faces all around for the award-winning young lady as she is congratulated by event officials. Shirley managed to extract 20.5744 mpg from her Dodge Coronet V-8 while driving under sometimes difficult conditions. (Photo Courtesy Chrysler. Chrysler is a trademark of FCA USA LLC.)

CHAPTER 6

AMC Comes KNOCKING

For 1969, Shirley switched from Chrysler Corporation to AMC.

It was an all-around better deal for more money and a new car that was incredibly powerful. In addition, Shirley raced mostly in California and the western states, which meant that she could spend more time at home. (Photo Courtesy the Patrick Foster Collection)

During the 1968 racing season, Shirley made a big change in her career path for the 1969 season.

"American Motors came along with a deal, and it included pretty good money along with a chance for us to stay at home a bit more, which was important to me because the kids were growing up quickly," Shirley said. "AMC arranged a deal for us to race under the Los Angeles American Motors Dealer Association banner. They put together a package where they would supply us with a car to run, the SS/AMX, along with a personal car for us to use, which I had to turn back in every 5,000 miles.

"I remember one car they gave me was a Rebel station wagon. Besides that, they also gave me a decent salary, plus any performance or service parts we'd need for the race car. One of the best parts was that they wanted us to race mainly in the Los Angeles area, which was perfect for us."

Racing for Rambler?

At first glance, it seemed like an unlikely partnership. Up to that point, the automaker, famous for marketing automobiles under the Rambler brand name, had stayed out of organized racing. Its president, Roy Abernethy, even authorized the running of an advertisement during 1964 that protested automakers' glorification of performance and speed. That kind of sentiment was unlikely to appeal to the hundreds of thousands of young drivers and car buyers who were interested in performance cars.

In fact, AMC actually was the very last of the major manufacturers to abandon the Automobile Manufacturers Association's 1957 decree that automakers should not be involved in racing or promote racing products for their cars. The mandate was created in the wake of the tragic 1955 Le Mans racing

BECAUSE THE ONLY RACE RAMBLER CARES ABOUT IS THE HUMAN RACE!

Racing has a real fascination as professional drivers unleash raw horsepower and flaunt death. It's a thrilling sport—in the right place.

Out of its proper place, racing is deadly. Yet there are those who are glamorizing and advertising race-track speeds in order to sell cars.

This is not in the public interest, and Rambler will have no part in it.

Glorification of horsepower tempts teen-agers to think high-speed driving is 'in'—and safety 'out'—makes irresponsible drivers even more irresponsible, contributes to the mounting carnage on the nation's highways.

While many people are still apathetic, growing numbers are joining Rambler's

> **IMPORTANT NOTE:**
> Rambler is strongly in favor of responsive horsepower and performance—offers engines up to 270 HP. But we are strongly against glamorizing raw horsepower and speed to the point where irresponsible drivers may be tempted to abuse them. We believe automobiles should have the best of both—a sensible and satisfying balance of performance and economy, as well as roominess and handling ease. That's the way we build Ramblers.

crusade against the promotion of excessive speed and horsepower.

Are Ramblers underpowered? Emphatically not! Every Rambler delivers spirited performance. Our Ambassador, for instance, offers a 270-hp V-8. It would be no trick at all to beef up that rating to 300-hp or more. *But it would serve you no better.*

Rambler's prime concern is for your safety, comfort, satisfaction, and savings.

That's why every Rambler balances turnpike performance with sensible economy.

It's why Rambler gives you strong *Advanced Unit Construction, Double-Safety Brakes* (separate systems, front and rear); a *Ceramic-Armored exhaust system* that protects against rust and fume leaks. Plus optional headrests that act as head-guards against whiplash if your car is struck from behind.

Rambler spends millions on testing cars *before* they go on sale, millions more on safety advances. *But not one cent to glorify speed.*

We welcome your comments, and invite you to join our crusade for safe motoring. *American Motors Corporation, Detroit 32, Michigan.*

No. 1 in Usefulness to the User

RAMBLER

American · Classic V-8 or 6 · Ambassador V-8

This 1964 advertisement, approved by then-AMC President Roy Abernethy, was heavily criticized by performance enthusiasts. Although AMC had a good-performing 327-ci V-8 at the time and could have competed fairly well, the company felt that its "practical" image was more important. We all make mistakes. (Photo Courtesy Chrysler. Chrysler is a trademark of FCA USA LLC.)

AMC *Gets Into Racing*

n 1967, AMC's brand-new Performance Activities Director Carl Chakmakian instrumented a $1 million agreement with Grant McCoon to build the Grant Rambler Rebel Funny Car. McCoon was the owner of the Los Angeles–based Grant Industries, which was a well-known manufacturer of piston rings, ignition systems, and steering wheels.

The idea was to demonstrate the performance of Grant racing parts as well as the AMC Rebel, which was all-new that year. The awesome Grant Rebel was designed to run in the NHRA's Experimental Stock (X/S) and Super Experimental Stock (S/XS) classes. Powering the Grant Rebel was an AMC 343-ci engine that was bored and stroked to 438 ci by "Famous Amos" Satterlee and then topped with a GMC 6-71 blower.

Initially driven by "Banzai Bill" Hayes in June 1967, the Grant Funny Car was soon taken over by the well-established drag racing star Hayden Proffitt. For 1968, a new car was built and named the Grant Rebel SST. This car was painted in AMC's new trademark red, white, and blue corporate racing colors.

Once Abernethy was replaced and Roy D. Chapin Jr. was in charge, AMC launched a program to introduce new sporty cars. The two-seat AMX became a symbol of a corporate revival. (Photo Courtesy Chrysler. Chrysler is a trademark of FCA USA LLC.)

accident in which 77 people were killed. This ban led to the brief but popular line of high-performance cars and equipment that were disguised as police packages and were offered by certain automakers who shall remain unnamed.

By the early 1960s, both Ford and GM's Chevrolet Division had decided to ignore the ban. AMC, battling perennial financial problems, finally decided to get into racing in 1967 by creating the Grant Rebel racing program to gain exposure, publicity, and a performance image.

Although most people who bought performance cars did it mainly for their own self image, it's important for any manufacturer to keep up with the latest industry trends. In the 1960s, the trend was definitely in favor of performance cars.

Car buyers were wild for performance, so the anti-racing Rambler magazine advertisement's appearance was greeted with hoots and hollers. Certainly, it won AMC no friends and almost certainly didn't help sell cars. However, AMC stuck to its guns even as its market share began to fall. Sales of the 1964 Ramblers were less than in 1963, and the following year, they fell again.

In 1966, AMC tumbled even further.

At one time a very successful automaker, AMC was on the verge of bankruptcy by 1967. While at one time its focus on economical cars had resonated strongly with buyers who were turned off by the Big Three's excessively gaudy and ostentatious big cars, the market had since evolved. Speed, performance, and glamour were what buyers wanted now, and shoppers felt that AMC didn't offer those virtues.

Roy Abernethy tried to put some distance between his Ambassador and Rebel models by removing the Rambler nameplate and selling them under the "AM" badge with some success.

However, one has to wonder about the confusion that the change in branding must have caused. Unlike its competitors, AMC didn't have a single performance-oriented car aside from the Marlin, which was an intermediate-size fastback with odd styling and a standard 6-cylinder engine.

Originally marketed as the Rambler Marlin, by 1966, it sold under the AM brand. Although it offered a fairly potent 327-ci AMC V-8, that simply wasn't enough displacement by 1966. AMC's competitors offered much bigger and more powerful engines.

Then, for 1967, the Marlin became a full-size sporty car, and the company discovered that there was no market for that type of car. At the end of the 1967 model year, the unfortunate Marlin was dropped.

Hot New AMC Cars

Because AMC's overall sales had been steadily dropping from 1964 to 1967, it was believed that only a complete change of management in 1967 could stave off the disaster that was coming. The board of directors asked Roy Abernethy to resign. In his place, the board appointed an industry veteran named Roy D. Chapin Jr as the new chairman and CEO.

Chapin realized that drastic measures were necessary to change the company's trajectory. He

The new AMX came with standard bucket seat, 4-speed transmission, V-8 power, and sports steering wheel. It was a beautiful, potent performer. (Photo Courtesy Chrysler. Chrysler is a trademark of FCA USA LLC.)

Do sporty cars get better looking than this? The new AMX was the only American two-passenger sports car on the market other than the Corvette. Even mighty Ford and Chrysler didn't have domestic-built two-seaters, and the AMX cost only a bit more than a prosaic Mustang or Camaro. (Photo Courtesy Chrysler. Chrysler is a trademark of FCA USA LLC.)

This is a 1969 AMX in a factory color choice that was dubbed Big Bad Blue. *Equipped with the new 390-ci V-8, it generated blinding clouds of burning rubber on takeoff. (Photo Courtesy the Patrick Foster Collection)*

authorized production of a new sporty car called the Javelin to replace the moribund Marlin. Surprisingly, Chapin also ordered up a second new AMC car, a two-seat sport coupe that was dubbed the AMX. Both cars would be introduced for 1968.

The Javelin debuted in the fall of 1967 with the rest of the new 1968 AMC cars, and it was targeted at the Ford Mustang and Chevy Camaro, which were the top sellers in the pony-car market segment. The two-seat AMX, which arrived some months later as a surprise introduction, was an all-out performance car with a standard V-8 engine, 4-barrel carburetor, dual exhaust, and a 4-speed transmission.

Larger engines along with additional performance equipment would be available as options to bring AMX's performance to an even higher level. The debut of the AMX shocked the automotive press, which never expected to see such a gorgeous, high-performance two-seater coming from the same company that built the prosaic Rambler. However, Chapin believed he had to completely change AMC's image, and two new sporty cars were a good, strong start. Notably, he insisted to the board that the AMX be authorized regardless of its acknowledged low-volume sales potential.

Chapin knew from experience that two-seat sports cars were seldom high-volume sellers, but he wanted the AMX to be a symbol of a resurgent AMC—in other words, a halo car. The AMX would be only the second two-seat American-made sports car on the market at the time; Chevrolet's Corvette was the other one. Ford and Chrysler offered no domestically built sports cars at the time.

At the introduction of the new AMX, writers were given the opportunity to drive several versions of the car. One writer reported the experience this way: "I'll never forget the first time I drove a 390 V-8 AMX. I was attending the drag-racing segment of the American Motors Mystery Trip (a special press introduction) at the Orange County International Raceway [OCIR] during the spring of 1968. My most vivid recollections were of side-stepping the clutch and hearing the throaty roar of the 390 AMC V-8 engine setting those E70x14-inch OEM Goodyear Custom Wide Treat Polyglas tires, howling like the proverbial banshee. Fighting to maintain control off the starting line, I thought 'Man, if they [AMC] could only get this thing to hook up and go straight, it would make a hell of a Super Stock car!'"

As it ended up, Hurst was the company to solve that little problem.

Carl Chakmakian was the AMC employee chosen to set up and run the company's performance activities. He quickly got the company into Trans Am racing, as well as drag racing. Chakmakian left the position after a year to go back to his regular job in product information, but the department he set up continued on to even greater success. (Photo Courtesy Chrysler. Chrysler is a trademark of FCA USA LLC.)

To further demonstrate the merit of the new sport coupes, Chapin dictated that AMC get into professional racing as quickly as possible. Since this was a complete reversal of the company's policy under Roy Abernethy, the process of creating and maintaining a factory performance department was going to take time because the company had to start from scratch.

AMC had no performance department, no performance parts in its parts catalogues, and almost no relationships with any racers. Getting things up to speed (pun intended) would also be much more expensive than cash-strapped AMC could easily afford, but Chapin knew that it must be done. In the end, it was decided that the quickest way to get into racing quickly was to supply financial backing to a few hand-picked teams and individuals that were likely to win races.

Obviously, an in-house racing department would need to be led by someone familiar with racing. It so happened that several people within AMC were interested in racing and had raced themselves. Among them, the most compelling figure by far was a handsome young driving enthusiast named Carl Chakmakian, who was a highly talented engineer.

Chakmakian had joined the company back when it was known as Nash-Kelvinator. After a short time on the job, he purchased a slightly used 1953 Nash-Healey (a two-passenger sports car that the company offered from 1951 to 1955) and raced it. However, Chakmakian decided that he wasn't content with the power of its factory-installed Nash Ambassador dual-carb inline 6-cylinder engine, which had been massaged by Donald Healey to develop 140 hp.

When the Nash-Healey debuted, that was enough horsepower for most people. Anyway, Nash didn't make a V-8 engine, so the big six was the best engine it could offer. However, the market changed rapidly, and by 1957, 6-cylinder performance engines were pretty much out.

Chakmakian wanted a fast car, so in 1957, he replaced the trusty Nash six with AMC's newest production engine: a 327-ci cast-iron V-8 that pumped out a solid 255 hp and 345 ft-lbs of torque at 4,700 rpm. (That V-8, by the way, has no relationship whatsoever to the Chevrolet-produced 327 V-8. And yes, the AMC one came out first).

The new AMC-built V-8 was a good choice. In independent testing, a 1957 Rambler Rebel hardtop powered by the same engine was shown to be the fastest American sedan that year. The company even considered offering optional Bendix electronic fuel injection on its 327 V-8, which would have increased horsepower even further to 288 hp and 350 ft-lbs of torque. Although, in the end, drivability problems prevented that from happening.

Because of his skill and experience, not to mention his tremendous enthusiasm to get AMC into racing, Carl Chakmakian was placed in charge of setting up AMC's new Performance Activities Department. He was the right man for the job. For the position of assistant manager of performance activities, Chakmakian chose a man he knew to be highly talented: Walter "Walt" Czarnecki, who was a young employee at the Hurst company. Chakmakian hired Czarnecki at the end of 1967. Together, the two men worked miracles with the small budget they were given.

Thankfully, by mid-1966, AMC began to replace its heavy V-8s (a 287-ci unit and the 327 incher) with a whole new slate of engines that were produced with lighter, more modern thin-wall block castings and offered greater horsepower and displacement. The initial engines introduced were 290-ci V-8s producing 200 to 225 hp (depending on whether 2- or 4-barrel carburetion was used) and a 343-ci V-8 that developed 235 to 280 hp. Both engines were larger and more powerful than their predecessors.

Then, for 1968, the company introduced the new AMC 390 V-8 in the new AMX. Developing an impressive 315 hp at 4,600 rpm and 425 ft-lbs of torque at just 3,200 rpm, the 390-ci V-8 was an engine built for performance.

However, the new engines weren't designed for professional, on-track racing. Initially, there were several failures during racing due to inadequate oil circulation, among other things. However, Chakmakian and the AMC engineering department were able to locate the right performance engine experts to iron out any weak points in the V-8s. In time, they produced a good, competitive engine.

Although AMC was a small company by auto-industry standards and was also short on cash from 1966 to 1968, Chakmakian maximized the tight budget. Somehow, he managed to put together an outstanding performance division.

Then, for 1968, the company introduced the new AMC 390 V-8 in the new AMX. Developing an impressive 315 hp at 4,600 rpm and 425 ft-lbs of torque at just 3,200 rpm, the 390-ci V-8 was an engine built for performance.

Having watched the racing scene for years, he knew who the best drivers were, and he tried to sign them. Because of AMC's position as the smallest domestic automaker, it sometimes took some fast talking, but in the end, Chakmakian signed the right drivers to get the new Javelin pony cars into Trans Am racing in a big way. He hired Peter Revson and George Follmer (both outstanding racers) to be the Javelin Racing Team's two official drivers.

The two men performed very well right from their first race at Sebring, Florida. Neither driver won the race, but they placed much better than anyone expected for any car and team engaged in a first-year effort. Amazingly, in their first-ever Trans Am race, the Javelins came in second and fourth, which was an outstanding showing and proof that AMC cars could be competitive in big-league racing.

In Funny Car racing, AMC had the renowned Hayden Proffitt driving the highly competitive Grant Rebel hardtop, and he was raising some eyebrows with his ability to win races.

Looking for Drivers

Hoping to make a splash across several racing venues at once, the AMC guys began to recruit drag racers. Again, they looked for the best. One drag racer that AMC offered to sponsor laughed at the idea, saying, "Why would I want to run a Kelvinator at the drags?"

This was a reference, of course, to the Kelvinator appliance division of the old Nash-Kelvinator Corporation, which was a predecessor of AMC. However, once racer Brian Higgins learned that Hurst would be building the cars and they would feature a potent new engine, he signed on, switching from Dodge to AMC.

The company also hired the husband-and-wife team of Craig and Lee Breedlove to set some records, which would demonstrate the capabilities of its new AMX when in basically stock form. Just prior to the AMX introduction at the Chicago Auto Show in 1968, the Breedloves set 106 national and international speed records in AMXs. That's not a typo. In a series of high-speed runs, a team of drivers set 8 International, 16 National, 66 American Closed Car, 14 American Unlimited, and 2 National Unlimited records. These included lap speeds topping 175 mph in Class B (for cars with engines ranging from 305 to 488 ci) and more than 160 mph in Class C (engines with 183 to 305 ci).

For reasons that aren't clear, Carl Chakmakian departed as head of AMC's racing efforts and was partly replaced by a corporate guy named John Voelpel. Walt Czarnecki was given the title of manager of performance activities and dealer marketing services.

AMC became even more involved in racing during 1969. First, the company introduced a special model of the Rambler that was powered by the AMX 390 V-8. Produced by Hurst for retail sale through AMC dealers, the so-called Hurst SC/Rambler, which was a 1969 Rambler two-door hardtop, was instantly nicknamed the Scrambler Rambler. It came with such factory standard equipment as a 4-speed transmission with Hurst T-handle floor shifter, dual exhaust, a Twin-Grip (Positraction) rear axle with a 3.54:1 ratio, a big hood scoop, and a Sun tachometer mounted on the steering column.

Other standard features included a sports steering wheel; heavy-duty shock absorbers; heavy-duty springs; a heavy-duty front sway bar; hood tie-downs; mag-style wheels with big (for the time) E70x14 Goodyear Polyglas Wide-Tread tires; and a wild red, white, and blue paint scheme that was impossible to ignore. The standard 390-ci V-8 had 315 hp and 425 ft-lbs of torque. It was, as the factory advertisements said, "A Rambler that Does the

The new AMX also launched a new V-8 engine for AMC: the 390-ci AMX V-8 was ordered by most buyers. It was a modern, thin-wall block design with high-revving capability and plenty of power in stock form. Developing 315 hp at 4,600 rpm and 425 ft-lbs of torque at 3,200 rpm, the 390-ci V-8 was an engine built for performance. (Photo Courtesy Chrysler. Chrysler is a trademark of FCA USA LLC.)

Quarter Mile in 14.3."

Although the Scrambler Rambler was aimed mainly at amateur racers, movie and television star James Garner's American International Racing team campaigned several specially modified versions of the SC/Ramblers in the grueling 1969 Baja 500 off-road race in Mexico and won.

In addition, a semi-factory team got into SCCA B/Production racing with a 1969 AMX. The racing team took for its name T.E.A.M., which stood for the Technical Employees of American Motors. However, the team was not officially sponsored by AMC because there wasn't anything left in the budget to support it.

T.E.A.M. was comprised of about 20 unpaid volunteer employees who came mainly from the engineering and product departments. The man who conceived T.E.A.M. and who managed it was Jim Alexander, who was a longtime racing enthusiast from AMC's product planning department. T.E.A.M. was a small, under-funded effort, but the crew worked wonders. With one great AMX car and an outstanding driver, Dwight "Ike" Knupp, T.E.A.M. managed to win three straight national points races against the seasoned Al Barker and his well-prepared Chevy Corvette.

Chakmakian's successor as liaison to the Trans Am Racing team was racer Ronnie Kaplan. Once again, the AMC racers faced tough competition, this time against the famed Penske Racing Team with the legendary Mark Donohue driving his oft-winning Chevy Camaro.

Can the AMX Compete in Drag Racing?

For 1969, AMC decided to also become heavily involved in drag racing on both the East and West coasts, and that's where Shirley came into the picture. Shirley was to be a key element in AMC's strategy to draw attention to its cars because Shirley was always a tremendous draw at racing venues. AMC management decided that it wanted the company to look hip and a little outrageous, and having the Drag-On Lady on its team went a long way toward accomplishing that goal.

Of course, AMC needed more than just a top-ranked driver. To effectively compete in professional drag racing meant that AMC needed a highly competitive car, and for 1969, it certainly had one: the new 1969 SS/AMX. It was prepared by Hurst Per-formance Research in Detroit with input and direction from American Motors Engineering and a good deal of special preparation by H.L. Shahan.

According to AMC Performance's Walt Czarnecki, Hurst initially suggested creating a Super Stock AMX. The company brought the idea to AMC and the company heads agreed to fund the effort. Czarnecki later noted that ". . . there was never [a thought] in my mind who was going to build more than 50 of these cars, as AMC certainly didn't have that capability. To do that required changes in procedure: for example, pulling these cars from the assembly line [in Wisconsin] and transporting them to the Hurst facility in suburban Detroit."

Before the program was approved by AMC management, a test car was built with an engine modified by Hurst. It was fully blueprinted, which the production SC engines wouldn't be, and had an Iskenderian cam, 12.4:1 pistons, and an Edelbrock manifold with a single Holley 3-barrel carb. This engine was given a thorough wringing out on a dyno and successively modified piece by piece to increase power and durability.

Initially some low-end oiling problems caused headaches, but the problems were solved. By the time testing was done, the engine was running strong. It was installed in a test AMX that delivered surprisingly good times. In the end, the 3-barrel carb was replaced by a dual-quad manifold with two Holley 4210 (615 cfm) carburetors, and Doug Thorley headers were installed. The results were everything they'd hoped for, and AMC gave its final approval for the program.

The first hands-on test of the SS/AMX prototype was conducted on Christmas Day 1968 at the Gainesville Raceway in Florida. Hurst Performance Vice President David Landrith was the driver, and he got some excellent times from the car. The crew was a little surprised when the AMX lifted its front wheels off the

This is the first SS/AMX prototype, as shown to reporters and magazine writers in early 1969 at the Orange County International Raceway in Irvine, California. This was where Shirley was introduced to the press as one of AMC's newest drivers. AMC also announced that she was being given the honor of receiving the very first SS/AMX to be assigned to a driver. (Photo Courtesy the Patrick Foster Collection)

Here's a side view of the experimental SS/AMX that was developed by Hurst and H.L. Shahan and painted in a red, white, and blue paint scheme with big Hurst decals on both doors. In demonstration runs, the AMX greatly impressed the journalists with Shirley burning rubber and pulling wheelies as she blasted down the track. (Photo Courtesy the Patrick Foster Collection)

ground on takeoff, but it was a relatively light car riding on a short wheelbase with gobs of power and the right axle and tires to get it to the pavement.

Shirley loved her new AMX. She was given vehicle number 34, which H.L. had ascertained was the best of the bunch. With the AMX, she was back to driving a stick shift, which she always preferred. Note the Hurst shifter and standard sports steering wheel.

Still, the idea of a Rambler pulling a wheelie was a little hard for some people to accept at first.

After the initial testing, it was Walt Czarnecki's job to go to the NHRA and convince them that the car should be considered homologated and be allowed to race in class SS/H or maybe SS/G. However, the NHRA insisted that the car be entered in class SS/E.

When Walt Czarnecki heard that, he replied that putting it in that class would destroy its chances to win in Super Stock. Apparently even then, the NHRA realized that the new AMX was going to be a seriously fast machine. They told Czarnecki not to worry, adding, "You guys have got a hell of a package here; you'll be surprised how well you do."

Czarnecki had to accept the NHRA's verdict, but even so, he left feeling worried. When he told some of the people at AMC about the class decision, the feeling was that the SS/AMX would get slaughtered by the Mopar products. However, it was too late to change anything. The program was in motion, and they would have to rely on H.L. Shahan's modifications and tuning of each car and on the skills of the people who would drive them, including Shirley Shahan.

Testing continued in January 1969 at the Miami Dragway in Hollywood, Florida. AMX number-1 was fitted with a 4.41:1 rear end plus a BorgWarner T10 transmission with a 2.65 low gear and a Hurst shifter. Using mostly stock suspension components, the crew ran into some traction problems, but in a series of test runs, several were in the 122-mph range, including eight that were in the 11-second range—excellent stuff! AMC Vice President of Marketing R. William McNealy was very pleased. He and Director of Merchandising Chris Scheonleb gave Hurst Performance the green light to proceed with the program as agreed.

Hurst Helps Out

Hurst Performance Vice President David Landrith continued to be the prime motivator for the project from the Hurst side. H.L. Shahan modified the cars that Hurst built. The dual efforts of Hurst and H.L. Shahan created a drag racer that featured a special AMC-produced 390-ci AMX V-8 engine equipped with two Holley 4584 650-cfm (cubic feet per minute) 4-barrel carburetors mounted on an Edelbrock dual-quad intake manifold feeding into ported and polished 390 heads.

To improve engine breathing, the stock valves were replaced by larger 2.065-inch intake valves and 1.74-inch exhaust valves. Special JE pistons were fitted, and a 12.3:1 compression ratio was used. In addition, special Doug Thorley headers were fitted (Shirley had used them on all of her Mopar cars) and a Mallory performance ignition system was installed.

AMC claimed with a straight face that all these modifications raised the engine's horsepower from the stock 315 to 340 hp. *Hmmm,* one would normally expect to see a lot more of a power increase from such extensive modifications. So, did AMC deliberately underrate the SS engine? The short answer is yes. Read on!

The SS/AMX Engine

Naturally, the engines that were installed in the SS/AMX race cars were not garden-variety AMC products, not by a long shot. The 390-ci V-8's bore was 4.165 inches, and the stroke was 3.574 inches. Each hand-built engine had a minimum compression ratio of 12.3:1 and featured Jahns (JE) forged aluminum pistons, which were domed and notched. The cylinder heads were modified by Crane Engineering for better breathing.

A camshaft with 266 degrees of duration was installed at the factory because it was expected that different racers and teams would want to install whatever camshaft they preferred for whatever type of racing they'd be doing. Thus, many (in fact, probably all) of the stock cams were changed out to more radical products by team mechanics. The bigger intake valves measured 2.065 inches, while the exhaust valves were 1.740 inches. The factory build also included Doug Thorley headers in the package.

Topping the engine was a dual-quad tunnel ram intake (part number 4486228) with the aforementioned 4584 Holley carburetors, which ensured more-than-adequate fuel delivery. The ignition system was by Mallory. The engines were deliberately not blueprinted or over-bored, which left those tasks to the personal preference of the buyer. As built, each engine weighed 579 pounds minus the clutch, bellhousing, and flywheel.

As stated earlier, the SS/AMX advertised horsepower was 340 hp with 417 ft-lbs of torque, but that was vastly underrated. It was common back then for an automaker to underrate the output of its racing engines to appear to be more like the stock production engines that came in the cars that people bought. In any event, the NHRA officials weren't fooled for one minute and determined that the engine was probably pumping out more like 405 hp. Later on, they raised their estimate to 420 hp.

Hurst installed a trick front crossmember that allowed for easy removal of the oil pan so that mechanics could inspect the rod and main bearings without having to remove the entire engine. With all of these modifications and upgrades, the SS/AMX engines proved to be very competitive.

Power from this well-tuned engine was fed to a BorgWarner T-10 4-speed transmission with a 2.23:1 first gear. The heavy-duty clutch by Schiefer was nestled within a Lakewood blow shield housing. Naturally, the gear shifter by Hurst, the racer's choice, was standard equipment on all manual transmission AMC cars. The Hurst shifter was considered the best you could get.

In addition to the engine modifications, AMC and Hurst Performance also slightly modified the body, chassis, and the balance of the drivetrain, all of which was within NHRA homologation rules and guidelines as long as a minimum of 50 cars were produced that way. Modifications included moving the battery to the trunk for better weight distribu-

Shirley lifts the front end in a controlled wheelie as she blasts off down the track.

The AMX, with its enormous power and short wheelbase, was more prone to wheelies than the big Dodge Coronet that she drove in 1967.

(Photo Courtesy Shirley Shahan)

Although the details are a little hazy, H.L. also did some work for AMC on its 1970 Rebel Machines. In this photo, we can see nine of them, which were part of a group that H.L. worked on for AMC. H.L. put on new Holly carburetors, manifolds, headers, and distributors. He, Shirley, and a group of friends delivered them to AMC dealers in Orange County. (Photo Courtesy Shirley Shahan)

tion, removal of all sound insulation and padding to reduce overall weight, installation of a steel hood scoop, and the opening up of the rear wheel wells so that bigger wheels and big slick tires could be fitted for maximum traction.

Various brackets and hinges were also removed for weight savings, but for some reason, the floor carpeting was retained as were the two stock AMX bucket seats. *Super Stock* magazine noted that there was no rear seat, apparently not realizing that the AMX was a two-seater only, so there never was a rear seat.

Only one horn was fitted rather than the two that were standard on production AMXs. No comfort or power options were available because they added weight, slowing the car down. In addition, as AMC explained, these cars were built for professional racing, period. They were never meant to be driven on the street as a regular car.

The suspension was a special design by Hurst, using Rockwell springs and Monroe shock absorbers. Hurst removed the front anti-roll bar entirely, revised the rear suspension geometry, and even relocated the right front rear leaf-spring pocket.

The Henry's Detroit Locker rear axle's gear ratio was 4.44:1 (some references claim that H.L. later

changed the axle to a 5.1:1 ratio), which was chosen because the aim of the car was to compete primarily in the SS/G category, with its low-11-second times. It was one of the categories that race fans especially enjoyed and in which AMC ultimately believed it would be most competitive.

In addition, special super tough Detroit Locker Hi-Tuf forged rear axle shafts handled the engine's extra power and the harsh punishment expected in a drag car. The rear tires were Goodyear 10.00x15 racing slicks; the front tires were Super Stock 7.00x15 skinnies.

Some of the subcontractors to Hurst included Vic Edelbrock, Doug Thorley, Holley Performance Products, Harvey Crane (Crane Cams), and Paul Schiefer. Earlier, Carl Chakmakian had developed a unique way to build a list of performance parts to be offered by AMC. He convinced some of the manufacturers to develop the parts and encouraged racers to buy and install them, then he purchased quantities for AMC, assigned them the special Group 19 performance parts numbers, and cataloged them so that more drivers could buy them.

Locked in the trunk of each SS/AMX prior to delivery were two carburetor velocity stacks, a Hurst

The manufacturer's suggested retail price for the SS/AMX was $5,994 plus tax, title, shipping, and dealer prep, so they went out of the showrooms at just over $6,000. This is an authentic Shirley Shahan trading card. Although it lists her 1970 accomplishments on the back side, the image itself is of the paint schemes used for 1969. (Photo Courtesy the Patrick Foster Collection)

**SHIRLEY SHAHAN'S "DRAG-ON-LADY"
1970 A.M.X. TOP STOCK**

OFFICIAL drag CHAMPS

AMERICAN HOT ROD ASSOCIATION

AHRA AMERICAN HOT ROD ASSOCIATION

DRIVER:	Shirley Shahan
CREWCHIEF:	H. L. Shahan
ENGINE:	390 cubic inch American
HORSEPOWER:	480
WEIGHT:	3100 lbs.
PERFORMANCE:	10.77 elapsed time, 128 M.P.H.
FUEL:	Gasoline
HOME:	Tulare, Calif.
SPONSOR:	Cragar Racing Equipment

Shirley Shahan is the only woman to ever win a national major drag racing event! For several years this young lady has been beating the men at their own game of professional Drag Racing. Her four speed equipped A. M. X. pulls the wheels off of the ground with brute horsepower as she shifts her way down the strip to another win. Having helped Cragar to develop their new High Performance Ignition Shirley is also an able automotive technician, with a great deal of experience. Blond and blue-eyed this California housewife truly represents the gentle female even at the wheel of her thundering race car.

Photo by Jon Asher   Fleer Corp. Mfg., Phila., Pa. 19141

T-handle for the shifter, and various decals from the companies that supplied performance parts for the car.

Hurst Performance OEM Sales Manager Don Morton said, "The AMX was a great race car—short wheelbase, lots of power . . . ."

The top guys at AMC were also pleased with how it turned out. Hurst company executives later claimed that the hardest part of the entire program was explaining the process of homologation to the top executives at AMC; they had a hard time understanding the reasoning and the complexity. The other big problem was selling the cars to the AMC dealer network because only 15 to 20 performance-oriented AMC dealers were interested in supporting AMC's racing efforts and could be counted on to purchase one or more cars each for resale. The company needed its dealers to order and sell all 50 cars built to meet NHRA homologation rules.

DECIPHERING *the 1969–1970 AMC VIN Code*

Here's a quick guide to deciphering the AMC VIN code for the 1969 SS/AMX.

After the SS/AMX prototype was constructed, the remaining 52 cars were made in a sequential batch. The VINs decode as follows:

For SS/AMX VIN numbers A9M397X213560–A9M397X213611:

Character(s)	Representation
A	AMC
9	1969
M	4-speed transmission
397	Code for two-seat AMX
X	390-ci 4-barrel engine
213560–213611	Sequential 1969 order numbers for SS/AMX

In 1970, AMC sent out complete change-over kits to all the owners so they could update their cars to resemble the newly styled 1970 model. The kits included a new VIN, though it was not matched sequentially to the 1969 VIN numbers.

For SS/AMX VIN numbers A0M397X183209–A9M397X183261:

Character(s)	Representation
A	AMC
0	1970
M	4-speed transmission
397	Code for two-seat AMX
X	390-ci 4-barrel engine

As far as body colors go, according to Mike Weaver, who is among the foremost experts on the SS/AMX cars, "All 50 or so SS/AMXs left the factory finished in Frost White. Some left the Hurst plant in the red, white, and blue combo. Others were just left white after the modifications because they probably were going to be custom painted anyway."

Massaging the AMX

In 2004, Bob McClurg asked H.L. Shahan to relay the story of how he went through and modified the Hurst-built SS/AMX cars.

"We had already signed with AMC to race with them by that point, and so they flew me back to Hurst's Detroit facility, where I converted all 52 of those cars," H.L. explained. "I pulled all the motors out, changed the pistons, changed out the camshaft, manifolds, carburetors, flywheels, clutches, pressure plates—the whole works. I also changed out the axles."

McClurg next asked H.L. if anyone helped him go through the cars.

"Well, I took my brother with me, and he lasted about three weeks before I burned him out," H.L. answered. "Then, I took another kid back, and he lasted for just about as long. Mainly, we had people come in and pull the motors out and set them on the floor for me. I didn't have to pull them out and put them back in.

"I did experience some problems though. It seemed that many of the crankshafts were scratched and the bearings were also scratched. So, I called AMC, [and soon] four quality control guys came in from Kenosha, and they said, 'Show me!'

"So, I said, 'Well, here's a crank right here that's scratched. You can see the bearings are also scratched.'

"Then, they said 'Well, pull the motor apart.'

"They picked one at random, and I tore it down right in front of them. By the next morning, I had 20 hand-picked crankshafts and cases of bearings!"

Writer A.B. Shuman described the scene inside Hurst Performance's assembly site this way, "Fifty-two brand-new AMXs are quietly being readied for yet another mind-boggling drag racing offering from AMC. Arranged in neat rows with their decklids popped open and their hoods stacked on their roofs, the all-white machines glistened under the fluorescent lights. Each engine and transmission had been pulled and now sat in front of the parent car on a wooden skid. Against the wall, the stock cast-iron exhaust manifolds were stacked like cordwood. All was in readiness for the 'go signal'!"

At the time, Hurst Performance had a sprawling 40,000-square-foot facility in Ferndale, Michigan. It was an indoor factory that some people have compared to Lockheed Corporation's super-secret Skunkworks. The building was massive and was buzzing with activity from one end of it to the other. So, H.L. came up with an idea to save time breaking in the engines by doing it inside the building rather than taking the cars to a remote test track.

"We used to break in those cars right there at the factory," H.L. said. "I would make a full-bore pass right down the center aisle between the two rows of cars. That's how we broke the engines in! While I was building those cars, I also race-prepared [ours] and had it painted, lettered, and ready to go. The first week or two, we set the record for that car at Indy!"

The first time Shirley took out her SS/AMX, she managed a 10.67-second ET (some references put it at 10.97 seconds) at 125.69 mph. (Photo Courtesy the Patrick Foster Collection)

Here's a section of the big Hurst facility where the SS/AMXs were built. H.L. not only built the Super Stock cars here but he also broke in the new engines by driving them flat out inside the building. (Photo Courtesy the Patrick Foster Collection)

AMC Performance Executive Walt Czarnecki confirmed H.L.'s story about breaking in the engines indoors.

"That's a true statement," he said. "H.L. came to Detroit and worked with the team at Hurst getting the basic car put together so we could ship them off to our dealers."

Interestingly, H.L. was also asked to help AMC with its 1969 SC/Rambler racing program. The SC/Rambler was a two-door hardtop factory equipped with an AMX 390-ci V-8, 4-speed transmission with Hurst shifter, and lots of performance modifications for drag racing. The company assembled 30 pre-

This large decal was issued by AMC for use by its various teams that were racing AMXs under the factory banner. The author received this from Carl Chakmakian, the man who set up AMC's Performance Activities group. (Photo Courtesy the Patrick Foster Collection)

production cars at its factory in Kenosha, Wisconsin, and shipped 15 of them to H.L. for preparation in advance of an important Long Lead Press Preview being held at the Orange County International Raceway.

H.L. made sure that the cars were tuned for maximum performance and then drag raced and road tested them to verify that they were ready. After the event, the car buff magazines raved about the performance of the SC/Ramblers, and the cars went on to enjoy a very successful racing season.

As stated earlier, the NHRA homologation rules at the time required a minimum of 50 cars

The 1969 SC/Rambler was another project AMC undertook with Hurst, and it's one that H.L. worked on. The formula was simple: take AMC's smallest car, the Rambler, and stuff the company's biggest engine, the AMX 390 V-8, into it, have it massaged by Hurst and H.L. Shahan, and see what happens. (Photo Courtesy Chrysler. Chrysler is a trademark of FCA USA LLC.)

SHIRLEY SHAHAN *The Drag-On Lady*

be built to qualify to race them. In the end, Hurst and AMC produced a reported 54 SS/AMXs, which consisted of 53 production cars plus the prototype. In the years since all this happened, that number has been called into doubt several times. Some sources claim that only 51 cars were built, while others say as many as 55 were produced. Although I firmly believe it was 54 cars, in all likelihood, it will never be entirely settled to the satisfaction of some people. What is known is that the cars received consecutive vehicle identification numbers that clearly indicate that 53 cars plus the prototype were produced. If more were built, they probably wouldn't have a consecutive number. There's more about this later.

The new SS/AMX was introduced at a press preview held in mid-February 1969 at the Orange County International Raceway in Irvine, California, where Shirley was also introduced to the press as AMC's newest driver. In addition, AMC announced that the honor of receiving the very first SS/AMX to be assigned to a driver would be given to her.

Although, many people assume that Shirley was given SS/AMX number-1, and some reference books make that claim, that's actually not the case. In fact, she was given the 35th car built.

The company had SS/AMX number-1 all decked out in AMC's trademark red, white, and blue paint scheme, which had a strong family resemblance to the company's newly introduced corporate logo, a stylish red, white, and blue square dubbed the A-Mark. Big Hurst decals were on both doors.

Performance maven George Hurst was in the audience, as was a very proud R. William McNealy, marketing vice president of AMC. After the surprise announcement was made that Shirley had agreed to become a driver for AMC, there was Shirley, smiling brightly, dressed in a white miniskirt, sleeveless top, and white go-go boots, and she looked absolutely fabulous.

After the usual speeches and remarks by various big wigs, Shirley climbed behind the wheel of the AMX prototype and drove it down the quarter-mile drag strip in a show of power and might. The engine growled at idle. Then, she floored the gas pedal and was off in a flash of smoke and noise. As they watched her slapping gears and pulling the wheels off the ground, the press writers were suitably impressed. Shocked might be a better word.

Naturally, a few members of the press asked Shirley why she had decided to jump from Chrysler to AMC; to them it probably seemed like a step backward. She demurred, saying only that she was proud and excited to be a driver for the hot new SS/AMX. However, when friends asked her the same question privately, Shirley provided more detail.

"When you're racing for Chrysler, you're racing for Chrysler, and that's all there is to it," she said. "There are no other opportunities that you're allowed to take advantage of. As a family, we had a lot of sweat equity invested in racing; H.L. had the shop, we had the kids, and I had quit my job at the gas company just to be able

R. William McNealy (left), vice president of marketing for AMC, and George Hurst discuss the new SC/Rambler. The hot little hardtop was built in limited quantities that one year only. This photo was taken at the Orange County International Raceway. (Photo Courtesy Chrysler. Chrysler is a trademark of FCA USA LLC.)

A Rambler that does the quarter mile in 14.3.

American Motors and Hurst have collaborated on the custom-built SC/Rambler.

It's a limited production car; only 500 units are planned at this time.

Enough to qualify the SC/Rambler for stock classes in drag racing.

The price is $2,998[1] Which is very little money when you see what it buys.

1. 390 cubic inch AMX V-8 Engine.
2. 4-speed all-synchromesh close-ratio transmission.
3. Special Hurst 4-speed shift linkage with T-handle.
4. A Sun tach mounted on the steering column.
5. Dual Exhaust system with special-tone mufflers and chrome extensions.
6. Functional Hood Scoop for cold-air induction.
7. Twin-Grip differential.
8. 10½" diameter clutch.
9. 3.54:1 axle ratio.
10. Power disc brakes (front).
11. Rear axle torque links.
12. Handling package (heavy-duty front sway bar plus heavy-duty springs and shocks).
13. Heavy-duty cooling system (heavy-duty radiator, power-flex fan and fan shroud).
14. A 20:1 manual steering ratio.
15. Special application of new Red, White and Blue exterior colors.
16. Two hood Tie-Downs with locking safety pins and cables.
17. Custom Tear-Drop racing mirrors (one each side).
18. Custom Grille.
19. Custom SC/Rambler-Hurst emblem on front fenders/rear panel.
20. Mag styled wheels, 14" x 6", painted specially to complement exterior color scheme.
21. Five E 70 x 14 Goodyear Polyglas™ Wide-Tread tires.
22. Sports steering wheel.
23. Custom-upholstered head restraints in Red, White and Blue vinyl.
24. All-vinyl charcoal seat upholstery with full carpeting.
25. Individually adjustable reclining seats.

There's more, but you get the idea. With this car you could make life miserable for any GTO, Roadrunner, Cobra Jet or Mach 1.

American Motors/Hurst SC/Rambler

1. Manufacturer's suggested retail price includes all items listed and federal taxes. State and local taxes, if any, and destination charges excluded.

to go racing full time. We were doing everything that was required of us by Chrysler and yet they still weren't paying us anything, just supplying cars and parts. We lived off of what H.L. earned from the shop and what I earned doing match racing, and sometimes it was slim pickings.

"Then, along comes American Motors, and they offered us some real money. They were more than generous. Driving for them, I would have a regular salary plus the winnings. It was also a chance to spend more time at home with the kids, who were growing up so quickly. When you're a mom and have to spend so much time on the road traveling to different racetracks around the country, you begin to really miss being home with your children. So, it was a great move for us as a family."

In addition to getting to drive the awesome SS/AMX, Shirley's SS/AMX Racing Program contract stated that she would receive a salary of $500 per month, which was pretty good money back then. It also provided the use of the Southern California AMC Dealers Association co-op Javelin, a fresh new AMC car for her personal use every 5,000 miles, along with all of the free parts that she needed for her race car. She could also earn a considerable amount of extra income from winning races, which she did with amazing regularity.

Shirley prepares for another run. Note the two shifters: the tall one is, of course, a Hurst shifter for the SS/AMX's 4-speed manual transmission. The other shift controls the line-lock. (Photo Courtesy Chrysler. Chrysler is a trademark of FCA USA LLC.)

This photo of Shirley was taken by a family member in 1969. With her blue miniskirt and red go-go boots, she could be mistaken for Wonder Woman today. Even in 1969, the sight of a beautiful woman driving a race car was very unusual. Shirley stood out from the crowd. (Photo Courtesy Shirley Shahan)

As soon as she received her car, Shirley went to work driving in the 1969 racing season. Fans were able to see her burning up the track, banging gears with the engine screaming and smoke pouring off the spinning rear tires. Shirley managed to establish new D/Super Stock records. From then on, AMC was really making news in the racing world. From late 1969 to early 1970, it seemed that new track and class records were being set almost on a weekly basis, and often enough, it was an AMX that set them. (Photo Courtesy Shirley Shahan)

Shirley reads the official time after a run with her AMX, and she looks pretty happy with it. Her SS/AMX was a very competitive machine. Shirley and H.L. helped propel AMC into third place in the NHRA standings for the year, which was an amazing result for a first-year effort. (Photo Courtesy Chrysler. Chrysler is a trademark of FCA USA LLC.)

  SHIRLEY SHAHAN *The Drag-On Lady*

Buying an SS/AMX

The SS/AMX cars were mainly built to compete in SS/C, SS/D, SS/E, and SS/G NHRA classes against such worthy iron as Cobra Jet Mustangs, big-block Chevy Camaros, and Super Stock Dodges. The AHRA classified the car in Formula One C/Stock.

The manufacturer's suggested retail price for the SS/AMXs was $5,994 plus tax, title, shipping, and dealer prep, so they went out of the showrooms at something more than $6,000. That was a ton of money compared to a stock AMX that was offered in 1969 with a $3,297 suggested retail price. All 53 of the SS/AMX cars that were built were sold, although it took some persuading to get some of AMC's hidebound dealers to accept them. The sale of the last one was held back a bit to keep it as a reserve in case of any mishap occurring with the delivery of the first 52 cars.

Like most production AMX cars that year, the SS/AMX cars had a production number stamped on a small badge that resided on the instrument panel center. For the SS/AMXs, these numbers ran in sequence starting with 12567 and ending with 12620. The SS/AMX VINs also ran in sequence starting with A9M397X213560 and ending with A9M397X213613. Both of these number sequences support the claim that 53 production SS/AMX cars were produced. Still, there is always a slight possibility that additional cars may have been produced. There are also rumors that some racers made look-alike clones of the SS/AMX.

At the 1969 AMC special SS/AMX press preview at the Orange County International Raceway, it was also announced that Shirley and H.L. Shahan

There's an interesting story about this photograph. It shows a one-page flier that Shirley autographs and sells at various vintage car meets. When I first met her, she didn't know me at all, and I'm sure we both never dreamed that 10 years later, we would collaborate on a book with her as the subject. (Photo Courtesy Shirley Shahan)

Shirley said, "I drove my Super Stock 390-ci AMX all through 1969, and it was a very competitive car. We won a lot of races with it. I also did some match racing with the AMX, mainly in the Los Angeles area. In addition, as part of my duties for AMC, I also served as a company spokesperson off-track." Shirley made appearances at AMC dealerships, telling the company's racing story. (Photo Courtesy Shirley Shahan)

THE SS/AMX

Below is a Q&A with author Patrick Foster, Shirley Shahan, and H.L. Shahan.

Author: We always heard that Hurst Performance built the SS/AMX cars, but it had some help with them, right?

Shirley: Oh yes! My husband, H.L., built the cars at Hurst. He was such a great engine builder. He became intimately aware of the relative strengths of each of the cars, so when I was given the honor of getting the first car assigned to a driver, H.L. picked the number 35 car. He had examined and worked on all of the cars, and based on his experience, he had a feeling that number 35 was the best of the fleet.

I think that he was probably right because after H.L. got my car tuned and ready to go for the first race at Madera, California, we set a new track record at that event. I remember how excited I was when I heard them announce the race results. I mean, it really shocked race fans everywhere and had them shaking their heads in disbelief saying "An AMC set a new track record? On its first time out?"

But that AMX really was a great car.

Author: We heard that Shirley did some gigantic wheelies at the Lions Drag Strip that were totally awesome. Can you tell us about that?

Here's Shirley burning up the track at the 1969 NHRA Winternationals. The SS/AMX boasted an advertised horsepower of 340 with 417 ft-lbs of torque, but that was vastly underrated. It didn't matter, because the NHRA officials weren't fooled for one minute; they determined that the engine was probably pumping out about 405 hp. Later, they estimated it to be closer to 420 hp. (Photo Courtesy Shirley Shahan)

Shirley really nailed it in the AMX at Lions Drag Strip, standing it up on its back bumper as the crowd went wild! The H.L.-prepared SS/AMX had gobs of power and a short wheelbase, which made it a little difficult to keep on the ground. (Photo Courtesy Shirley Shahan)

H.L.: Yeah, she did those on Firestone tires. At the time, we were sponsored by Goodyear, but Firestone wanted us to try a set of their newest tires. However, I didn't feel comfortable doing that, so I went over to Goodyear and asked them if it would be all right if we made a few runs with the Firestones, and they said, "Go ahead. Try 'em!" That's when Shirley put that AMX up on the back bumper!

Shirley: Yes, that's right. That AMX was a real kick to drive, and I think everybody was amazed when I stood that car up on its bumper.

Author: You drove that AMX for two seasons, right?

Shirley: That's right. I raced the car for two years, although it looked somewhat different for the 1970 race season. The first year, 1969, it was white with the hood painted red. Then, for the second year, we had the lower half of the body painted a navy blue color with the *Drag-On-Lady* name done in gold across the doors. The rest of the body was fairly close to the original paint scheme with a white top and red detailing around the window frames. But also, the second year, the hood was painted blue. By the way, that second paint job was done by Doyce's Paint and Body, a shop in Tulare, California, the same ones who did the original painting. As a matter of fact, we had Doyce paint nearly every race car we ever had.

would campaign their new racer in the NHRA Division 7 Super Stock Eliminator category under the sponsorship of the AMC Southern California Dealer Association. The announcement caught some of the reporters by surprise for two reasons: first, because AMC fielded an entry in such a highly competitive drag racing class; and second, that they were relying on a woman to bring home the wins for them.

Soon enough, the reporters were able to see the wisdom of having Shirley on the team. The first time that Shirley took her SS/AMX to the track, it delivered the goods with a 10.67-second ET (some references put it at 10.97 seconds) at 125.69 mph at

Shirley talks with a race fan who is leaning on an AMX. This photo shows how casual things were in the 1960s' racing world, where a fan could just walk up and speak with a famous racer without having to go through a series of "handlers." (Photo Courtesy Shirley Shahan)

TOP: *Here's a copy of a poster done by artist Tom Frederick showing the famous* Pete's Patriot *SS/AMX racing against the* Drag-On Lady *SS/AMX. Notice who's out front! The poster is signed by the drivers of both cars; the great Loren "Lou" Downing drove* Pete's Patriot. *(Photo Courtesy Shirley Shahan)* **RIGHT:** *One of the many manufacturers that hired Shirley to promote its products was wheel maker Cragar. In this advertisement, Shirley wears a Cragar jacket. The advertisement refers to her as the "Queen of the Super Stockers" and notes that she uses Cragar G.T. mag wheels on her personal car and Cragar S/S wheels on her Super Stock AMX. (Photo Courtesy the Patrick Foster Collection)*

Here's a press photo of Shirley and H.L. talking with the newest members of the AMC racing family. Pictured left to right is the great Mark Donohue (his name is misspelled in the label on the photo), Shirley, team owner Roger Penske, and H.L. (Photo Courtesy Chrysler. Chrysler is a trademark of FCA USA LLC.)

Another view of the meeting of lions of the racing world: Mark Donohue, Shirley Shahan, Roger Penske, and H.L. Shahan. The two cars are AMC Javelins that Donohue and Penske were campaigning. (Photo Courtesy Chrysler. Chrysler is a trademark of FCA USA LLC.)

the 1969 Orange County International Raceway Super Stock meet. To illustrate how much faster Shirley was than other drivers in equal cars, that same day, another SS/AMX driver, David Kempton, had a final ET of 12.41 seconds at 112.50 mph.

When it came to stomping on the loud pedal and banging gears, few drivers were quite as good as Shirley Shahan. As H.L. noted, they took the AMX down to Indianapolis the following week and set a track record with it there as well.

Of course, Shirley wasn't the only one who was setting the world on fire with the SS/AMX. Loren "Lou" Downing was another record setter with his famous *Pete's Patriot* AMX. He became the NHRA Division 5 S/S world champion in both 1969 and 1970 and held the NHRA speed record at 126.96 mph for a time. Down in Norfolk, Virginia, driver Nat Thompson campaigned his AMX-1 Super Stock car and held the SS/D class national ET record at 11.04 seconds and 124.50 mph. Lancaster, Pennsylvania's Ross Gilbert, at the wheel of the NOLT Rambler SS/J AMX, consistently ran under the record at 11.71 to 117.0 mph, and there were others.

In a way, all of the "regular" buyers of 1969 AMC Javelins and AMXs benefited from the company's sponsorship of the SS/AMX series. Because of the Hurst connection, it was decided by management that henceforth all 4-speed-equipped Javelin and AMX production cars would be fitted with the Hurst shifter right from the factory.

The racing program also turned up minor weaknesses in various suspension and chassis parts that were subsequently beefed up on production cars. Carl Chakmakian wrote a report for management summarizing the updates and titling it "Racing Improves the Breed."

AMC also continued to sponsor racer Hayden Proffitt and his Grant Rebel Funny Car, primarily

WHEELIES

As a drag racer, Shirley naturally experienced quite a few wheelies in her career. Below is a Q&A with author Patrick Foster and Shirley Shahan.

Author: What's the deal with wheelies? Do you do that to wow the crowd or is it just part of being fastest?

Shirley: No, you don't want to be doing wheelies (at least not big ones) because they cost you time. It's just that to get off the line really quick, you've got to pour on the gas and dump the clutch, and you've got so much power [that] the front wheels pull up off the ground. If they do lift, you don't want them too high, or you can't see where you're going to land.

I remember one time I was racing my AMX and stood the car almost straight up, and when I came down, I was facing the guardrail. You don't want that to happen. It's okay if the wheels lift a foot or two, but more than that and you can get in trouble quick. Usually, the wheels come down within 100 feet or so, which sounds like a lot, but at the speeds you're going it's really not. But to answer your question, well, yes, the crowd loves to see you doing wheel-stands.

(Photo Courtesy Shirley Shahan)

in the eastern half of the country. Proffitt had raced Chevrolets but, like Shirley, was recruited by AMC. The effort actually began with AMC in 1967, when the company wanted to show off its handsome new Rebel intermediate with the new 343-ci V-8. It was dubbed as the Grant Rebel because AMC had Grant Industries in Los Angeles engineer and build the car with AMC's input.

Driven by Bill Hayes for 1967, Hayden Proffitt took over and drove for the 1968 season. From its first race in June 1967 to the end of the year, the Grant Rebel SST toured and raced in 19 cities around the country, setting a national speed record and six track records. At the 1967 NHRA Summernationals in Indianapolis, it ran 172 mph to make the top 10 qualifiers.

On the West Coast, AMC's most visible effort was having Shirley Shahan drag race under the AMC banner. For AMC, the investment in having Shirley race for it saw palpable results that no one would ever have predicted. She and H.L. helped propel

The photo is a little fuzzy, but Shirley poses with the newly painted AMX for the 1970 season. It was the same car as in 1969 with a different paint job. This one looks a lot more aggressive. (Photo Courtesy Chrysler. Chrysler is a trademark of FCA USA LLC.)

One of Shirley's sponsors was Fram filters, and it used her in advertisements. It also produced and sold a 21x28-inch poster of her that today is highly collectible. The posters sold for only a buck when new! (Photo Courtesy the Patrick Foster Collection)

Shirley takes off at the 1970 NHRA Supernationals and gets the jump on her competitor in a Mustang.

(Photo Courtesy Shirley Shahan)

AMC into third place in the NHRA standings for the year, which was an amazing result for a first-year effort. Race fans loved to see Shirley stand her AMX racer on its back bumper and roar down the track at incredible speeds. In fact, she was so popular that a poster of her with her SS/AMX was offered to fans by Fram Filters. Today, it's a very desirable collectible item.

Did Shirley enjoy her time at AMC?

"Oh yes," she recalled. "I drove my Super Stock 390-ci (6,400 cc) AMX, and it was a very competitive car. We won a lot of races with it. I also did some match racing with the AMX, but we stayed pretty close to the Los Angeles area. In addition, as part of my duties for AMC, I also served as a company spokesperson off-track."

Shirley made appearances at dealerships and motor shows and told the AMC racing story.

The sponsorship program offered by AMC was a pretty good deal for Shirley. AMC paid her a regular

Fun on
THE ROAD *Part III*

Shirley has many stories about the fun (and the hazards) of life on the road as a traveling drag racer.

"We had a really close call once on our way to Seattle," she said. "We were driving in the mountains, and, of course, after a while, we had a line of cars behind us because we could only go just so fast with the truck. So, H.L. decided to pull over to the side of the road to let the faster drivers pass. But just as he pulled to a stop, one of our tires rolled past us. Somehow, the lug nuts had worked themselves loose from the wheel during the drive, and H.L.'s moving to the side of the road was just enough for it to let go on its own.

"We collected the wheel and tire—it hadn't gone too far—and H.L. put it back on the truck. He took one lug nut off of each of the other wheels and put it on the one that had come off. It was a little scary driving on that, but it was the only way for us to make it to the next town where we could buy some more lug nuts."

This glamour shot of Shirley was taken in Las Vegas during the 1969 racing season. (Photo Courtesy Chrysler. Chrysler is a trademark of FCA USA LLC.)

Shirley (right) poses for a photo with her kid sister Kathy. This was probably taken at Irwindale Racetrack. Kathy is dressed in red, white, and blue because she was asked to serve as the hostess of the AMC/Hurst tent. Shirley took her to the mall and bought her the clothes so that she would fit in. Shirley believes that this was for a Rambler Scrambler event. (Photo Courtesy Shirley Shahan)

Shirley's SS/AMX is shown, circa 1970. A large percentage of these race cars have survived, and they are quite valuable. Some are still used in vintage racing events.

salary (unlike Chrysler) and she was given a new AMC car for her own personal use. She was able to remain closer to home and also go back to work for the gas company, which in turn meant that she'd have two regular incomes as well as H.L.'s income. As if that wasn't enough, there was icing on the cake: the SS/AMX was a stick shift, which she always preferred to drive.

Shirley raced often for AMC in the 1969 racing season. Fans were able to see her burning up the track and banging gears with the engine screaming and smoke pouring off the spinning tires of the AMX. It wasn't long before Shirley established new D/Super Stock records. She went on to set new high marks for the same class in 1970.

Shirley drove at the 1969 NHRA Winternationals, where she qualified at number 8. However, it was a disappointing day. Things were looking hopeful at first, but she was eliminated in the semifinals by the number-11 qualifier, Ed Terry.

The 1970 Season

Not surprisingly, Shirley and H.L. signed on for a second year with AMC to drive for the 1970 season. They continued to race their 1969 SS/AMX because it was a proven winner. However, the 1970 AMC production AMX cars looked a little different from the 1969 models, and AMC wanted to convert Shirley's 1969 model to look more like a 1970.

"For the second year, we did try to change the appearance of the car to make it look like a '70

Shirley drives the AMX at the 1970 NHRA Winternationals. In this event, Shirley managed to score a class win. Over the course of the racing season, she set both the low ET and top speed records for the class. (Photo Courtesy Shirley Shahan)

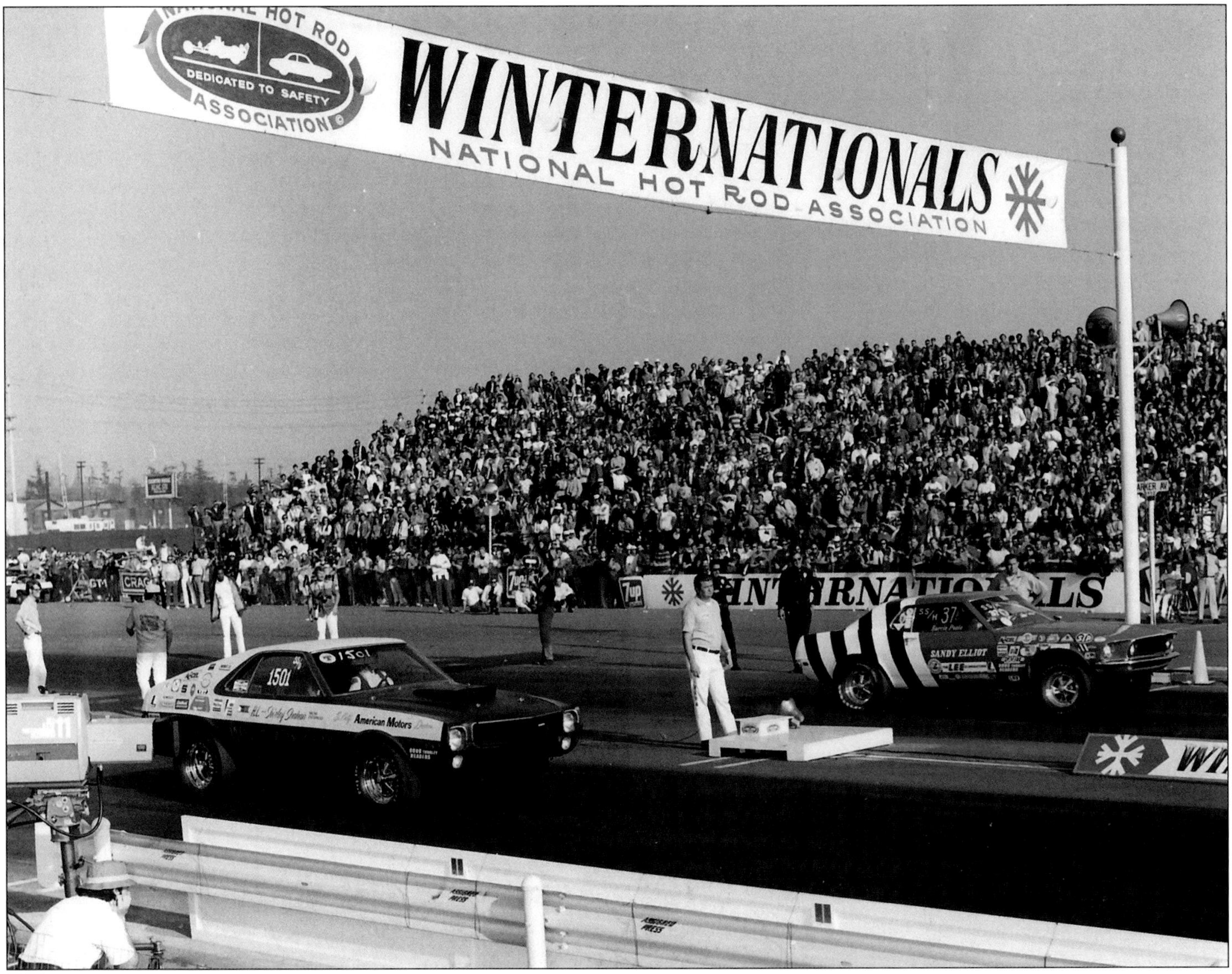

Just look at the size of the crowd! This action shot was taken at the 1970 NHRA Winternationals. The car in the background is Sandy Elliott's Ford Mustang, while Shirley is in the lower left. (Photo Courtesy Chrysler. Chrysler is a trademark of FCA USA LLC.)

Another day, another trophy for the shelf.

H.L. and Shirley Shahan pose with their award for being named the Superstock D Class winner at the 1970 NHRA Winternationals. (Photo Courtesy Shirley Shahan)

model," Shirley said. "The 1970 AMX production cars had been given a new look up front with a longer, peaked hood plus a hood scoop, so we asked AMC for the parts needed to make our racer look like a 1970. They sent out new bumpers, a new grille, headlights, taillights, and the new hood with the hood scoop, and we tried to change the car to look like a 1970. We even changed the paint scheme a little, painting the hood black. But in the end, the NHRA just wouldn't go for it. So, we ended up having to replace all the parts we'd swapped out to make it a 1970 model and change it back to a 1969 model."

One thing they could do, however, was repaint the car in a different paint scheme so that it looked different. For the 1970 season, Shirley's SS/AMX boasted a paint scheme with the lower half of the car plus the decklid and rear roof painted a dark blue. As usual, the painting job was handled by her favorite shop: Doyce's Body and Paint.

Things became even better for Shirley in her second year with AMC. She managed to score a class win at the 1970 NHRA Winternationals, driving her trusty AMX, and set both the low ET and top speed

Shirley poses with sons Steve and Bobby at Orange County International Raceway while an unidentified AMC dealer looks on. What's happening is some sort of raffle for the console television set. Apparently, the boys have been chosen to spin the raffle drum and select the winner. (Photo Shirley Shahan)

records for the class over the course of the season. While Shirley managed to qualify for the 1970 US Nationals, she was disallowed due to a technical infraction. However, Shirley and the AMX managed a class win at the 1970 NHRA Winternationals. Over the course of the 1970 racing season, Shirley also set low ET and top speed records. To the best of her recollection, Shirley said that her best run with the trusty AMX was 10.77 seconds at 128 mph.

Author: You did fairly well during the first half of the 1970 racing season.

Shirley: Yes, well, like the previous season I was driving stick shift, which was always my preferred choice, and that AMX was such a kick to drive! We had a lot of fun. I think everyone was a little amazed when I stood that AMX up on its bumper.

In 1970, we won our class at the Winternationals, and we even set new records for both ET and [top speed], which was really nice. We also did a good deal of match racing with the AMX, but for that, we stayed pretty close to the Los Angeles area.

Author: You were going strong throughout most of the 1970 racing season. You easily qualified for the 1970 US Nationals but then you were disallowed due to some sort of technical infraction. Can you tell us what was that all about?

Shirley: Well, to the best of my recollection, I think it was the CCs. We didn't have enough CCs because AMC had given the NHRA the wrong specifications.

The Game Changes for 1971

Things changed dramatically for 1971. H.L. and Shirley came up with an idea to get AMC into Pro Stock Eliminator racing. The NHRA's new Pro Stock Eliminator category had debuted at the 1970 NHRA Winternationals in Pomona, California, which opened the door to a new breed of race cars and a new category of racing. Featuring wheel-standing performances from gasoline-fed big-inch engines with 4-speed transmissions and mid-9-second times, it seemed ideal for someone with Shirley's skills.

After considering it, Shirley and H.L. put together a detailed program for how they could do it. A very helpful collaborator with the idea was none other than David Landrith, their friend and former manager of Hurst Performance. By this time, Landrith had left Hurst to start his own performance business, the Landrith Corporation, of which he was CEO.

In a series of planning sessions, Landrith, H.L., and Shirley decided that the best approach was to field a team of three AMC cars. They'd have liked to have more cars, but AMC was focusing its attention elsewhere, and budgets were, as usual, very tight. One of the proposed cars was a 1971 AMC Gremlin subcompact and the other two were 1971 AMC Hornet two-door compact sedans.

The first thing H.L. decided was to have the Gremlin's body acid-dipped to reduce weight. Weighing in at a mere 2,200 pounds, the little AMC was designed and engineered for match racing, while the two Hornets were created to run in NHRA

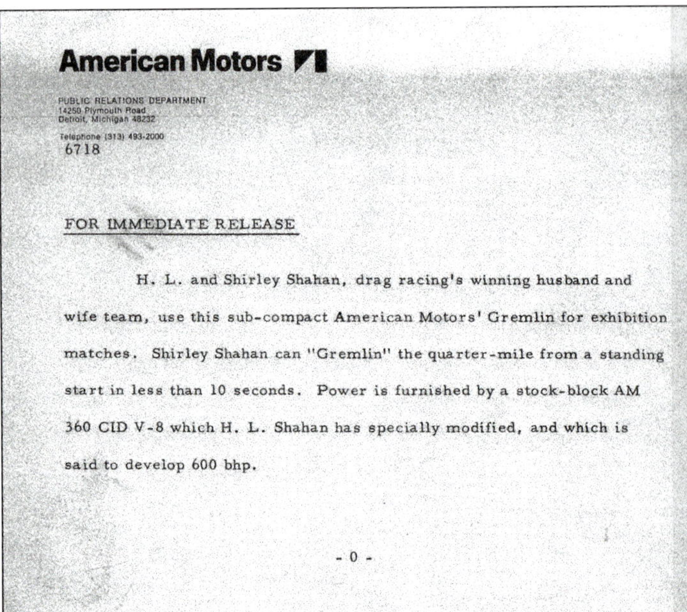

American Motors

PUBLIC RELATIONS DEPARTMENT
14250 Plymouth Road
Detroit, Michigan 48232

Telephone (313) 493-2000
6718

FOR IMMEDIATE RELEASE

H. L. and Shirley Shahan, drag racing's winning husband and wife team, use this sub-compact American Motors' Gremlin for exhibition matches. Shirley Shahan can "Gremlin" the quarter-mile from a standing start in less than 10 seconds. Power is furnished by a stock-block AM 360 CID V-8 which H. L. Shahan has specially modified, and which is said to develop 600 bhp.

- 0 -

In this press release from AMC, the new Gremlin race car is announced. It was used for "exhibition matches" (i.e., match racing). The power from the stock-block AMC 360-ci V-8 was said to be 600 hp. (Photo Courtesy Chrysler. Chrysler is a trademark of FCA USA LLC.)

For 1971, Shirley and H.L. decided to campaign a pair of AMC compact Hornets and a Gremlin. The NHRA's new Pro Stock Eliminator category debuted a year earlier at the 1970 NHRA Winternationals, which offered a new breed of race cars and a new category of racing. (Photo Courtesy Chrysler. Chrysler is a trademark of FCA USA LLC.)

1971 GREMLIN Dragster—The noted husband-and-wife team of H. L. and Shirley Shahan used this Gremlin for exhibitions and special match drag races. They also drove two Hornets in Pro Stock racing.

The Gremlin's body was acid-dipped to reduce weight. Now weighing a mere 2,200 pounds, the little Gremlin was designed for match racing while the two Hornets ran in NHRA Pro Stock Eliminator. The Gremlin was fitted with an H.L.-prepared 366-ci V-8. (Photo Courtesy Chrysler. Chrysler is a trademark of FCA USA LLC.)

Pro Stock Eliminator. The Hornet bodies were also acid dipped. Then, both Hornet and Gremlin bodies were extensively modified by H.L. The modifications included triangulating every corner of the body for strength and installing full roll cages per NHRA Pro Stock guidelines.

As with the Gremlin, the two Hornet compacts were fitted with specially prepared 366-ci V-8s. Those 366-ci V-8 engines were built at H.L.'s performance shop in Tulare using a bare 360-ci block as a starting point. To get to 366 ci, the engine's stock 4.187-inch bore was increased by 0.107 inch. Then, the stroke was reduced to 3.2960 inches, which resulted in 366 ci.

The crankshafts were specially made from raw forgings that H.L. obtained from AMC. These forgings were shipped to the Moldex Crankshaft Company in Michigan (a firm that is still in business today). Moldex then Tuftrided the forgings and cross-drilled them, then hard-chromed and micro-polished them before shipping them back to H.L.'s shop in California.

American Motors

PUBLIC RELATIONS DEPARTMENT
14250 Plymouth Road
Detroit, Michigan 48232

Telephone (313) 493-2000
21717

FOR IMMEDIATE RELEASE

DETROIT -- When Shirley Shahan opened the 1971 drag racing season, she introduced a new car to professional super stock competition.

It's the compact Hornet of American Motors.

In fact, the Shahan team consists of two '71 Hornets for Pro Stock racing and a 1971 sub-compact Gremlin for exhibition appearances and special match races.

All three of the models are powered by stock-block 360-cubic-inch American Motors V-8 engines which have been specially modified for racing.

"Changes in the rules this year have permitted us to use smaller engines with lighter cars," explained Shirley's husband, H. L., who both tunes and maintains the cars.

For the first time, it is possible to run cars weighing a minimum of 2,400 pounds, or 7 pounds per cubic inch of engine displacement in the National Hot Rod Racing Association and 6.8 pounds per cubic inch in the American Hot Rod Association. The Hornets are being campaigned with both major sanctioning bodies.

Thus, in NHRA meets, Shirley's Hornet weighs 2,520 pounds and 2,448 for AHRA competition. This is considerably less than most of her rivals who have cars with much bigger engines that weigh in at 3100-3200 pounds.

- more -

SHIRLEY SHAHAN *The Drag-On Lady*

In contrast, last year the minimum weight was 2,700 pounds.

"We felt this combination would get the job done," said H. L. Shahan. "We're putting out 600 horsepower and its mainly a matter of power to weight."

H. L. estimated the competition is getting 660 to 670 horsepower with 430 and 440 cubic inch engines for their heavier machines.

Top Pro Stockers in this category will cover the quartermile distance from a standing start in 10 seconds or slightly less, hitting a terminal speed of 136-140 mph.

L. D. (Dave) Landrith of Landrith Corporation, a Detroit-based automotive firm which prepared the three vehicles, said the Pro Stock Hornets use total American Motors components in engine, transmission and rear end.

The cars are equipped with four-speed transmissions.

H. L. Shahan said it was necessary to build two Hornets because of Shirley's busy 1971 schedule.

"While she is racing one Hornet, the other one can be on its way to the next meet," he said. "Shirley then just hops a plane and a 'fresh' car is waiting for her."

And if both Hornets are at one place at one time?

"Well, I drive the other one," H. L. said with a sign of hesitation.

Imagine, racing against your wife!

This is the press release created by John A. Conde of AMC that introduced the new Pro Stock Hornets along with H.L. and Shirley Shahan. The press story explains that the cars would be run at both NHRA and AHRA events. H.L. explained, "Changes in rules this year have permitted us to use smaller engines with lighter cars." Unfortunately, the Hornets were less competitive than the AMX. (Photo Courtesy Chrysler. Chrysler is a trademark of FCA USA LLC.)

The 1970
RACING SEASON

Below is a Q&A with author Patrick Foster and Shirley Shahan.

Author: During the 1971 racing season, you and H.L. campaigned an AMC Hornet for American Motors, correct? How did that come about?

Shirley: [AMC] arranged to have two of the race-prepared Hornets available, and I was assigned one of them. But as things ended up, the Hornet two-door sedans just weren't very competitive. A little later on, they gave a Hornet Hatchback to Wally Booth, and I think that car might have been a little better, but the car I got just wasn't competitive.

Author: The books say you qualified number-22 for the 1971 Supernationals but were eliminated in round one by the 1971 Plymouth Barracuda of the number-6 qualifier (and ultimate event winner) Ronnie Sox. Tell us about that.

Shirley takes a break after a race and talks with one of her fans. Today, some 50 years later, she still has legions of fans. (Photo Courtesy Shirley Shahan)

Shirley and H.L. entered the Hornets in the US Nationals in Indy in 1971. Ultimately, the couple achieved a best time of 10.01 seconds and 139.52 mph with the Gremlin and 9.89 seconds and 139.52 mph with one of the Hornets. (Photo Courtesy Chrysler. Chrysler is a trademark of FCA USA LLC.)

Shirley: That was at the Ontario Motor Speedway, I believe. I was driving an AMC Hornet, and, as I said, the car just wasn't competitive. It needed a bigger, more powerful engine than what we had.

Author: You think that was the problem?

Shirley: Yes, I think it was the engine, mostly. It just didn't have enough cubic inches. The truth is, we weren't happy with the Hornets that AMC provided. Although H.L. did all he could to beef up the engines, in the end, those 360-ci/366-ci engines just weren't as competitive as the AMXs had been.

Author: Shirley, can you tell us how long you and H.L. ran with those cars?

Shirley: It was all through 1970 and 1971, but I have to say it was a struggle all the way. We really wanted to get one of the newer Hornets, but for some reason, AMC wanted us to continue to run the same car, and we just weren't competitive enough to win. By the middle of 1971, H.L. and I had already decided that if we couldn't get a new car from AMC we would no longer race. I would simply retire from racing while H.L. would go find a job with another team. Soon after that, he got an offer to go to work for a performance shop in Denver, and I took the kids and went home."

A surprising but true fact is that the larger, heavier AMC Hornet was actually faster than the Gremlin because its longer wheelbase and greater rear overhang helped it get off the line faster than the stubby little Gremlin. (Photo Courtesy Shirley Shahan)

As he put the engines together, H.L. installed a set of F77 Federal-Mogul main bearings in each along with a Milodon Engineering 392 Chrysler four-bolt main girdle adapted to fit the AMC tall-deck block. Nestled inside were Venolia forged-aluminum pistons on Chevy-length Carillo connecting rods using 7/16-inch rod bolts.

The valvetrains were from Crane Cams and were 0.628 inch with a duration of 324 degrees. H.L. ported and polished the AMC cylinder heads and then installed offset valve guides along with Manley 2.165-inch stainless-steel intake valves and 1.860-inch stainless-steel exhaust valves along with Crane needle bearing 1.6:1-ratio rocker arms springs and keepers.

Induction was handled by H.L. He fabricated dual-quad tunnel-ram intake manifolds fitted with two 750-cfm Holley carburetors. As usual, Doug Thorley headers were specified. H.L. liked to give the business to friends, and Doug's Headers were outstanding. Mallory ignition was also specified, firing Champion spark plugs. At the time, Champions were OEM on AMC production cars.

"We built those cars right here in town," H.L. said. "We built the motors right here in my shop. We sent the bodies down to L.A. and had them acid dipped to reduce the weight. But, in the first race we ran in Dallas, the engine sucked a piston, and we didn't have any spare parts yet."

All of that engine power was channeled to a 10.5-inch Lakewood Schiefer clutch and a lightweight aluminum flywheel. The transmissions were

The Hornets were not competitive. Shirley said that they needed bigger, more powerful engines. "We weren't happy with the Hornets AMC provided. Although H.L. did all he could to beef up the engines, in the end, those 360-ci/366-ci engines just weren't as competitive as the 390-ci AMXs." (Photo Courtesy Shirley Shahan)

Shirley performs last-minute checks on one of her AMC race cars. Shirley was a pretty decent mechanic in her own right, having learned from her father and from H.L. (Photo Courtesy Chrysler. Chrysler is a trademark of FCA USA LLC.)

tough Doug Nash–modified slick-shift BorgWarner T10s with a Hurst shifter. The super-strong Henry's Detroit Locker rear end featured 5.21:1 gears.

The rear suspension was special. It featured H.L.-fabricated 2-inch by 3-inch box-tube subframes with SS/AMX rear springs and traction bars and Hurst-Gabriel shock absorbers. The front suspension consisted of specially wound Super Stock–spec coil springs with Hurst-Gabriel shock absorbers and AMC spindles.

The braking system was comprised of lightweight Hurst-Airheart Pro Kit racing disc brakes. The rear wheels were by Halibrand, the front wheels were American Racing, and all four were rolling on Goodyear racing tires.

The 1971 racing season was one of disappointments. Their first race with the Hornet was at Dallas International Motor Speedway; the Hornet suffered engine damage, and the team didn't have any spare parts to fix it.

"Bill 'Grumpy' Jenkins came by, looked at the engine and said, 'Well, heck, it'll still run on seven cylinders, won't it? Go out there and get that round money,'" H.L. said. "So, I did. In the first round, I treed Ronnie Sox and beat him to the first light before that big Hemi motor of his came to life, and he roared right by me."

Then, at the US Nationals at Indy two months later, Shirley and H.L. entered both of the Hornets. Shirley qualified for the 16th spot, where she once again raced Ronnie Sox in round one. H.L.'s Hornet suffered mechanical problems, so he failed to qualify. Ultimately, the couple achieved a best time of 10.01 seconds and 139.52 mph with the Gremlin and 9.89 seconds and 137.20 mph with one of the Hornets.

Shirley qualified at number-22 for the 1971 Supernationals but was eliminated in round one by the 1971 Plymouth Barracuda of her old friend (and ultimate event winner) Ronnie Sox, who was the number-6 qualifier.

After that, she reached the semifinals at the 1971 AHRA Gateway Nationals. In the end, she was eliminated by the 1970 Dodge Charger of event winner Tom Haller.

At the 1971 US Nationals, Shirley and H.L. got their two Hornets into the Pro Stock field. Shirley's car qualified in the 31st slot. However, both were eliminated in round one. Ironically, H.L. lost to his old buddy Butch Leal. Shirley lost her opening-round race to "Fast Eddie" Schartman's red-hot Mercury Comet. As things turned out, it was 21 years before another woman won a round in NHRA Pro Stock competition.

After it became clear to everyone that the Hornets were not competitive, H.L. and Shirley again asked for an updated car, something with more power. However, the request was turned down by AMC.

"We wanted to get one of the new 1972 Hornets, but AMC wanted us to run the same cars, and we just weren't competitive enough," Shirley remembered.

The reason for AMC's reluctance to fund the building of new cars was that the company was putting so much of its racing money behind Roger Penske's Mark Donohue–driven NASCAR Matador coupe that it simply didn't have anything left in the budget to give Shirley the kind of car that she deserved.

She was understandably more than a little annoyed because racer Wally Booth was given better cars, and she felt short-changed. As a small company that was only marginally profitable at the time, AMC couldn't put in all the money it would have liked.

SHIRLEY SHAHAN *The Drag-On Lady*

Shirley Shahan (upper right) is on the cover of a 1970 catalog for Doug Thorley Headers. The upper left photo shows Doug Thorley with Shirley and H.L (left to right). The lower left photo shows their friend Hubert Platt. (Photo Courtesy Shirley Shahan)

1970
Supersedes any prior catalogs
DOUG THORLEY HEADERS
CITY DODGE

Women 'N Wheels

An Interview with Shirley Shahan

by Barbara Nielson and Anne Scott

Shirley Shahan is a unique and remarkable woman. Unique because she is one of the few women Drag Racers in the United States. Remarkable because between her frequent trips to races she plays on a woman's soft ball team (center-field), rides horses, goes bowling, finds time to work part time for the Gas Company in Southern California and helps her husband keep his books at his auto repair center. Somehow Shirley also has found time to raise three children: Janet 15, Steve 10 and Bob 11.

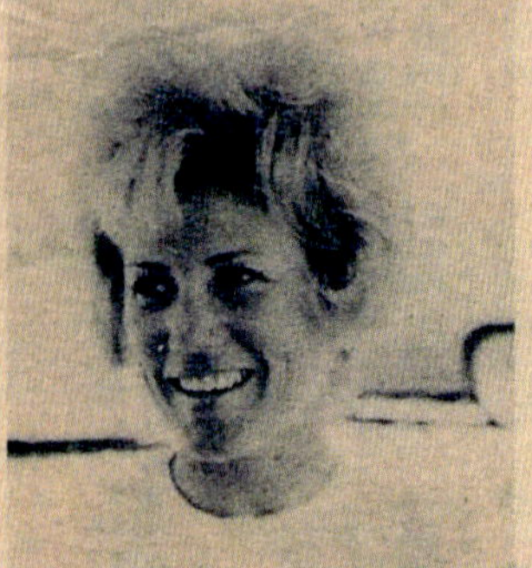

Shirley has been racing ever since she was married 16 years ago. Her husband, H.L. started doing mechanical repairs at races as a hobby and he eventually talked Shirley into doing the

Shirley races her American Motors Sponsored car in Pro Stock. When asked who was her toughest competitor, she replied, 'the Hemi-powered cars, any of them'. She likes the people involved in racing. Even though she feels racing is more unusual for a woman

than a man, she has the same goals as the men who race. She strives for 'a sense of achievement or a feeling of accomplishment'. Shirley never has had much of a problem racing men. No one 'ever bothered her or tried to stop her'. She believes that 'it takes a real man to admit that a woman can do something as well as him'. Her greatest moment in Drag Racing was when she won the Winter Nationals in '66.

The Shahan children attend races in the summer

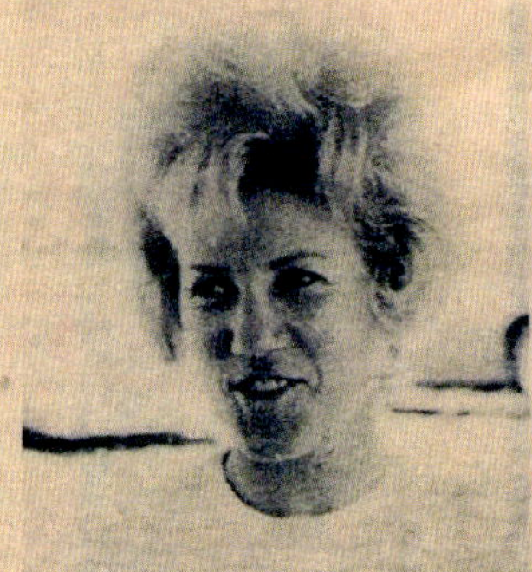

'mostly to collect the decals'. One of the boys already has expressed a desire to become a driver like his mother. The children have grown up around racing and they love it.

Shirley feels as many other women in racing do, that there are many broken marriages in racing because the wives don't take an inter-

est in their men. Women should 'help in the pit crew or just watch and keep track of the times of the competition, but generally BE THERE'. You can bet the Shahan family will 'be there'

Around that time, there were some significant changes in the management of AMC's Performance Activities. Walt Czarnecki left the company to work for the legendary race team owner Roger Penske. In his place, AMC hired Jim Hennel, who only stayed in that position for a few months before being replaced by Bob Swaim.

As things turned out, right around this time, AMC drastically scaled down its participation in drag racing for 1972. So, when H.L. was offered the opportunity to build racing engines full-time at a race shop in Denver, Colorado, his attention was diverted to that, and Shirley decided that she would quit racing. That, sadly, was the end of the Drag-On Lady as an active racer.

"That was it," Shirley explained. "By that point, we decided that if we couldn't get a newer car, we'd quit racing. It was in 1972. My daughter Janet was a teenager by then, and the boys were like 10 and 12 years old. I just felt that it was a good time to leave racing and go back to being a full-time mom again."

The 1971 season was a season of disappointments. At their first race at Dallas International Motor Speedway, the Hornet suffered engine damage. Then, two months later at the US Nationals at Indy, Shirley and H.L. entered both Hornets. Shirley qualified in the 16th spot. H.L.'s Hornet suffered mechanical problems and failed to qualify. (Photo Courtesy Chrysler. Chrysler is a trademark of FCA USA LLC.)

Shirley and H.L. struggled through 1970 and 1971 to win races with the Hornets. They really wanted to get a newer, more competitive Hornet, but AMC wanted them to continue to run the same car. By the middle of 1971, H.L. and Shirley decided that if they couldn't get a new car from AMC, she would retire from racing and H.L. would find a job with another team. He soon received an offer to go to work for a performance shop in Denver. (Photo Courtesy Chrysler. Chrysler is a trademark of FCA USA LLC.)

Shirley sometimes served as a spokesperson for AMC and made personal appearances at AMC dealerships and at cars shows. As a top competitor and a beautiful lady, she was always a popular attraction. (Photo Courtesy Chrysler. Chrysler is a trademark of FCA USA LLC.)

SS/AMC
SURVIVOR CARS

As noted earlier, there's some disagreement as to how many of the factory Super Stockers were built. However, most people can at least agree that it was between 52 and 55. The number had to be at least 50 to meet NHRA and AHRA eligibility requirements for competition, plus one prototype. The VINs indicate 52 production cars plus the prototype.

The big question nowadays is: How many of the SS/AMXs have survived? After all, race cars from the 1960s and 1970s often were so used up from racing that they were parted out or junked once they had reached the end of the line.

One of the better websites covering the SS/AMXs is SSAMX.com. It includes a record of each SS/AMX built along with the name of the dealership/organization that first purchased the car. The site also lists many of the names under which each car was originally raced and, most importantly, the surviving SS/AMXs that have been found so far.

As of this writing, 39 of the original SS/AMX cars have been located, including Shirley Shahan's number-35 AMX. Current owners periodically gather the cars for reunions.

The SS/AMX site also includes lots of photos, SS/AMX documentation, a list of unique parts used on the cars, plus lists of SS/AMX toys, and even some video clips. Although we've heard that it hasn't been updated in a while, it's still worth a visit.

Another, more up-to-date SS/AMX website is Tom Benvie's SuperstockAMX.com. This site also hasn't been updated in about four years, but it still is a wealth of information. Tom Benvie is a noted expert on the SS/AMX series, and it shows on his website.

The
DRAG-ON *Lady's SS/AMX Today*

Shirley's *Drag-On-Lady* AMX was discovered in a forlorn warehouse by an enthusiast named Gordon Gibson. Gibson purchased the car and arranged for its restoration. Reportedly, Gibson has now passed on, but the legendary drag car is still cared for by a family. A family spokesman relayed the following to a journalist: "This car looks exactly like it did when Shirley raced it. We ran it one year after several years of inactivity."

The car is so powerful, Gibson once said, that his driver, Dale Herley, got it up on the rear bumper, and when it returned to earth, the oil pan was banged up. Thankfully, the engine was not damaged. Gibson also owned a second SS/AMX, the one car No. 36, which was originally campaigned by Jimmy Walker. Also in his garage was a second *Drag-On-Lady* car, this one being one of the pair of 1971 AMC Hornets.

Looking back, the signs seemed clear enough. Shirley could have gotten over the disappointing 1971 race season if that was the only concern. However, H.L. was offered a good job building engines in Denver starting in 1972, which he accepted. That meant Shirley wouldn't have him to prepare and fix her cars anymore. There clearly also wasn't as much interest at AMC in drag racing as there once was. It seemed that having proved its point, the company decided it would soon bow out of sponsoring race teams.

In addition, Shirley's kids were growing, and they were now at the age when a child really needs a parent close at hand for guidance. Shirley looked at all these things and decided to close out her driving career after 19 years with a few very nice spots in the record books. She went back to work for the Southern California Gas Company, where she remained until she retired.

Shirley Shahan, the legendary Drag-On Lady, stands next to one of her final race cars. It's too bad that the Hornets were not competitive, as she may have decided to continue racing. (Photo Courtesy Shirley Shahan)

CHAPTER 7

Fame and Glory

AFTER 1971

and working on the special investigations desk. She enjoyed the job and decided to grow with the company, taking business management classes at the College of Sequoias in Visalia.

In 1983, she became a meter reading supervisor, managing 30 employees, and then in 1986 was promoted to service bureau supervisor. Promotions kept coming. She later became the district manager for Kings County, responsible for communications with city, county, and elected officials on issues pertaining to the gas company.

She continued to do well. By the time she took early retirement from the gas company, she was a supervisor in charge of a $6 million budget and 100 employees. I wonder how many of them realized that their boss was a legendary drag racer. Every time Shirley received a promotion, an article would appear in the local papers, and the reporters seldom failed to mention that she was an ex-professional racer known to the world as the Drag-On Lady.

Looking back, Shirley was a true pathfinder, a pioneer in the world of drag racing. Because of her ability and her amazing wins, she opened the door to more women competing in drag racing. In 1977, more than 10 years after Shirley's landmark win at the Winternationals, a woman named Shirley Muldowney became the first woman to win a major NHRA event in the Professional class. As with Shirley Shahan, Muldowney was a wife and mother, and she also faced some pushback from male drivers

Life, as they say, happens. When H.L. was offered a good job building engines in Denver, Colorado, in 1972, he decided to take it. For her part, Shirley decided to retire after 19 years of competitive driving to focus more time on her three children. Sadly, in 1975 she and H.L. divorced.

Shirley had been working part-time for the Southern California Gas Company since signing on with AMC in 1969, but in 1976, she returned to full-time work there after the divorce. She worked in the customer service department, where her various positions included telephone services representative, billing clerk, counter clerk, special ledger clerk,

---

Gas office manager races

Southern California Gas Co.'s new district manager in Hanford has had a lot of experience with natural gas — and with gasoline.

Twenty years ago, Shirley Bridges was the first woman to win a nationally ranked drag race.

At the 1966 Winter Nationals in Pomona, sponsored by the National Hot Rod Association, she drove a superstock Plymouth — powered by a 427-cubic-inch V-8 with dual four-barrel carburetors — down the quarter-mile track in 11.2 seconds, reaching 127 mph.

"After that I got offers to do personal appearances, TV and radio shows, and match races," she recalls.

Even though she was breaking new ground as a woman driver, she says she never encountered any discrimination from the men she raced against.

She raced Chrysler automobiles from 1966 to 1968, and in 1969 she went to work for the American Motors dealers' association of southern California. Driving for that firm required less traveling than she had to do with Chrysler, and she took a part-time job with Southern California Gas Co.

She had worked for SoCal on two previous occasions, leaving the first time to have children and leaving the second time to take up full-time drag racing.

A native of Visalia, she is a graduate of Mt. Whitney High School and is married to Ken Bridges, fire chief of Tulare.

Shirley Bridges

Until taking over as district manager in December with the retirement of Wayne Taulbee, Bridges had been responsible for 28 gas meter readers in Kings, Tulare and Kern counties.

She supervised the company's service bureau in Visalia for the last nine months.

Like Taulbee before her, her responsibilities in Hanford include public relations with the communities in the district, taking part in civic and service organizations and representing the company at meetings of city councils and boards of supervisors.

A 1986 press release from the Southern California Gas Company announced their new district manager, Shirley (Shahan) Bridges, boasting that she was the first woman to win a nationally ranked drag race. The company was proud of its employee and mentioned her racing career several times during her employment. (Photo Courtesy Shirley Shahan)

SHIRLEY BRIDGES

SoCal Gas has new district manager here

Southern California Gas Co. has announced a new district manager for Fresno and Kings County areas. She is Shirley Bridges of Hanford.

Mrs. Bridges has worked for SoCal Gas Co. since 1957, with some time off and then steady since 1975.

Bridges was known as the "Dragon Lady" back in 1966 for her ability and success in drag racing. She was the first woman to win a national drag racing event. For nearly five years, she and her family traveled all over the United States, Mexico and Hawaii. She drives Chrysler, Dodge and Plymouth cars.

Bridges will be active in the communities of her general district. She will be visiting in Reedley at intervals. The position is one of public relations to keep the public informed about SoCal Gas services.

A smaller press release was made for Shirley Shahan's promotion to district manager. After her racing career, Shirley put her considerable determination to work learning new skills and advancing her career. By the time she retired from the gas company, she was a supervisor in charge of a $6 million budget and 100 employees. (Photo Courtesy Shirley Shahan)

This photo was taken at an AMC show after the AMX was found in a warehouse. At the time, the car was still wearing its 1970 color scheme, but it looks a little worn. (Photo Courtesy Shirley Shahan)

who didn't like being beaten by a woman. Regardless, she went on to enjoy a brilliant career racing Top Gas dragsters and Funny Cars.

At some point, Shirley Shahan met Ken Bridges, the fire chief in Tulare. Before long, they became a couple. Shirley and Ken were married on July 3, 1976, in Carson City, Nevada. As of this writing, they have been married for more than 44 years, and it's a very happy marriage. Ken is a good sport; he travels with Shirley whenever she goes to classic car meets or vintage racing shows. Ken has even gotten used to being known as the Drag-On Lady's husband.

Shirley retired from the gas company in 1992; her husband, Ken, retired from the fire department in 1991. The couple has a fifth-wheel trailer, and they travel a great deal. On the way back from one extended vacation trip in 1995, they stopped at the Ponderosa Ranch in the little town of Incline Village, Nevada, near Lake Tahoe. They liked it so much they decided to put in applications for jobs there.

The Ponderosa Ranch, which has since closed, was a theme park based on the popular 1960s television program *Bonanza* and the affluent land-, timber-, and livestock-owning Cartwright family. The amusement park operated in Incline Village for more than 30 years from 1967 until 2004.

At the Ponderosa, they both dressed in Western clothing and were provided with red and white

Fram Filters commissioned an art poster of Shirley with her SS/AMX as it looked in 1969. She was presented with the original painting. The poster, which sold for $1 back in 1969, is a sought-after collectible today and rather hard to find. (Photo Courtesy Fram Filters)

Count fast! How many ladies do you see in this photo of top race car drivers? Yes, just one. In 1969, Shirley was a pioneer, although more and more women were getting into drag racing. At the time, she was the best of the best. (Photo Courtesy Fram Filters)

As a woman who loves to travel around America, Shirley has been to many places and been greeted by many different people. Here, she is being serenaded by the Philadelphia Mummers, an ancient organization with roots to Egypt in the time of the pharaohs. The Mummers hold a parade on each January 1 in Philadelphia. They devote an entire year to crafting their costumes. (Photo Courtesy Shirley Shahan)

checkered shirts. At first, they did mundane jobs, such as guarding the front gate, cooking Hossburgers, and driving the wedding couples to the church in the park's 1948 Packard convertible. However, in later years, Ken had the job of driving guests in a hay wagon up the hill to an outdoor breakfast. Ken also bartended in the saloon and entertained folks with his guitar/singing.

"My first year, I sold entrance tickets and worked in the fudge/ice cream store," Shirley said. "We made our own fudge. The next year, I worked in the office [as a] receptionist and booked weddings, ordered the minister, flowers, [and] photographer. The park did weddings every hour on the hour, eight of them a day on weekends. After that, I moved into the cash cage where the money was counted; only two people were allowed in there other than the bosses. I became the head auditor, issuing the cash for all the stores and balancing them the next day. I also provided relief to all the stores. Both Ken and I bartended in the Saloon for night parties."

Shirley and Ken ended up working there for nine years.

After the ranch closed, they went to work for the owner of a ranch in Wellington, Nevada. Mainly, they just kept the place clean and provided security.

"We were the only ones there," Shirley said. "The owner had a large log home, plus a small one that we lived in."

The Drag-On Lady in Retirement

Today, Shirley Shahan Bridges lives in Tulare, California, not far from her old hometown of Visalia. It's been a blessed life; for much of the time, all three of her children have lived nearby. Daughter Janet and her husband compete in tractor pulls, operating a Lucas Oil–sponsored tractor puller called *Git-R-Done* with one of Shirley's grandsons at the wheel.

Her oldest son, Steven, has a silk-screening and monogramming business in Tulare and has also served as a sometime crewmember for several drag racing teams, including NHRA drag racers Ed McCulloch and Steve Faria. Her youngest son, Robert (called "Bobby"), worked for the city of Tulare and often raced a tribute replica of Shirley's 1968 *Drag-On-Lady* Dodge Dart. Sadly, during the writing of this book, Robert passed away suddenly as a result of an accident.

With her love of family, Shirley Shahan enjoys being both a grandmother and great grandmother. She is also a charter member of Tulare County Women's Trade Club and volunteers for both the World Agricultural Expo and the Calvary Chapel Church Motor Sports Show in Tulare.

"As of today, we have 16 grandchildren and 26 great grandchildren, happily with most of them living in the local area, and that keeps us pretty busy," Shirley said.

Awards and Records

Shirley can look back with pride on a life well lived and on a slew of records and accomplishments. In addition to the family she raised, the children, grandchildren, and great grandchildren, there's also her place in history.

"After I won the 1966 NHRA Winternationals, *Sports Illustrated* magazine did honor me and sponsored a luncheon in my honor," Shirley said. "I also

Shirley's son Bobby built and raced a clone of his mother's Dodge Dart Super Stock racer, as seen here at the historic race-track in Bakersfield. Sadly, Bobby passed away during the time this book was being written. H.L. watches in the background. He also passed away in 2020. It was two months before Bobby's passing. (Photo Courtesy Shirley Shahan)

Shirley Shahan with her late son, Bobby, posed for this photo at the Hot Rod Reunion. Notice the T-shirt that Bobby is wearing, which shows Shirley's SS Dodge racer. Racing has been a family activity with the Shahans, starting with Shirley's father. (Photo Courtesy Shirley Shahan)

received a small little trophy from them, and they ran an article on it in one of their issues. But other than being inducted into both the International Drag Racing Hall of Fame and the *Super Stock* Magazine Hall of Fame in 1997 and then being inducted into the Don Garlits Museum Hall of Fame (also in 1997), and then being honored with a Lifetime Achievement Award at the Bakersfield racetrack in 2002 during the Goodguys meet and serving as the grand marshal at the 2005 California Hot Rod Reunion, that's about it."

Whew!

We'd say that was more than enough for one person! Shirley is being overly modest because the fact is, as we've recounted in this book, she was the first driver, male or female, to win the famous March Meet. She was the first woman to win a major drag racing event: the 1965 NHRA Winternationals. Besides that, Shirley also was named to and received the *Hot Rod* Magazine Top 10 Drivers of the Year Award in 1966. Yes, it's true that she had a relatively brief career, as things go in professional racing, but it was an extremely important career.

"At the induction to the hall of fame, I was trying to find eight motel rooms and couldn't," Shirley

In 1997, Shirley was inducted into the International Drag Racing Hall of Fame, a great honor that was perhaps overdue. That same year, she was also inducted into the **Super Stock** Magazine Hall of Fame. In 2002, she was honored with a Lifetime Achievement Award at the Bakersfield racetrack during the Goodguys meet. (Photo Courtesy Shirley Shahan)

Shirley gathers with family outside the International Drag Racing Hall of Fame in March 1997. The people are (left to right): her husband Ken, daughter Janet, daughter-in-law Kim Shahan, son Steven, Shirley, Bobby, his wife Lynee, Shirley's brother Jerry Epperson, and his wife Joanne Epperson. Kneeling in front are Shirley's brother Jackie Epperson and her sister Kathy Trimble. Located in Ocala, Florida, the International Drag Racing Hall of Fame was created by racing legend "Big Daddy" Don Garlits. (Photo Courtesy Shirley Shahan)

said. "They had sent us a list of motels and I started calling, but I couldn't find any rooms, so I went to the bottom of the list and started calling, and found a motel that had enough rooms: the University Inn. My brother got there a day early and called my husband, Ken, and told him 'Don't tell Shirley, but these rooms are horrible.' Well, we got there and sure enough, I wouldn't have stayed if I wasn't in dire need. I wouldn't wish those rooms on anybody.

"Anyway, we went to Walmart and bought scented candles, room spray, towels, soap, bug spray, deodorizer, anything we could find. We slept on the towels and didn't take our shoes off. We were booked for a week and had to stay at least two nights because of the event. It was horrible and embarrassing. After two nights, we moved to the Embassy Suites and went to Disney World."

In addition to the honors she mentioned, in 2010, Shirley was inducted into the River Way Sports Park Pillars of Fame in her hometown of Visalia, California. To this day, she remains a very popular speaker and guest at drag racing reunion events. She is admired by the scores of women drag racers who came after her; they understand and appreciate her pioneering efforts.

The AMC enthusiast crowd loves her. The various clubs often ask her to speak at their National meets. She and Ken appear at AMC club meets where she sets up a table to sell signed photographs,

One of the honors bestowed on Shirley Shahan by the California Hot Rod Reunion in 2005 was the placement of her name on this bench. Notice that old friend and competitor Dick Landy was also so honored that year. (Photo Courtesy Shirley Shahan)

SHIRLEY SHAHAN *The Drag-On Lady*

SUPER STOCK MAGAZINE
DRAG RACING HALL OF FAME MEMBERS

1995

DRIVERS

Arnie Beswick
Phil Bonner
Malcolm Durham
Maverick Golden
Bruce Larson
Bill Lawton
Roger Lindamood
Don Nicholson
Hubert Platt
Ronnie Sox

MECHANIC

Bill Jenkins
Jake King

TEAM OWNER/MANAGER

Buddy Martin
Tasca Ford

MANUFACTURER

Dodge
Ford

SPONSOR

Nalley Chevrolet
Mr. Norm's Dodge

AFTERMARKET MANUFACTURER

Hurst Corporation
M & H Tires

1996

DRIVERS

Jim Dunn
Leroy Goldstein
Jim Liberman
Ed McCulloch
Tom McEwen
Don Prudhomme
Dale Pulde
Don Schumacher
Richard Tharp
Doug Thorley

MECHANIC

Keith Black
Ed Pink

TEAM OWNER/MANAGER

Roland Leong
Ramchargers

MANUFACTURER

Chevrolet
Plymouth

SPONSOR

Bob Banning Dodge
Revelle Models

AFTERMARKET MANUFACTURER

Cragar Industries
Simpson Safety Products

1997

DRIVERS

Wally Booth
Tommy Ivo
Butch Leal
Art Malone
Ron Mancini
Herb McCandless
Ken Montgomery
Kenny Safford
Clare Sanders
Shirley Shahan

MECHANIC

H. L. Shahan
Ted Spehar

TEAM OWNER- MANAGER

Harry Schmidt
Barry Setzer

MANUFACTURER

Pontiac
Mercury

SPONSOR

Army
Yenko Chevrolet

AFTERMARKET MANUFACTURER

Goodyear Tires
Stahl Headers

1998

DRIVERS

Gordie Bonin
Bunny Burkett
Wayne Gapp
Don Garlits
Bob Glidden
Judy Lilly
Eddie Schartman
Gene Snow
Arlen Vanke
Jack Werst

MECHANIC

Gene Adams
Ralph Moody

TEAM OWNER/MANAGER

John Mazmanian
The Rod Shop

SPECIAL AWARD

Jon Lundberg
Dave Strickler

SPONSOR

Pepsi Cola
Royal Pontiac

AFTERMARKET MANUFACTURER

Lenco Transmissions
Edelbrock Intakes

Drag-On-Lady toy cars, and other paraphernalia. I have set up my own tables next to her and watched with envy as she sits there signing autographs for hours with a line of fans waiting patiently to see her, shake her hand, and say how much they appreciate her.

Shirley Shahan Bridges and her brother Jerry have dinner at the International Drag Racing Hall of Fame in 1997 when she was inducted. (Photo Courtesy Shirley Shahan)

In 2014 came another great honor: Shirley was inducted into the Mopar Hall of Fame. In a happy coincidence, another one of the inductees that year was her old friend Butch Leal. Some of the other inductees that year included such greats as Don "the Snake" Prudhomme, Keith Black, Norman "Mr. Norm" Krause, and Tom McEwen. That's pretty good company, and it illustrates exactly how important Shirley Shahan has been to the sport.

Visiting the Racetracks Today

Shirley was asked if she missed drag racing.

"Most days, I don't miss it," she said. "But then, when Ken and I visit the local racetracks and I can smell the fumes and clutches burning and hear the engines roaring and the tires screeching—that's the point when I really miss it because those smells and those noises sure bring back a lot of very good memories.

"H.L. and I were young and having so much fun racing and traveling from track to track. But

Vintage racing at Bandimere Speedway pits Shirley's SS/AMX against another SS/AMX. Bandimere Speedway is in Morrison, Colorado, and this exhibition race took place in 2007 during an American Motors Owners Club event. (Photo Courtesy Shirley Shahan)

you know, for many years after I remarried, I didn't have much of anything to do with racing. Then, the nostalgia craze really started to take off, and people began to get interested in racing from back in the day, and then they started calling me to go out to some of the vintage car shows, and so I got interested again.

"I especially enjoy going back to the American Motors clubs national events, because they're a lot of fun, and I've been invited to speak at some of them, which is also fun. Living in such a small, quiet town, I really had no idea that people were so interested in stuff that happened back in the 1960s. It was a lot of fun to be racing back then—I really

Even though it's an exhibition race, the two drivers are quite serious. Look at Shirley's SS/AMX popping a wheelie just like the old days. Shirley said, "This was the first time we went to an AMO International Convention. Even though the two ran the same class, we never raced against each other in the old days. Later that day, my AMX raced a Gremlin so that the audience would have a show. I wasn't driving; Gordon Gibson's mechanic was driving my car." (Photo Courtesy Shirley Shahan)

Shirley stands with Rambler Ranch owner Terry Gale. During one of her appearances at the American Motors Owners Club National Meets in Colorado, Shirley and a group of AMC enthusiasts took a short drive to visit the world-famous Rambler Ranch, which is a private museum that is loaded with AMC cars. (Photo Courtesy Shirley Shahan)

*Shirley received this letter concerning
her induction into the International Drag
Racing Hall of Fame in Ocala, Florida.
(Photo Courtesy Shirley Shahan)*

October 8 , 1996

Shirely Shahan Bridges
1400 Colorado Street
Boulder City, NV 89005

Dear Mrs Bridges,

Preparations are underway for the Seventh Annual Banquet
and Induction Ceremony of the International Drag Racing
Hall of Fame to be held on Thursday, March 6, 1997.

As Museum Secretary, I will be your contact here in
Florida, coordinating your participation in the program.
If you have any questions at any time, please do not hesitate
to call on me for assistance.

Following are a few things that we need from you immediately:

1) An 8 x 10 color or black/white head shot of yourself.
    This can be a photo from any time in your career and
    of any style (formal or casual). This photograph will
    be used for press releases, on the presentation plaque,
    and in the program of the evening. We also need any
    available video footage of yourself and your cars for
    the ESPN broadcast, Banquet room monitors, and home
    video.

2) If you haven't already done so, please give us an idea
    as to how many seats you will be needing at the Banquet.

3) Let us know if you require and assistance for lodging in
    the Ocala/Gainesville area. (List enclosed)

I look forward to meeting you and consider it an honor to work
on your behalf.

Sincerely,

Meredith L. Clark

MUSEUM OF DRAG RACING
13700 SOUTH WEST 16TH AVENUE • OCALA, FLORIDA 34473 • (352) 245-8661

Goodguys 43rd March Meet — Grand Marshal

She's a drag racing pioneer, a winner, a champion, and, her name is Shirley. Shirley Muldowney, right? No, try again. Shirley, ah…ah…ah…Geez, I don't know? Shirley who?

Shirley today, retired and living life to the fullest with husband Ken Bridges.

Don't feel bad if the name Shirley Shahan doesn't leap to mind, for Shahan's gender-bending quarter-mile success came long time before Cha-Cha charged onto the scene. Way back in 1966 Shahan was NHRA's first-ever female champion, winning Super Stock class at the Winternationals in her Drag-On-Lady '65 Plymouth. Her performance opened the eyes of guy racers everywhere; suddenly drag racing was no longer the sole domain of men.

Born in the sleepy agricultural town of Visalia in California's San Joaquin Valley, Shahan picked up an interest in racing from her father, who drove circle-track cars on dusty ovals across the Valley. "I was the oldest daughter, so I got to go to the track with dad," she remembers. "I got to hand dad the wrenches and learn about cars. I also remember taking an aptitude in test in school when I was 8 or 9. It said I should be a mechanic!"

Shirley, however, preferred racing to wrenching, and began competing at age 17. It makes sense she would marry racer, as her future husband H.L. was a drag strip regular too. Together they formed a formidable team, terrorizing valley drag strips in Visalia, Madera, Raisin City, and Bakersfield.

Bakersfield, in fact, was the scene of one of her most important early triumphs: in '59 she drove her '58 Chevy to the Super Stock class win at the first "Smokers" meet at Famoso. And to prove that even if you race in a straight line, life sometimes comes full circle, Goodguys will honor Shirley this March as Grand Marshall of the 43rd Annual Smokers Meet, a fitting tribute to one of drag racing's true pioneers.

Shirley launches her new 1967 Dodge at famed Lion's Drag Strip circa 1967. Dig that metallic open face helmet!

Following the victory at the Smoker's meet, Shahan took a few years off, when she had two children, but she returned to competition in 1963. She earned some success in the next couple years, before picking up a factory sponsorship from Chrysler in 1965 — a coup for any racer, let alone a woman.

She didn't disappoint her corporate backers. In 1965 she had strong runner-up finishes at the Hot Rod Magazine Championships and the AHRA Winternationals, two results that set the stage for the '66 Winternationals breakthrough.

The Winternational's win changed her life as well as the competitive landscape at NHRA. In the 11.26 seconds it took for Shahan zip down the Pomona quarter mile she went from struggling racer to national celebrity, increasing the exposure for her and the entire sport. Super Stock & Drag Illustrated dubbed her Mrs. Stock Eliminator. National wire services spread the news. ABC's Wide World of Sports aimed their cameras. Shahan got her fifteen minutes of fame and more, and NHRA went along for the PR ride.

"Winning that race really turned things around for me," she told NHRA's National Dragster recently. "Right after we won, we began getting calls from back east for match-race appearances. I quit my job at the Gas Company and traveled back easy with H.L. to race from April through October before returning back home to Visalia for the winter.

Throughout the 1960's Shahan's life was a blur of match races, NHRA and AHRA competition, and personal appearances. She set NHRA SS/AA track records in a Hemi Dodge Dart and appeared on television game shows "To Tell the Truth" and "Hollywood Squares." Performance products companies recruited Shahan to endorse their products. Hot Rod Magazine named her one of the Top Ten drivers of 1965, her name appearing next to that of Don Prudhomme. She was hot as a Top Fuel open header.

Her credibility was so strong Chrysler recruited her to represent Mopar in non-racing events, such as the then-prestigious Mobil Economy Run. In three years of competition, she finished first, second and fourth. "It was like driving with an egg under your gas pedal," she remembers.

Pushing the as pedal to the floor was more Shahan's style. After record setting efforts in the Dodge Hemi Darts, she switched to AMC in 1969 to drive a SS/D AMX. A year later she participated in the inaugural year of NHRA Pro Stock, wheeling an AMC Hornet, which stung the competition with E.T.s in the 9.80s. She campaigned the Hornet in Pro Stock through 1972. But in 1973 trouble loomed. AMC focused its racing budget on Trans-Am (Roger Penske and Mark Donohue) and refused to provide Shahan with new equipment. So, rather than compete in a year-old, non-competitive car, Shahan hung up her racing gloves and retired. Quietly, with hardly a notice in the racing trades, a drag racing legend tripped the lights for the last time.

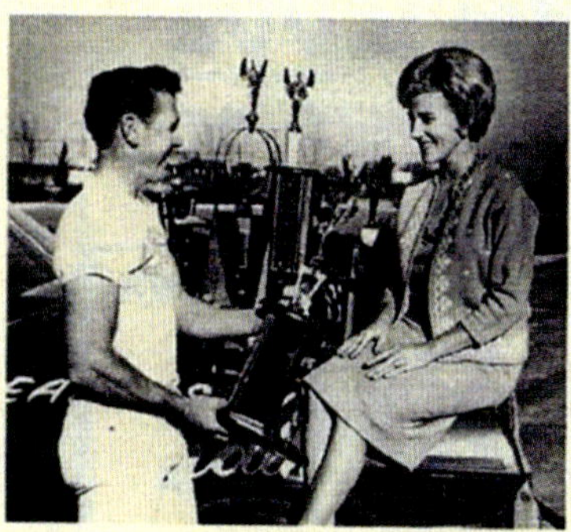
The years of 1963 & '64 were fruitful for H.L & Shirley Shahan. Their 1963 Chevy won just about everywhere they took it as evidenced by the numerous trophies stacked on the hood.

Shahan returned to Visalia and took a job with the Gas Company. Shirley and H.L. parted ways in 1975, and she married Ken Bridges a year later. A normal, racing-free life followed, so normal Mrs. Shirley Bridges retired from the gas company in 1992. These days Shirley enjoys more leisurely motorized pursuits, traversing the links in golf carts and seeing America through the windshield of an RV. She hasn't completely lost touch with the racing world, however, as she regularly visits the Hot Rod Reunion in Bakersfield and attends the NHRA National events at Pomona and Phoenix. It helps that her sons, Steven and Bob, have wrenched on big-time Funny Cars driven by Ed McCulloch, Raymond Beadle and Louis Sweet.

Like many hot rod heroes of yesteryear, Shahan hasn't been able to out-race her legacy. The older she gets, the more fans, both young and old, appreciate her accomplishments. In 1997 Shahan was named to both the Super Stock Magazine and International Drag Racing Halls of Fame. Moreover, Super Stock Collectibles recently released a diecast replica of her 1969 AMX. And now Goodguys has named her Grand Marshall of the Smoker's Meet. Whoever said fame is fleeting didn't know much about racing.

Thirty-five years after that historic pass at Pomona, Shahan is happy with her life, and well aware of the ripple she caused in the racing world. "I never saw myself as some sort of female pioneer, I just loved to go racing," she explained. "I had been racing against the guys for a long time before winning the Winternationals. And I wasn't even the only woman. Paula Murphy also was a well-known racer. The guys always respected me, so I didn't think much about it.

"But I do remember driving the return road after I won at Pomona. The fans were cheering, and Paula came up and handed me a beer. Then it finally hit me, 'wow, maybe I did something here.'" Yes, Shirley, you sure did. You made history, and all us race fans, men and women, are the better for it. See ya' at Bakersfield!

The year 1997 was a big one for Shirley because she won several awards, including being inducted into the Super Stock *Magazine Drag Racers Hall of Fame. Shown is the letter informing her of the honor. (Photo Courtesy Shirley Shahan)*

working with the people at Chrysler Corporation and American Motors. I do have to admit that I'm surprised at the number of fans who still remember me after all these years. I'm still in contact with some of the old racers who were such good friends, and we remain that way, even after all these years.

"My experience in drag racing was really fantastic and is something I will never forget. With all of the records being broken by lady racers today, I'm proud that my career may have helped pave a path for a lot of what has happened and what continues to happen."

I asked Shirley what drag racing has meant to her.

"As you know, my dad was into cars, and I have one sister who drove quarter midgets back then and one brother who also drove quarter midgets," she said. "So, when I got into the sport with H.L., I just really enjoyed doing it, and it seemed like it was a natural thing for me to be able to do that. I realized early on that it was something that I could do that was an accomplishment for me."

Was Shirley ever scared at the wheel? She can recall only a few times. The worst one was when she, H.L., and son Bobby were driving on the 23-mile-long Pontchartrain Causeway bridge on their way into New Orleans. Their family station wagon was running fine one moment, and then

don't know how it is today, but back then it was really great fun. I know they talk about racing being one big happy family today, but I'm sure it just can't be as close and friendly as it was back then because there's so much money involved nowadays."

Of the time she spent in drag racing, Shirley said, "I really enjoyed the years when I was racing and

Everywhere she goes, people ask Shirley for her autograph and to have their picture taken with her. (Photo Courtesy Shirley Shahan)

it died completely with no warning. H.L. hopped out and got under the hood to determine the cause of the problem while Shirley (with Bobby in hand) stood at the back of the car trying to wave people to slow down to avoid them on the narrow causeway. Cars were whizzing by at highway speeds.

"It was really terrifying," Shirley said.

Luckily, H.L. figured out that the points had somehow been stuck together. He pried them apart, reset them by eyeball, and they were able to resume the drive into the Big Easy.

This is a copy of the folder for the 1997 International Drag Racing Hall of Fame induction ceremony. (Photo Courtesy Shirley Shahan)

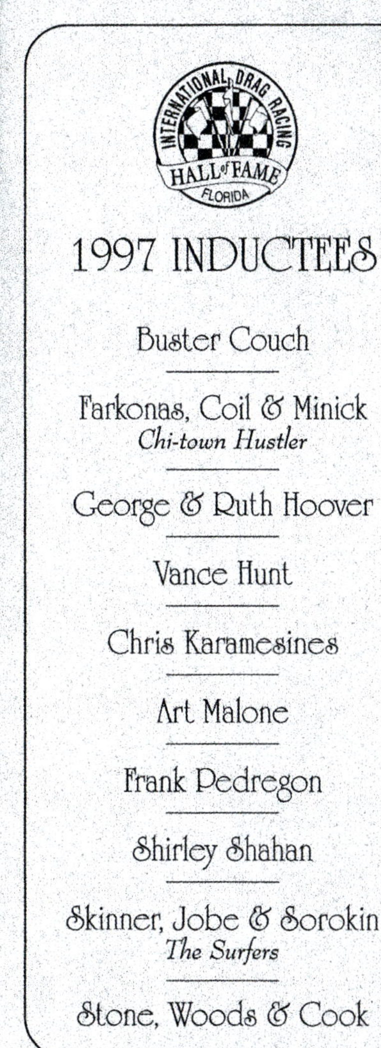

1997 EVENTS

INTERNATIONAL DRAG RACING HALL OF FAME

THURSDAY
MARCH 6, 1997

8:30 am - 5:30 pm	Museum of Drag Racing Open
7:00 pm	Banquet at the Gainesville Radisson
7:30 pm	Dinner
8:30 pm	Induction Ceremony

Televised Nationally on ESPN

SATURDAY - SUNDAY
MARCH 8 - 9, 1997

9:00 am - 7:00 pm	Museum of Drag Racing Open (Extended Hours)

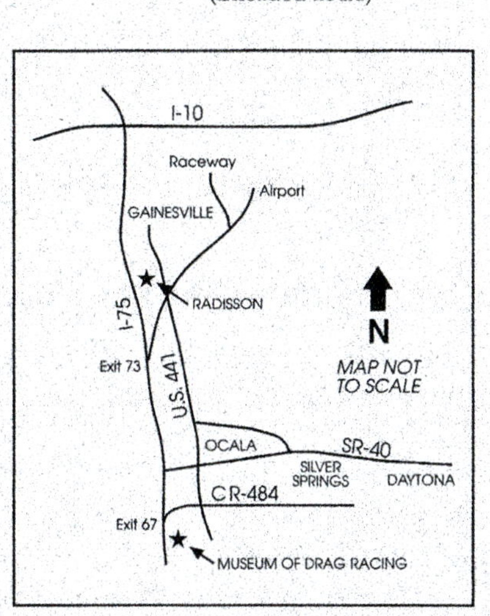

1997 INDUCTEES

Buster Couch

Farkonas, Coil & Minick
Chi-town Hustler

George & Ruth Hoover

Vance Hunt

Chris Karamesines

Art Malone

Frank Pedregon

Shirley Shahan

Skinner, Jobe & Sorokin
The Surfers

Stone, Woods & Cook

HALL OF FAME MEMBERS

Sydney Allard
Art Arfons
Zora Arkus-Duntov
Joaquin Arnett and the Bean Bandits
Keith Black
John Bandimere
Lou Baney
Raymond Beadle
Willie Borsch
John Bradley
Joe Bush
Don Carlton
Larry Carrier
Art Chrisman
Jack Chrisman
Emery Cook
Bud Coons
Bruce Crower
Ted Cyr
Ed Donovan
Vic Edelbrock, Sr.
Scotty Fenn
Lyle Fisher
Kent Fuller
Don and Pat Garlits
Woody Gilmore
Ray Godman
Gary "Red" Greth
Barb Hamilton
Jack Hart
C.J. Hart
Ernie Hashim
Chet Herbert
Doris Herbert
Joe Hrudka
George Hurst
Ed Iskenderian
Tommy Ivo
Bill Jenkins
Howard Johansen

Bobby Langley
Jim and Alison Lee
Tommy "T.C." Lemons
Jim Liberman
Buddy Martin
Don Maynard
Bob Metzler
Ak Miller
George Montgomery
Paula Murphy
Tony Nancy
"Jazzy" Nelson
Jim Nelson
Don Nicholson
Jimmy Nix
Danny Ongais
Gary Ormsby
Herb Parks
Wally and Barbara Parks
Robert E. Petersen
Ed Pink
Joe Pisano
Setto Postoian
Calvin Rice
Eric Rickman
Marvin Ritchin
Pete Robinson
Paul Schiefer
Lloyd Scott
Ralph Seagraves
Lee Shepherd
Mike Snively
Ronnie Sox
Mickey Thompson
Jim Tice
James Warren
Phil Weiand
John Wiebe
Jack Williams
Ed Winfield

By Shirley Shahan

A SPECIAL DAY at MCACN

In 2019, Ken and I were invited to the Muscle Car and Corvette Nationals (MCACN) in Chicago.

Ian Webb and the group, Nash Nutz, went to great lengths to get both the Hornet and AMX to the show. It was to be a reunion of the cars, myself, and Gordon. Sadly, Gordon passed away a few months before the show. Gordon's wife, Mary, and stepson Tony made sure that the cars made it to Chicago anyway.

The MCACN show is special in that you have to be invited to attend. Only special and unique cars are allowed.

Ian's group went above and beyond getting the display set up with both cars and the old Hornet door, providing a place for me to sign autographs and take photos.

The first day, as I was signing autographs, I looked up , and my daughter Janet and husband, Clarence, and son Bob and his wife, Carla, were standing in front of me. They had flown in from California to surprise us. Everyone knew but Ken and me. It was a great weekend. There is a photo of me sitting in the AMX; it was the first time in 50 years that I had been in the car.

Shirley reunited with her AMX at the event. For the 1970 race season, H.L. and Shirley first tried to convert their race car to a 1970 model. There were only minor styling differences, but the NHRA wouldn't allow it. So, the couple decided to change the color scheme to this flashier red, white, and blue paint job. (Photo Courtesy Shirley Shahan)

Shirley's Hornet made an appearance at the event. The Hornet bodies were acid-dipped and then extensively modified by H.L. The Hornets were then fitted with specially prepared 366-ci V-8s that were built at H.L.'s performance shop in Tulare. (Photo Courtesy Shirley Shahan)

Shirley reacts to the surprise visit from her family at the 2019 Muscle Car and Corvette Nationals show.

Shirley receives so many requests to make appearances and sign autographs that she has stacks of photographs printed and sells autographed copies at various car shows and get-togethers around the country, as seen here at MCACN in 2019. It was at one such event, an American Motors Owners Association in St. Louis, Missouri, that I first met the Drag-On Lady and her husband, Ken. Ten years later, we met again at the same event, and that led to this book being written. (Photo Courtesy Shirley Shahan)

Shirley sits in the AMX for the first time in 50 years. Over time, further safety measures were added to the car, including an upgraded roll-bar assembly. Shirley noted that getting in and out of the car used to be much easier than it is now.

Pictured at MCACN in 2019 are (left to right) Shirley's son-In-law Clarence, daughter Janet, Shirley, Ken, daughter-in-law Carla, and son Bob.

Sadly, all that remains of one of Shirley's Pro Stock Hornets is the driver-side door, complete with the special lettering (albeit faded). Here, the hard-working crew from Nash Nutz, which was responsible for setting up the display, poses next to the door.

Joining in on the fun was Pontiac drag racing legend Arnie Beswick, whom Shirley had not seen in decades. Here, they are joined by the models working in the display.

Shirley is often asked to sign pieces of automobilia, such as the sign seen in this photograph. AMX owners often ask her to autograph their cars (usually under the decklid). (Photo Courtesy Shirley Shahan)

This is Shirley's son Steve, who competed in off-road racing.

Shirley remains very active in retirement.

"Ken and I still travel to some nostalgic car events," she said. "I'm still in contact with some of the old racers, folks who have remained such good friends all these years. We also play golf, travel around the country in our fifth-wheel trailer, and try to stay close with the family. You know, we retired folks are always busy."

Old Friends and Family

She also stays close with old friends such as Erline Myers, the lady who used to do her hair for her when she was in town. Erline also worked on some of the wigs Shirley wore during the Plymouth racing days. Erline remains one of her best friends.

She remembers good times with friends Doug and Bette Thorley of Doug's Headers, the folks who installed headers on all of Shirley's cars. Doug ended up being instrumental in Shirley getting the offer to race for AMC because he had some good friends who worked at AMC in the Performance Activities Department. The couples first met in 1963 at the old Inyokern Dragstrip near Inyokern, California, which was, in its time, the oldest dragstrip in the country. Shirley remembered that day because it was also the day she met race announcer Bernie Partridge, who a few years later was the announcer when she won the Winternationals.

Doug and Bette Thorley lived in Long Beach, California, at the time. Shirley and H.L. stayed at the Thorley's home a lot because it was near Lions Drag Strip and because the Thorleys were such great friends. Doug's brother Dick lived with them and had a bed upstairs of which he was very protective; for some reason he couldn't stand anyone sitting on it or sleeping in it. One night, a few of Doug's racing pals decided to put a full-size blow-up doll in his bed. Shirley recalls that when Dick came home and found it, "You could hear the swearing for a city block!"

Shirley remembers old friends who've passed away, such as Dave and Norma Kempton. Dave was a drag racer and also worked as the tech advisor at the Irwindale Dragstrip. His wife, Norma, worked the timing tower recording ETs and top speed for each car. The Shahans and the Kemptons were acquainted with each other from racing but became great friends when Shirley spotted Dave stalled along the side of the freeway and stopped to help. She still keeps in touch with their kids Mark and Laura.

Shirley and Ken also still attend some drag racing events, and they've been active in the old car hobby by attending National Meets of the American Motors Owners Association, a club dedicated to owners of vintage AMC vehicles. Shirley is a hero to the entire AMC crowd, and when she appears at

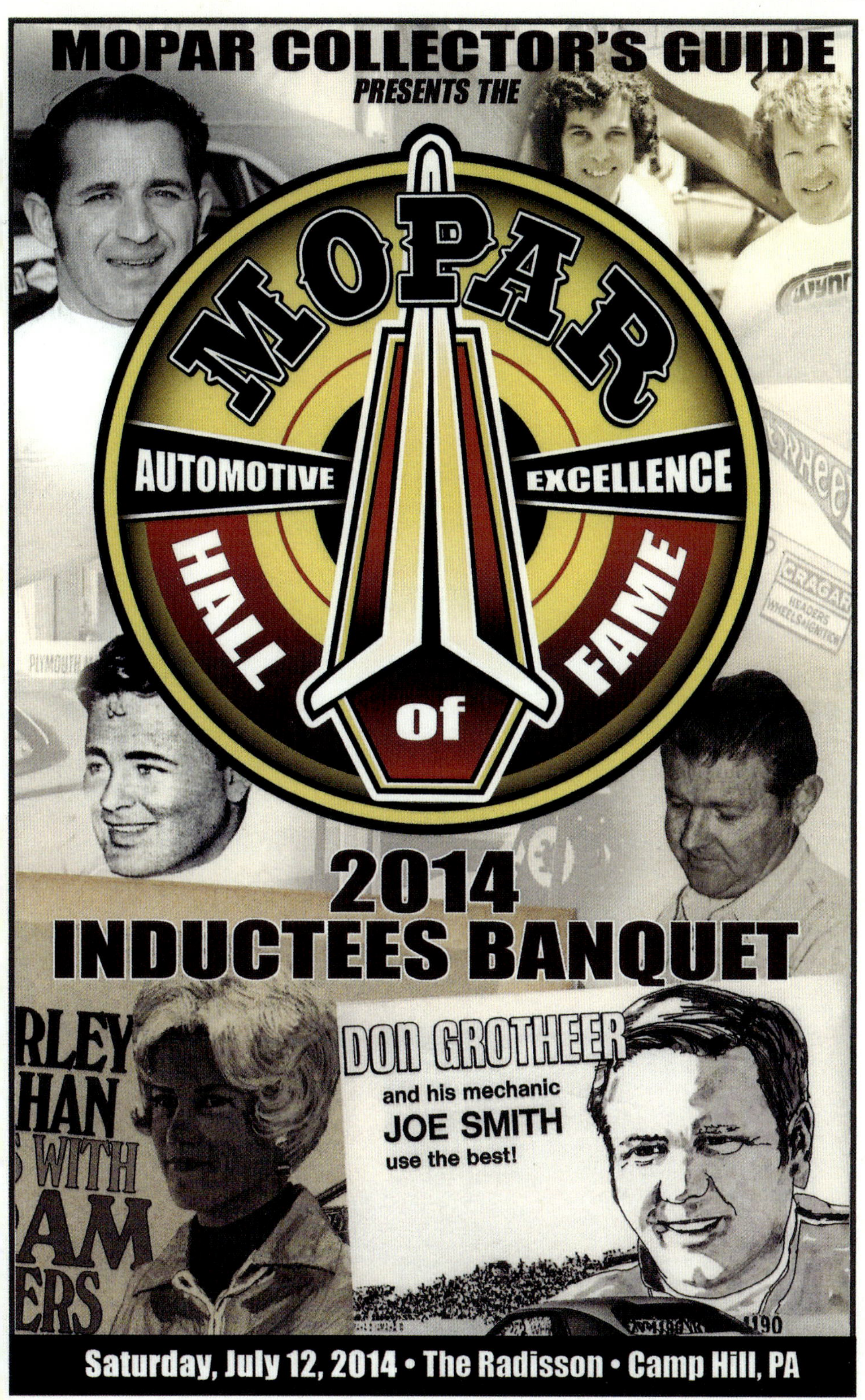

Here's a 2014 poster announcing the Mopar Hall of Fame, which inducted Shirley Shahan for her outstanding career in professional drag racing at the wheel of her Plymouth Belvedere, Dodge Coronet, and Dodge Dart racers. (Photo Courtesy Shirley Shahan)

diecast toy websites. The largest sizes, the 1/18-scale replicas, are the most desirable and the most expensive by far, but they are well worth the money because they feature amazing detail.

Sadly, tragedy has visited her life recently. Shirley's first husband, the famed race car preparer and driver H.L. Shahan, passed away on June 19, 2020, in a nursing home in California. He'd been ailing for some time. Then in September, her youngest son, Bobby, died in a tragic accident. Strongly religious, Shirley has relied on her faith and her family to get through these very difficult times.

Reflecting on her relatively short but amazingly successful racing career, Shirley sometimes wishes she'd done a few things differently.

"You know, my first big victory at Pomona came about five years too soon," she said. "If it had happened later, in the women's lib era, things might have turned out differently. I might have stayed in racing longer than I did, and my racing career might have turned out differently.

"A professional manager probably would have been a great asset for me at that time. A manager could have helped in negotiating better contracts, getting me better deals, and helping to promote me. The ladies that are racing now are doing such a fabulous job, I take my hat off to them."

events, her fans gather around to see her and to get her autograph.

Over the years, the toy industry has produced toy replicas of each of her famous race cars in a variety of sizes. Brands include Johnny Lightning, Matchbox, Ertl, Yat Ming, and more. You can usually find them for sale on eBay as well as on vintage

Shirley is forever grateful for all of her fans, who

over the years have stood and cheered her on whenever and wherever she raced and who still remember her today. In the course of a year, she still shakes a lot of hands and signs a lot of autographs. People still love her.

I asked Shirley if she ever races people on the street.

"No," she replied with a smile. "But my husband says I do!"

Drag On, Drag-On Lady, Drag On!

This drawing of Shirley was done years ago and has since been posted on the internet with the added wording that you see here. (Photo Courtesy Shirley Shahan)

This is one of the 1/18-scale toy models of Shirley's Plymouth Belvedere race car.

These are hard to find today and very popular.

(Photo Courtesy Shirley Shahan)

Fresh and new from Auto World is this toy model of a Shirley Shahan racer. This Super Stock AMX is dressed in the color scheme that it wore during the 1970 racing season. (Photo Courtesy Shirley Shahan)

Shirley, a pioneer for women in drag racing, poses with Angelle Sampey, a current star and talented driver in the field of Pro Stock motorcycle racing. (Photo Courtesy Shirley Shahan)

Shirley wipes the dirt and grime off her face after a successful run. You can see the quiet determination in her eyes and the satisfaction that she had when she performed well. (Photo Courtesy Chrysler. Chrysler is a trademark of FCA USA LLC.)

Shirley and Ken Bridges are a lovely couple who travel in retirement and enjoy each day. (Photo Courtesy Shirley Shahan)

Additional books that may interest you...

HEMI UNDER GLASS: Bob Riggle and His Wheel-Standing Mopars
by Rich Truesdell & Mark Fletcher
Bob Riggle campaigned wheel-standing Mopars for more than 60 straight years. This is a new must-have history book on *Hemi Under Glass*. 8.5 x 11", 176 pgs, 350 photos, Sftbd. ISBN 9781613255612
Part # CT670

DON "THE SNAKE" PRUDHOMME: My Life Beyond the 1320
by Don Prudhomme & Elana Scherr
Don "The Snake" Prudhomme reveals for the first time ever his incredible life and career on and off of the drag strip. He shares lessons about business and life and the importance of family. 8.5 x 11", 176 pgs, 400 photos, Hdbd. ISBN 9781613255186 Part # CT662

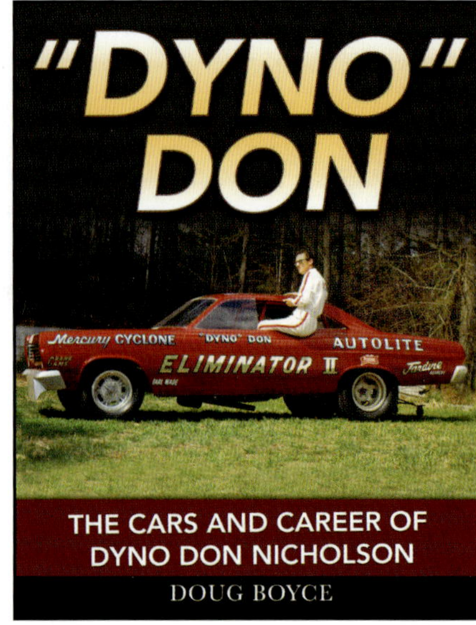

DYNO DON: The Cars and Career of Dyno Don Nicholson *by Doug Boyce*
If you are a fan of a certain era of racing, a Ford fan, or certainly a "Dyno Don" fan, this book will be a welcome addition to your library. Follow his Hall of Fame career on the match race circuit. 8.5 x 11", 176 pgs, 330 photos, Sftbd. ISBN 9781613254059
Part # CT631

DRAG RACING'S WARREN "THE PROFESSOR" JOHNSON: The Cars, People, & Wins Behind His Pro Stock Success *by Kelly Wade*
Go behind the scenes for a look at Warren Johnson's path to becoming *The Professor of Pro Stock*. This new book illuminates the life and career of one of the most prolific engine builders and racers ever to compete in the ultra-competitive Pro Stock category, drag racing's most technologically advanced class. 8.5 x 11", 176 pgs, 350 photos, Sftbd. ISBN 9781613255704 Part # CT672

Check out our website:

CarTechBooks.com

✓ **Find our newest books before anyone else**

✓ **Get weekly tech tips from our experts**

✓ **Featuring a new deal each week!**

Exclusive Promotions and Giveaways at www.CarTechBooks.com!

www.cartechbooks.com or 1-800-551-4754